POLICING BODIES

Policing Bodies

Law, Sex Work, and Desire in Johannesburg

I. INDIA THUSI

STANFORD UNIVERSITY PRESS
Stanford, California

STANFORD UNIVERSITY PRESS
Stanford, California

Printed in the United States of America on acid-free, archival-quality paper

Library of Congress Cataloging-in-Publication Data

Names: Thusi, I. India, author.
Title: Policing bodies : law, sex work, and desire in Johannesburg / I. India Thusi.
Description: Stanford, California : Stanford University Press, 2021. | Includes bibliographical references and index.
Identifiers: LCCN 2021016526 (print) | LCCN 2021016527 (ebook) | ISBN 9781503629226 (cloth) | ISBN 9781503629745 (paperback) | ISBN 9781503629752 (ebook)
Subjects: LCSH: Prostitution—South Africa—Johannesburg. | Law enforcement—South Africa—Johannesburg. | Sex workers—Legal status, laws, etc.—South Africa. | Prostitution—Law and legislation—South Africa. | Human rights—South Africa.
Classification: LCC HQ262.J6 T48 2021 (print) | LCC HQ262.J6 (ebook) | DDC 306.74096822/15—dc23
LC record available at https://lccn.loc.gov/2021016526
LC ebook record available at https://lccn.loc.gov/2021016527

Cover design: Angela Moody
Cover: vpanteon | Adobe Stock
Typeset by Newgen North America in 10/14.4 Minion Pro

Contents

Acknowledgments

This study would not have been possible without invaluable support from numerous individuals and organizations. The work was emotionally draining and challenging, and I relied upon several individuals to guide me through this process. First, I offer my profuse gratitude to my mentors Catherine Albertyn and Julia Hornberger. Professor Albertyn, you have been an intellectual, emotional, and administrative guide to me. I am sincerely grateful for your contribution in making me a more intellectually and emotionally mature scholar. You answered calls in the middle of the night as I navigated the Johannesburg sex industry and pushed me to delve deeper into the historical roots of sex work. Professor Hornberger, I thank you for providing me with your invaluable expertise in policing and for ensuring that my research was methodologically and theoretically rigorous. Your insights forced me to reexamine my assumptions about policing and to truly consider the theoretical implications of my research on the policing literature. Your contribution is extremely appreciated. I also appreciate both of you for your patience with me during this process and guidance after late night emergency phone calls, delays in research approvals, and general uncertainty during the research process.

I am grateful to Professor Kelly Gillespie for invaluable feedback at the early stages of my research. Thank you Dr. Jo Vearey for pushing me to thinking critically about how to engage my research participants and be sensitive to the realities of researching sex work. I am also grateful to the Andrew W. Mellon Foundation for supporting my project and endeavors, to the staff of the University of Witwatersrand Research Office for their reliable support and guidance, and to the staff at the Social Science Research Council who selected me for a Next Generation African Scholars award that provided much needed support, mentoring, and networking opportunities. Thank you Thomas Asher for your encouragement as I encountered some of the most challenging moments while conducting my research. I am also thankful to the W.E.B. Du Bois Institute for African and African American Research at Harvard University for providing me with intellectual resources and support while I was writing the final drafts of this book, and the Law & Society Association's Graduate Student Workshop for providing me with an intellectual space in which to revisit concepts I had not previously realized needed to be revisited.

I am grateful to Aziza Ahmed for thoughtful feedback on this book. Kimberly Bailey, I. Bennett Capers, Jessica Clarke, Edward De Barbieri, Nicole Crawford, Cynthia Godsoe, Phyllis Goldfarb, Andrea Freeman, Jing Geng, Darrell Jackson, Neha Jain, Joan Howarth, Ramona Lampley, Eric Miller, Eboni Nelson, Catherine Powell, Sarah Rogerson, Shakirrah Sanders, Nirej Sekhoun, and Rachel van Cleave have all provided feedback on various projects that contributed to the theoretical foundations of this book, which I deeply appreciate. I am grateful for conversations with Guy-Uriel E. Charles and Richard Ashby Wilson that pushed me to think broadly and that encouraged me as I was writing. I am grateful to former Stanford University Press editor Michelle Lipinski for believing in my work and encouraging me to write this book, and my current editors Marcela Maxfield and Sunna Juhn for their guidance and support throughout the writing process. I would also like to thank members from the production team at Stanford University Press, including Susan Karani, June Sawyers, and Stephanie Adams. I am grateful to Alan Bradshaw and his team at Newgen for excellent editorial assistance. My former colleagues at the California Western School of Law were a source of inspiration as I wrote this book, and I would like to especially thank Daniel Yeager, Laura Padilla, Catherine Hardee, Donald Smythe, and Hannah Brenner for being supportive as I traveled back to South Africa and spent part of my summers working on this project. I am indebted to

Marcus Glover, Catherine Ghipriel, and Ani Nalbandian for their invaluable research assistance. Thank you all. This book also benefited from discussions at the Albany Law School, California Western School of Law, Howard Law School, Oxford University, and the University of Wisconsin School of Law. I am grateful to the Black Women Collective Junior Legal Scholars Writing Workshop for being a continual source of inspiration for me. We have become close friends during challenging times, and I owe so much to you. Thank you, Jamelia Morgan and Ngozi Okidegbe.

I owe my husband, Mothusi, a huge amount of gratitude for his understanding and patience during this process. Mothusi, I am grateful for the sacrifices you made while your wife wandered Johannesburg brothels and streets in the middle of the night. I thank you for being my escort when I needed one and for encouraging me when I needed it. I thank my parents for being supportive of my decision to do this research and my father for his consistent words of encouragement. I would also like to give a special thanks to two friends: Rukariro Katsanda, for his guidance, and Nancy Ginindiza, for being a good friend as I was writing this book.

Finally, I am grateful to the numerous sex workers who shared their stories. Thank you for participating in this study. Thank you for sharing your lives with me and allowing me to enter into your world. Thank you to the members of South African Police Service for permitting me to conduct this controversial research and giving me access to your members. I also offer my profuse gratitude to the police officers who participated in this study. To protect identities, I will not specify names or levels of assistance, but I am extremely grateful for your contributions. Thank you for allowing me to enter into your workspace and allowing me to become a part of your everyday work environment. Thank you for accommodating me. I am grateful to you for allowing me to enter into your world for a small bit of time. Thank you!

POLICING BODIES

INTRODUCTION

I WAS CLERKING for the Constitutional Court of South
Africa the first time I visited the Hillbrow community in Johannesburg, South
Africa. The Constitutional Court is just adjacent to Hillbrow, yet many of my
native South African co-clerks had never even entered this area. Several of
my colleagues warned me about the danger that lurked right behind us in
the Hillbrow community. There is a mythology about Hillbrow as a "den of
iniquity"[1] that was enough to frighten young lawyers from ever daring to enter this space, even during the daytime.[2] Nevertheless, one day, disappointed
by the lunch options near the Court, I decided to take a walk through this
community. Immediately, I was struck by the hustle and bustle of its streets.
Hillbrow is filled with high-rise apartment buildings with laundry hanging
outside, graffiti sprayed on the sides of buildings, and the honking of minibus
"taxis" polluting the air. Groups of young men chat outside apartment building entrances, and hawkers sell goods as diverse as bananas, chewing gum,
and live chickens.

The streets are crowded with Africans from around the continent, filled
with various African vernaculars as you walk down the street. During this
initial visit, I saw no White people (which is unusual for many parts of Johannesburg), just many Black African faces on the pulsating streets. Hillbrow is
vibrant and full of life. I ended up eating at a fish and chips spot down the
road from the Court.

This visit sparked my interest in the area, clouded by its reputation for illegality and crime. Hillbrow's high-rise buildings include residences, hotels with transient housing, business offices, strip clubs, and bars; at times, they are managed by sophisticated criminal syndicates that charge cheap, daily rents.[3] Hillbrow is one of the most densely populated areas in Africa and has an estimated population of 75,000 people crammed into just 1.08 square kilometers.[4] It is well known as a red-light district, although it is no longer a site for visible street-based sex work. In a 2002 survey of local hotels, 27 percent of women living in those hotels admitted to working as sex workers.[5]

The sense of vibration, movement, and new settlement in Hillbrow illustrates Edgar Pieterse's view that "urban territories are as much nodal points in multiple circuits of movement of goods, services, ideas and people, as they are anchor points for livelihood practices that are more settled, more locally embedded and oriented."[6] While this book focuses on Johannesburg, it also describes "elements or processes in cities, or the circulations and connections which shape cities," more generally, uncovering a story about sex, policing, and urban spaces common to other cities around the globe.[7] This book contributes to comparative yet global perspectives on policing, feminism, and sex work, following Jennifer Robinson's suggestions for a comparative methodology that is still global.[8] Much as Kimberly Kay Hoang's book *Dealing in Desire* provides global insights about Western decline and capitalism through an ethnography about prostitution in Ho Chi Minh City, this book provides global insights about feminism, race, and policing through an ethnography about prostitution in Johannesburg.

Although I began my research ambivalent about whether sex work should be (de)criminalized, the limitations of promoting human rights by policing and criminalizing conduct became evident as my research progressed. I began to seriously question whether a human rights approach to sex work should ever contribute to more policing of sex work, even if the policing is limited to sex workers' clients. This issue is important, as there is growing concern about the appropriate role for police, if any, in society. Many people around the world are critically examining policing in response to various incidents of police violence within marginalized communities. In the past several decades, police have taken on additional responsibilities as administrators of social welfare and adopters of community policing. Yet, it remains an open debate whether policing and criminalization bring additional security and human rights protection, especially when it comes to populations that have been historically stigmatized.

It is within this social context that I examine the policing of sex work in Johannesburg. In Hillbrow, the commanding Hillbrow police station spans multiple buildings and is charged with maintaining public safety in this bustling community. The main building is six stories high. The upper levels include the offices for ranking members of the police. There are also meeting rooms on multiple floors, and brightly colored flyers near the elevator for each floor advertise the current police meetings. When people walk into the main building, they see police officers seated behind a long front counter, addressing community complaints and needs. There are usually around eight police officers behind the counter, and an endless flow of community members waiting to file complaints, certify documents, and meet with detectives. During my ethnographic fieldwork, I met with my police officer "partners" in this front lobby area to accompany them on their daily patrols of various brothels.

One evening, I interviewed Zolo, a young police officer who filed community complaints and certified documents. I began my interview by asking for his thoughts on "prostitution" (the term for sex work used by the police) and, soon after, asked him whether prostitution should be legal. Zolo conceded, "It is legal . . . mostly."[9]

This comment about the "mostly" legal nature of sex work illustrates how sex work occupies a liminal space[10] because the government has made the commercialization of an ordinary occurrence—sex—criminal. Sex work is difficult to regulate and is at the literal and figurative margins of proper society, occupying a place where legality and illegality often blur into one another. The policing of sex work in Johannesburg straddles the line between formal and informal. On the streets, police often appear to be acting in an informal and ad hoc manner. However, high-level organizational directives intended to regulate the obligations and duties of the police toward sex workers also influence police action and tilt the exercise of discretion to the formal. These obligations themselves reflect the tension between the law and human rights: the police must respect the human rights of sex workers, but they must also enforce the laws of the country. Sex work is illegal, but it is also time-consuming to regulate and difficult to prove that a sex work transaction occurred. Sex work involves activity that occurs in private transactions in spaces that are ordinarily private. But the illegality of sex work makes it a matter of public concern.

In this liminal space, this book examines the history of sex work in South Africa and reveals the continuities and contradictions between the discourses that have both informally and formally policed sex workers, as well as the current conditions that constitute the contemporary policing of sex workers in Johannesburg.[11] Achille Mbembé and Sarah Nuttall have complained about the descriptions of the urban African metropolis as a site of terror and vice—arguing that the "loathing of Johannesburg in the social sciences should be seen as part of an antiurban ideology that has consistently perceived the industrial city, in particular, as a cesspool of vice."[12] However, even in the world of vice, there is space to contemplate resistance, alternate visions of the world, and the liberatory potential of the body. Vice is not all bad. And sex work is a site for the contestation of femininity and masculinity, desire, and—in the context of South Africa and countries like it—race. Of course, Johannesburg is not all vice, and in this book I reveal how the framing and conception of vice is itself contestable. Moreover, I aim to disrupt the tendency to treat "Africa as an object apart from the world, or as a failed and incomplete example of something else." In searching out the realities of sex work and its policing, my study acknowledges that there are "multiple elsewheres of which the continent actually speaks" to offer insights that transcend the borders of Africa.[13]

This book encapsulates nearly two years of fieldwork that I carried out in Johannesburg, South Africa, and it addresses three questions about the policing of sex workers. The first two are descriptive questions about the way the policing of sex work currently occurs. The final one is a normative question about how the policing of sex work should occur. First, I examine the various discourses regarding sexuality and gender that act to informally police sex workers and to formally shape how police officers interact with sex workers. Second, I provide an ethnographic description of the relationship between the police organization and sex workers in Johannesburg. The ethnographic chapters (chapters 2, 3, and 4) expose the complexities of the state's interactions with vulnerable citizens through this relationship. They show the possibility of negotiation between police and sex workers, which can provide provisional security for sex workers through police protection. And this relationship is often formulated in a human rights language and adopts legal language and terms. However, it is never a lasting security because it is unregulated, and police "greed," the structural effect of working for an institution that police officers perceive to be underfunded, can tilt the relationship very quickly. Thus, the law is not the primary issue in the policing of sex workers; the informal practices that remain despite changes in the law—and that are informed by popular discourses and competing rationales—constitute the everyday practices, norms, and understandings that make up the everyday reality of the policing of sex workers. The ethnographic chapters about the nature of sex work provide the foundation for answering the final question concerning how sex work *should* be policed.

Practiced in the face of competing discourses and social practices, the policing of sex workers in Johannesburg demonstrates the limitations of the law as a tool for reform and its fluidity at the margins, providing context for considering how sex work should be policed. The final question is normative in that it considers what it means to adopt a human rights framework for the policing of sex work. This question goes beyond the formalistic legal treatment of sex work and is concerned with (1) how sex work should be treated from a rights perspective, (2) how it should be treated as a discursive object that reflects popular notions about sexuality and gender, and (3) how it should be treated within the dominant discourses as the subject of the gaze of feminists. In this book, I adopt a feminist theoretical approach, which is akin to a radical feminist framework insofar as it centers the role of structural discrimination and patriarchy when examining how sex work should be treated. I move away from an analysis based solely upon the individual liberty interests of atomistic sex workers. However, I arrive at a very different conclusion from radical feminists, who often argue that we should strive for a society where sex work is no longer an acceptable form of labor. This book considers how even partial criminalization of sex work reinforces notions about sexuality that are rooted in patriarchy, even when deployed by feminists. I am deeply skeptical of the feminist reliance on policing and punishment to eliminate social injustice—here, purportedly, the existence of sex work—when policing and punishment have been the state's primary technology for facilitating social injustice. Women who face intersectional forms of discrimination are constantly negotiating various risks and constrained choices, and they should nevertheless be able to pursue the options available to them that they deem to be beneficial, including the sale of sex. Moreover, the feminist debate must go beyond questions of criminalization if it is to be concerned with the lived realities of sex workers, because their policing occurs despite the mandates of the actual law.

It is important to emphasize that I initially began my research resolutely focused on how sex workers were being policed, with little concern for whether selling sex in exchange for money should be criminalized. Sure, the question naturally arose on several occasions, but I was more interested in exploring the complexities of the relationship between police and sex workers, the possible role of transactional sex in that relationship, and whether the relationship truly was "all bad."[14] However, the question of legality became a prominent feature of my informal conversations with sex workers, police, and various actors in the industry. My own feelings about the topic naturally evolved, and my views on how we, as a society, should treat sex work began to develop. Sex work is difficult. It is messy. It triggers our emotions, as citizens of the world, concerned participants in our local spaces, as women, men, wives, husbands, mothers, fathers, daughters, and sons. It challenges much of what we have been taught about human relationships and frustrates many of our own notions of morality. It is not a neutral subject, and we all bring preconceived notions of what it is and how it looks to our debates about sex work. Academic discourses about sex work are often emotional and passionate because sex work makes us feel so uncomfortable and is the antithesis of what so many have been taught, from both a radical progressive and ultraconservative perspective.

Conservatives argue that sex work is an affront to the traditional nuclear family. It sanctions non-procreative sex. It happens outside of the marital relationship. Sex work commercializes sex. It presumably destroys marital relationships and infects spouses with venereal disease that has been harvested in the sex worker's body. The radical progressive position is concerned with systemic reform and rejects theories of citizenship that overemphasize the individual. It is concerned with protecting vulnerable classes from the systematic oppression of a racist, heterosexist, male hegemonic patriarchy. The sex worker does not simply represent the sex worker. She represents woman-kind, and her choices may be detrimental to women even when they are ben-eficial to her. Sex work represents violence against women because it some-how victimizes the sex worker. The conservative and progressive positions are inapposite in their reasoning. However, they share one thing in common: At their very core, these arguments are premised on an understanding that sex is different and potentially oppressive for participants and outsiders alike. And so sex work, the commercialization of sex, is questionable. Sex work has no procreative value and may in fact disturb the public.

Consequently, sex work has been hotly debated among feminists and has created seemingly irresolvable divisions between scholars, most of whom are committed to a society that treats women fairly but struggle with conflict-ing visualizations of such a society. In between the conservative and radical views is a continuum of arguments regarding sex work—some highlight the autonomy of the individual; others emphasize the importance of economic empowerment; others recognize individual autonomy while adopting social-ist and materialist feminist approaches; and any combination of any of the varying viewpoints. This range of opinions reflects how research about sex work must contend with the inherent moral subjectivity that we all bring to this research object. This subjectivity is not necessarily a flaw but rather a natural result of conducting research on such a sensitive topic.

South Africa is a particularly interesting nation to explore sex work, given its cultural identity and political history. Catherine Albertyn has out-lined South Africa's transitional period:

> In December 1993, after two years of intensive negotiations, the South African Parliament ended white political domination by enacting an interim Constitution. Opening the door to the first non-racial govern-ment in South Africa, this Constitution enshrines the principles of liberal democracy and constitutionalism by establishing universal suffrage, an elected Parliament, a regionally based Senate, a strong central govern-ment with nine regional governments, an independent judiciary and a justiciable Bill of Rights.[15]

Given its history of minority political domination, human rights dis-courses are in many respects fetishized and valorized in South Africa, as they arguably should be. However, the discourse around human rights has created tensions between morality and rights preservation. For example, what is a human rights approach to sex work? Should sex work be decriminalized? Given the lack of scholarly (and feminist) consensus concerning how we should approach sex work, it is not surprising that there is a lack of coherence in the everyday policing of sex workers.

While sex work in South Africa has been explored in a variety of contexts,[16] there is very little research on how police members themselves conduct and perceive the task of policing sex workers. The policing of sex workers in Johannesburg involves a variety of policing mechanisms that move far beyond the mandates of the law. Michel Foucault argued that popular discourses regulate human behavior, and people who are vocal participants in shaping popular discourses are exercising power.[17] In the unique and particular area of sex work policing, both human rights discourses that have come to dominate narratives relating to the law in South Africa and activist attempts to decriminalize sex work in South Africa influence police behavior.

Popular understandings about gender and appropriate female behavior also influence police reactions to sex workers. As a general matter, South Africa is a society with complicated gender relations. On the one hand, women are frequently the heads of households, charged with providing for their families and raising children on their own.[18] On the other hand, South African women are subjected to some of the highest levels of domestic violence and rape in the world.[19] The society both relies upon women and in many ways subordinates them.[20] Mohamed Seedat, Ashley Van Niekerk, Rachel Jewkes, Shahnaaz Suffla, and Kopano Ratele have discussed the various forms of masculinity in South African society and how they are expressed through violence as an exercise of male sexual dominance: "The dominant notions of masculinity are predicated on the control of women, and infused with ideas of male sexual entitlement. Physical violence is used to manufacture gender hierarchy (i.e., teach women their place) and to enforce this hierarchy through punishment of transgression."[21] This is especially the case when referring to the sex workers,[22] as the approach to policing them is consistent with their ability to remain in "private" spaces that police deem appropriate for sex work.

Robert Morrell, Rachel Jewkes, and Graham Lindegger argue that South Africa has at least three forms of hegemonic masculinity that dictate the patriarchal nature of South African society:

[South Africa has not] one masculinity that was hegemonic, but at least three—a "white" masculinity (represented in the political and economic dominance of the white ruling class); an "African," rurally based masculinity that resided in and was perpetuated through indigenous institutions (such as chiefship, communal land tenure, and customary law) and finally a "black" masculinity that had emerged in the context of urbanization and the development of geographically separate and culturally distinct African townships.[23]

These forms of masculinity reflect the complex manner in which class and race have contributed to how women experience various forms of sexism and how men are similarly affected by it. The expression of the three types of masculinity in South Africa are context-determinate and are themselves subject to hierarchization and marginalization dependent upon class and social context. These various forms of masculinity were readily apparent as I spent countless hours on patrol with Johannesburg police members while discussing their perceptions of policing sex workers. A police member's need to assert masculinity would often lead to moments of friction between the police and sex workers who attempted to challenge a police member's masculinity.

DEFINING SEX WORK

In this book, *sex work* means the provision of sexual services for monetary reward.[24] Even within this narrow definition, there is great diversity in how sex work appears. C. Harcourt and B. Donovan describe at least twenty-five types of sex work.[25] Their typology highlights the various forms sex work can take, including street-based sex work, brothel-based sex work, escort services, private sex work, and dance hall and hotel sex work, as just a few examples. Each of these forms of sex work occurs in Johannesburg, and this book focuses on two of them: street-based sex work and brothel-based sex work. The brothel-based sex work in this study actually lies somewhere between the lines of brothel-based and hotel-based sex work. These hotel-brothels are not brothels per se, in that they do not directly receive a portion of the sex workers' income for services rendered. Instead, they are venues where clients are aware that sex workers are available for hire, and where sex workers pay rent for private rooms to render services. This quasi-brothel-based sex work is prevalent in Hillbrow. The street-based form of sex work was observed in central Johannesburg and on Oxford Road in the suburbs of Rosebank and Illovo. Although sex work in Johannesburg has been explored in these locations, there is very little research on how police officers themselves conduct and perceive the task of policing sex workers, as a state function. The existing research on sex work in Johannesburg and South Africa focuses primarily on public health concerns, efforts to rationalize the movement to decriminalize sex work, and the gathering of demographic information about sex workers. An exception is a paper published by the South African Women's Legal Centre that addresses police abuse of sex workers, finding that one in three sex workers who approached the Women's Legal Centre had been harassed by the police.[26] Several academic studies employ in-depth interviews and focus group discussions. These studies rarely rely upon extensive ethnographic participant observation or extended fieldwork to explore the experience of sex workers. None of the research is focused primarily on the policing of sex workers, although several earlier studies mention that police abuse is an issue of concern for sex workers.[27] This book partially focuses on Hillbrow although several earlier studies have focused on sex workers in Hillbrow and police officers there.[28] Moreover, as Kimberly Hoang has observed, there are few global sex work studies that focus on "multiple markets that cater to different clientele from diverse socioeconomic and racial/ethnic backgrounds."[29] This book undertakes to describe a variety of sex work markets in Johannesburg, demonstrating the diversity of sex work even within a single city.

A complete understanding of how South African sex workers are policed today and how they should be policed benefits from insights derived from the history of the national and local police, the history of policing sex work in South Africa, the everyday policing of sex workers in various field sites, and how various social orders and perceptions influence how sex workers are policed. Viewing the "everyday"[30] may reveal resistance in a potential site of oppression—such as the relationship between police and sex workers. Moreover, past description of that relationship has been somewhat reductionist, categorizing police as mere roadblocks to sex workers' human rights.[31] There is undoubtedly plenty of evidence that police exploit sex workers, and this abuse is not to be taken lightly. However, the relationship between sex workers and police is more complicated than the narrative of police as rights-abusers and sex workers as victims would suggest. Researchers have indeed found that sex workers are harshly policed and suffer abuses at the hands of police.[32] Some sex workers complain that police officers frequently ask for bribes, and many have been raped and physically assaulted by police officers.[33] However, I also found that sex workers did at times call upon police officers for assistance, some sex workers had a patronage relationship with police, and still others viewed them as occasional allies.

My intent in exploring the rich history of social conditions and circumstances surrounding the policing of sex workers is to develop a conceptual framework for understanding how the law is lived and experienced in this peculiar area, where popular norms about gender, sexuality, legality, and space are influential. The debates regarding the criminalization of sex work are often missing the perspective and depth that can be provided by an intensive ethnography. Indeed, they can at times appear completely lacking in on-the-ground evidence. This book aims to address this gap.

Although focused on Johannesburg, the research I carried out offers globally relevant perspectives on the various expressions of sex work policing, the limitations of the (de)criminalization of sex work, the limitations of relying on policing to regulate marginalized populations, and the relevance of a theory (and policy) that is grounded in the local realities of sex work. Within Johannesburg, this is a multi-site study, examining how sex workers are policed in both indoor and street-based environments. This comparative approach reveals how perceptions of public and private, patriarchy, the visibility of female sexuality, and gender norms influence this peculiar area of policing.

METHODOLOGY

The Hillbrow police force is one of the largest police forces in the country, with 498 members. I gained access to the police by submitting a request to the national office of the South African Police Service to conduct research at both the Rosebank and Hillbrow police stations. Obtaining approval was a challenging process. After I submitted the formal research request application to the national office, I then waited through a lengthy bureaucratic process before receiving the final research approval. During this time, I called the police on several occasions and spoke to the head of the research department. Eventually the national department granted its approval, and the request was submitted to the provincial police. After the provincial police received my request, the approval was submitted to a similar lengthy bureaucratic process, requiring signatures from various officers, some of whom were on vacation or on sick leave. I submitted my initial application on November 12, 2012, and I received final approval to begin my research on May 14, 2013, after approximately six months and after some gentle nudging from me. The fieldwork research was conducted between June 2013 and February 2015. The majority of the participant observation was conducted between June 2013 and August 2014, whereas follow-up interviews were conducted until February 2015. (More detail on methodology can be found in the appendix, "A Note about Methodology.")

Studying the policing of sex workers presents unique challenges because sex work is illegal. The activities of the authorities while policing sex workers are frequently illegal and corrupt. The discussion of the sale of sex and sexual desires is often considered taboo. The two groups I needed to work with appeared to be antagonistic to each other, complicating my relationships with the participants and ability to gain access. And the dominant social norms that dictate how people are supposed to act when talking and thinking about sex and sexuality made the research participants hesitant to discuss this topic openly with a researcher who was essentially a stranger to them. Given these challenges, I adopted a legal ethnography as my primary methodology. This allowed me to consider temporal shifts in the treatment of sex work in the research sites and gave me adequate time to establish trust with research participants who might have been hesitant to participate in the research project, given the frequent illegality of their conduct and the embarrassment many people experience when discussing topics related to sex and sexuality. It also facilitated observation of the gap between what research participants state is the nature of a research object and their actual behaviors in connection to the research object.

Within this overall methodology, I adopted several methods of gathering data, to allow a multifaceted analysis: participant observation, semi-structured interviews, and a focus group discussion. I spent twenty months among sex workers and in police stations in order to appreciate the perceptions, values, behaviors, and norms that govern the relationship between sex workers and police.[34] As Richard Schwartz notes, if we are "[t]o make law a more effective instrument of policy . . . it is necessary to understand why it develops, what forms it takes, and especially what are its consequences."[35] By spending time with the police, the organ of the state charged with enforcing the law, I was able to understand why the police exercised discretion and chose to enforce or not enforce prostitution laws at the research sites. The arguments regarding the policing of sex workers in South Africa, examining a "human rights approach" to sex work, have this empirical research as their support and context.

An ethnographic approach is particularly useful in obtaining a greater understanding of the policing of sex workers because deeply engrained cultural values inform this policing. Police officers often incorporate their personal moral and cultural values while policing. Understanding how and whether these values influence the policing of sex work—a topic subject to value-based judgments and cultural marginalization—is significant. However, as Monique Marks finds, such values, such "deep level assumptions," cannot be determined from "structural arrangements or quantifications of police attitudes. Instead, researchers need to take an ethnographic approach, whereby they prioritise the social actor and his/her subjective orientation."[36] Thus, as the researcher participates in and observes the everyday occurrences that form policing, they can explore the ways in which subjective values influence that policing. For example, I was able to study how popular discourses about sex workers, such as perceptions of public health and public hygiene, influence the everyday policing of those workers. I could gather data for the actuality of policing and also observe the inconsistencies between police practice and police policy. With an ethnographic approach, I could reach understandings available only through in-depth observation of the research object over time.

As I was observing the behaviors of the police and the sex workers at my research sites, I was also intent on understanding and interpreting their behaviors in light of the legal, historical, and social contexts in which they were taking place. This ethnography studies the natural setting of the research object and interprets the subjective interactions that occur within it.[37] It allows the empirical to become theoretical through interpretation of the ethnographic data and explanation of why certain behaviors occurred. Collecting ethnographic data through participant observation required me to both actively participate in and observe the natural environment of the research subjects. Although time-consuming and not always specific to the research aim, participant observation is critical in revealing the distinctions between expressed conduct and actual conduct. It is capable of exposing biases, routine behaviors, and understandings that research participants would rather not explicitly express. It also requires more than sitting back and watching. It requires that the researcher actively participate in the conduct of the informants, observe both the spoken and unspoken conduct and circumstances of those informants, and continuously engage in data collection through extensive field notes. Through participant observation, I observed the gaps between what police officers said the law required, and how they actually practiced their roles as enforcers of the law. Moreover, sex work can be an uncomfortable subject for strangers to discuss. I expected that police officers might be less willing to openly share how they really felt about the topic and might feel judged if their opinions deviated from dominant social mores. With a topic like this, and with an institution reputed to be insular and secretive, participant observation became a tool to pierce the blue veil. Law is socially situated, and participant observation provided me with a tool to see how the law regarding sex work was actually expressed and lived.

I joined police officers during their routine patrols of sex workers, and I came to appreciate the exhaustion police experience during the twelve-hour shifts that stretch between 6:00 p.m. and 6:00 a.m. This appreciation allowed me to see how quickly an acrimonious encounter with a sex worker could turn into an instance of police harassment or worse. I also spent significant time inside police stations in order to contextualize the policing of sex workers within the larger policing task and to understand how the police worked with their communities. Although I did not literally participate in policing by directly responding to community complaints or carrying a firearm, I did accompany police officers during routine patrols to respond to complaints and during traffic stops. I attempted to maintain as much proximity to the policing task as was legally permissible.

Over time, participant observation proved to indeed be the most appropriate methodology for exploring the sensitive subject of how sex workers are policed. The police were initially hesitant to speak candidly with me about their experiences with sex workers. They were suspicious of me—a

Black American woman—and speculated about my intentions. They would frequently question me about my origin and my family background in an attempt to "place" me. Several of them thought I was young and would speak to me as if I were their child. They frequently questioned the purpose of my research and often told me I would learn nothing from joining them on their patrols. In many respects, this was an exercise of masculinity, as these male officers thought it was their right to put me in my place and lecture me about my research object.[38] Some officers worried that I would place myself in danger. They would frequently put on a performance to assert their masculinity, such as bragging about the danger of the job or displaying their firearms for me.[39] There was a constant performance of Black, urban male masculinity in the form of bravado and displays of physical strength. In addition, some officers viewed me as a woman who needed protection, and they provided unsolicited guidance during the course of my research project.

However, as the police officers grew familiar with me, their concerns dissipated. They became natural with me and would speak casually with each other in front of me. They were no longer stiff around me. This evolution occurred rather quickly, and within a few weeks of our working together, they had become comfortable with me. Given the sexual topic of my research, police officers often relied on innuendo and suggestion when talking to me and when admitting to unlawful conduct or confirming that they had previously engaged sex workers. They told many dirty jokes and became comfortable discussing their perceptions of the various sex workers and brothels with me. While patrolling with the police, I was careful to wear clothing that was dark and loose fitting, as a way of masking my femininity. I wanted to appear as neutral as possible and did not want them to perceive me as a potential mate. I was a researcher and needed to be perceived as such. This approach helped me to be perceived as a (nonsexualized) colleague.

Nonetheless, there were uncomfortable moments. For instance, one married police officer suggested that I act as his girlfriend to protect him against the advances of sex workers. In moments like this, I would often subtly deflect the conversation, because I did not want to appear uptight and did not want the police to become less comfortable around me, but I also did not want to pave the way for future sexual advances or suggest that my pretending to be an officer's girlfriend would ever lead to a romantic relationship.

Maintaining this balance required me to constantly negotiate my position and monitor the officers' perceptions of me.

I conducted participant observation with sex workers by adopting the role of a friendly patron, spending significant time at sex work hot spots, drinking at sex work venues, and socializing with sex workers. Negotiating the parameters of participant observation with sex workers proved trickier than it was with the police. Sex workers were initially hesitant to speak with me, and many of them feared I was a journalist who would expose them to the public. I randomly approached several sex workers near Rosebank, wearing jeans and a dress shirt, and was met with a tremendous amount of suspicion. I believe many of them perceived me as a judgmental female member of the Black South African community intending to expose them for their conduct. I do not think many of them had encountered Black, female researchers, and they assumed I was there to harm them in some way. In their minds, if I was not a sex worker advocate, I was a threat. They viewed me as both an insider and an outsider. I was an insider insofar as I could pass judgment on them as a Black community member and potential acquaintance. But I was also an outsider because I was not a sex worker and did not fit into the roles they attributed to women within that world.

On the advice of a retired sex worker, I at first wore "sex work attire" to adapt to the surroundings, and then approached sex workers regarding my research. In response, several sex workers were hostile toward me and perceived me as potential competition. I received very little participation adopting this approach, and I felt uncomfortable. I received favorable feedback from sex workers only when I began dressing in a "masculine" uniform of baggy jeans and oversized plaid shirts. Soon after this shift in wardrobe, sex workers began to approach me and participate in the research project without prompting. The sex workers treated me as a potential client and were more receptive to me because I had found a role in their world that made sense for them and was nonthreatening. They were no longer suspicious of me and were incredibly friendly and receptive to my research. By adopting this uniform, I positioned myself within a group that sex workers view rather favorably—clients—rather than suspiciously, as they would a journalist or Black female community member. Although some researchers might be offended by my approach, my particular identity and positionality as a

Black, female, American researcher required that I adopt this uniform and approach for my interest in this research to make sense to the sex workers. Gaining meaningful access to sex workers was practically predicated by my negotiating how I could fit into their world without offending them.[40] As a friendly patron, I "made sense" to them.

Participant observation strives for partial immersion. I achieved this by living within a block of one of the sex work hot spots in Rosebank. This allowed me to make frequent visits to Rosebank sex workers while they were working and to respond promptly to calls during the evening working hours. However, I did not live near all my research sites during the course of my project and so I had this level of immersion only in Rosebank. This proximity to Rosebank often made it difficult to establish clear boundaries, and I was often fielding calls from sex workers in the middle of the night in response to some encounter they had had with the police.

Furthermore, I was juggling two types of relationships, which required adopting two personas and lexicons. With sex workers, I referred to their work as *sex work*; with the police, I referred to that work as *prostitution*. To do otherwise would have been a distraction in our interactions. More fundamentally, I had to internally shift my perspective during my different encounters, because I formed personal relationships with the participants and thus was considered a confidant. Even though the police and sex workers were more closely aligned than I had anticipated, there were still moments when I felt I had to take sides and decide on my loyalty. It was difficult to manage this process of moving back and forth and split identity. But this constant shifting also allowed me to gain a holistic perspective on the issues and factor in matters that would otherwise seem irrelevant.

To explore sex work in Hillbrow brothels, I relied heavily upon my key informant, Emily, whom I met through a friend who frequents brothels. Emily had previously worked in Hillbrow Inn and then retired from sex work to take a job as a domestic worker. We visited Hillbrow brothels together, and she introduced me to sex workers whom she knew. I also visited these establishments alone to become acclimated with the scene and meet additional sex workers. Most of the brothel-based sex workers had very limited interactions with police. In general, the brothel-based sex workers I encountered were suspicious and mistrusting of strangers.

Sex workers are generally considered to be a vulnerable group and discussing their concerns regarding police may expose them to psychological damage. I had to be sensitive to this fact during my questioning, and was able to refer sex workers who required therapeutic services to outside providers. However, maintaining a respectful researcher-participant relationship was tricky. The sex workers began to view me as a friend, and the boundaries began to get blurry. It was important to maintain our professional relationship without sacrificing their hard-earned trust and our natural rapport. I sometimes received phone calls from sex workers in the middle of night, and they relied upon my immediate response. The research was blurring into my personal life, and it became difficult to maintain my personal space. I wrestled with the difficulties of doing research with a vulnerable population, particularly when sex workers came across financial difficulties and viewed me as a friend. I also had similar challenges with the police.

I had to be sensitive to the illegal nature of sex work. When working with the police, I did not want to encourage unnecessary police interactions with sex workers, that is, interactions that would not have occurred in my absence. For example, when I first began my research with the police, one of the officers asked me whether he should arrest some sex workers and question them for the research project. He promised that after he had arrested them, I would be allowed to interview them. I vehemently opposed the suggestion because I did not want to create a harmful situation for the sex workers or promote unnecessary friction in the relationship between police and sex workers. However, I also had to be sensitive to the fact that in exploring the everyday interactions between police and sex workers, I could not shy away from interactions that would also have occurred in my absence. I had to walk a fine ethical line.

I also was careful when observing illegal conduct by the police. On several occasions that I witnessed, officers solicited illegal bribes or admitted to patronizing sex workers (or explained the rationale for either behavior) while engaged in police work. These occurrences presented ethical challenges for me. As a concerned individual, I may have wanted to report the police misconduct. As a researcher, I understood that police officers had confided in me and trusted me to protect such confidences. I even observed an incident of extreme police abuse, as the police tortured an arrestee by cutting off the circulation to his hands by tightening his handcuffs. I was casually informed that this was routine, presenting a challenge for me in my research. I had to ask myself serious ethical questions. Do I report the police misconduct? Do I jeopardize this *and future research projects* by compromising the officers' trust in me? Have I placed the police in a compromising position by creating a relationship so transparent that they believe torturing an arrestee in my presence is appropriate? How should my ethical obligations as a researcher guide me? I regularly consulted my research advisors as such ethical challenges presented themselves, and we discussed suitable approaches. We were continually engaged in a dialogue about the appropriate methods for conducting this type of sensitive research. I signed a waiver that detailed the risks of observing police work, and I also adopted safety protocols to reduce my risk while in the field. While patrolling with the police, I was provided with clear safety instructions, and I followed the instructions of my partner officer during the patrols. Police work is inherently dangerous, and on several occasions, I accompanied police officers as they responded to complaints unrelated to sex work. This meant that I sometimes accompanied the police on high-speed chases and routine traffic stops.

Given the nature of my research, safety was also an issue while I was in the field without police protection.[41] During my nighttime visits to Hillbrow brothels, I brought companions who were already familiar with the Hillbrow brothel scene to ensure my safety. I would make these evening visits to the brothels only when I had at least two companions. This ensured that I would not be a target for robbery and also provided me with comfort. During my daytime visits, I dressed as a patron and left the venue by 3:00 p.m., while it was still daylight outside, to avoid traveling alone in the evening through Hillbrow. During my visits to central Johannesburg, an escort always accompanied me. In Rosebank, I was much more casual, because of its close proximity to my home. I felt comfortable in the neighborhood but still exercised reasonable caution. I frequently interviewed sex workers in Rosebank, and in this pursuit, I spent time on Rosebank street corners without any escort and at all times of the evening.

NARRATIVE, STORYTELLING, AND KNOWLEDGE

The subjectivity of the research process, and a view of research as studying "transitive objects"[42] is apparent throughout this study. I incorporate my personal experiences with the policing of sex work and comment on how others' perceptions of my personal identity shaped the research, making a conscious choice to interfuse reflexivity within the text. This choice illustrates how the knowledge was being produced and acknowledges that my unique positionality influenced the type of data I was able to collect. Reflexivity often adopts first-person accounts of the experience during research and, as Douglas Foley remarks, is a method for understanding "historical, socially constructed reality in a partial, provisional sense through an intensive, experimental encounter with people who live by these cultural constructions of reality."[43] This approach recognizes the multiple subjectivities that may occur during the research process, rejecting a methodology premised on a singular objectivity. I also recognize that especially in studying a topic such as sex work, which relies upon trusting relationships with individuals engaged in a range of illegal activities, my identity influenced my access, and ultimately provided unique insights as I explored the research questions. In short, this study recognizes my unique positionality in relation to the research participants, the shifting temporalities encountered while I was studying the policing of sex work, and the subjectivities in my interpreting the mapping of the urban landscape.

At the same time, this subtle realism recognizes that the rubrics of research experiences are limited by the environment and the nature of the research object. I triangulated my data by interviewing multiple sources, referring to police work schedules and outlines, reviewing official policies and manuals, and reviewing newspaper accounts of stories that participants shared with me, recognizing that certain pieces of data are verifiable. The next chapter provides a historical analysis of the regulation of sex work in South Africa to contextualize its contemporary policing.

1 | POLICING AND SEX WORK
IN HISTORICAL PERSPECTIVE

SEX WORK REGULATION and policing in South Africa have a lengthy history, shaped by discourses on public health, public hygiene, public nuisance, racialized morality, and sexual morality. In addressing this history, I offer an expansive conceptualization of policing that extends beyond the activities police officers frequently do that may lead to state punishment and imprisonment. Thus, I begin with a discussion of how policing is interwoven with moralistic norms; understandings of gender, race, and ethnicity; perceived threats to masculinity; and accepted expressions of female sexuality. A "policing of sex" occurs in public and private discourses, and power emanates, not from the repression of sex, but from the discursive technologies of sexuality. The discourses around sexuality do not serve to repress it but rather place the state's gaze upon it; and the regulation of sex work and its connection to maintaining White racial dominance in South Africa illustrate the power of discourses to discipline sex workers for deviating from the racialized moral order of the time. This history reveals that sex work has long been inconsistently regulated, and that regulation is based on popular understandings and ideas about sex.

This genealogy of sex work reveals that the body of the sex worker has been the site for the exercise of *biopower* concerned with disciplining female sexuality. It is through morality discourses about the appropriateness of sex work that norms about the contours of male and female sexuality are spelled out. Men are presumed to be more sexual and in less control of their sexual appetites, as was reflected in the preamble of the British Contagious Diseases Act, which led to similar Acts in Britain's colonies, and in the treatment of sex work as a necessary evil during the Victorian era. Contemporary discourses reproduce, resist, and adapt historical social orders and norms.

THE DUTCH EAST INDIA COMPANY AND SLAVERY

The Dutch East India Company established a settlement in Africa's Cape Peninsula in 1652, as a refreshment station for vessels traveling between the Netherlands and what was then called Batavia and later became Jakarta. This small refreshment station eventually grew into a settler colony, as company employees sought land there and then began to retire to the colony. Company employees could lease plots of land from the company for labor-intensive farming. From about 1658, slaves were imported from Madagascar, east Africa, and Asia to meet the labor requirements of the settlement, thus increasing the number of inhabitants of the colony.[1]

As "thousands of single Company soldiers and sailors disembarked each year at Cape Town for ten days to three weeks of recreation," sex work naturally evolved as a method for entertaining these visitors near the port.[2] Sex workers catered to both the seamen, who were temporary visitors, and the settlers of the colony, and a lively community of taverns and houses of ill fame developed near the colony's dock.[3]

Several factors contributed to the active sex trade in the Cape Colony. First, there was a gross imbalance in the gender population of the colony. Sex work provided an opportunity for enterprising women to capitalize on the lonely situation of the relocated men.[4] In many ways, sex work was viewed as a necessary evil. Saheed Aderinto has examined how prostitution was similarly a feature of the emerging urban centers and ports in colonial Nigeria.[5] In South Africa, engaging sex workers boosted the morale of seamen after their long voyages. The Cape hosted many Dutch and, later, British seamen and troops—many of whom arrived in the Cape without their wives—who would frequent "houses of ill fame."[6] Although there is scant information about the indigenous Khoi women engaging in sex work, records clearly indicate that slave women routinely participated. The Company Slave Lodge, which was described as the "finest little whorehouse," employed slaves who also worked as sex workers.[7] Company employee Otto Mentzel described the Company Slave Lodge:

> Female slaves are always ready to offer their bodies for a trifle; and towards evening, one can see a string of soldiers and sailors entering the Lodge where they misspend their time until the clock strikes 9. After that hour no strangers are allowed to remain in the Lodge. The Company does nothing to prevent this promiscuous intercourse, since, for one thing, it tends to multiply the slave population, and does away with the necessity of importing slaves.[8]

Luise White has detailed how prostitution was likewise core to the economic interests of the colonial government in Nairobi, Kenya, because it facilitated reproduction and maintained the labor force.[9] Otto Mentzel claimed that the motto of the slave sex worker was "Kammene kas, kammene kunte," or "No cash, no cunt,"[10] and sex work became a means for some of these sex workers to purchase their freedom.[11] During this period, there was no formal policing or legal regulation of sex work: "On the whole, apart from some legislation to control disorderly conduct in public, the authorities did little to interfere with the practice of prostitution" in the Cape Colony.[12]

In fact, there are reports of opportunistic sex workers and madams lining the Cape port to welcome arriving Company seamen and to direct them to their respective establishments.[13] Sex work became a mode for these women to transform their economic realities and provide an income that was higher than what could be earned through other available opportunities. It also enabled widowed women to provide for themselves and their families. Historian Henry Trotter has discussed the Cape Colony sex trade, which frequently catered to passing seamen:

> After months at sea in an all-male environment, many seafarers desired female companionship when they reached Cape Town. For a long time, there were few women to provide this service. Only when the society stabilized and grew did a notable prostitution sector emerge. White women were initially scarce at the settlement, but some ended up prostituting themselves due to the loss or absence of their husbands.[14]

In 1795 and then again in 1801, the British took control of the Cape Colony and abolished slavery in 1834. Soon thereafter, the British annexed Natal, and the "ports of Cape Town, Port Elizabeth, and Durban were then all under imperial control. During this time . . . 'prostitution remained a casual profession. It had become an offence, but was relatively rarely prosecuted.'"[15]

In her seminal piece on prostitution in the Cape Colony in the 19th century, historian Elizabeth van Heyningen argues that government officials viewed sex work as "inevitable in a seaport town [as it] provided a form of controlled release for the antisocial energies of unruly sailors."[16] The sexual appetite of these "unruly sailors" was a concern in several of the European colonies as the empire expanded. For example, in the Dutch colony of Gombong, an officer warned about the potential for unrestrained homosexuality given that there were restrictions on male seamen's sexual interactions, stating: "Far more than half of the young men quartered [in a barrack that banned concubinage] were guilty of practicing unnatural vices [including male-male sex]."[17] In general, European colonists worried about the sexual morality of seamen, and "[t]he dangers of a homosexual European rank and file were implicitly weighed against the medical hazards of rampant heterosexual prostitution: both were condemned as morally pernicious and a direct threat to racial survival."[18]

Throughout the British Empire, sex work was in this way encouraged, although feared, because colonial authorities did not want men to resort to homosexuality because they were not provided with an alternate form of sexual release. As in the Dutch colony, in the subsequent British colony, sex work was thus considered necessary and was largely tolerated. Engaging sex workers ensured that men would not lose all their "sensibilities" by delving into homosexual behaviors due to their prolonged absence from Europe.[19] The irony in this tolerance of sex work is that the very act of engaging in sex work was viewed by many as the very loss of those "sensibilities" that were so highly prized in the colonial state. The result of this approach was a regulatory scheme that treated the sex workers as deviants while ignoring the men who engaged sex workers. This reproduced deeply entrenched sexual double standards, according to which men were expected to be sexual beings, whereas women who were engaged in "deviant" sexual conduct, such as sex work, were viewed suspiciously.

The later years of British colonial rule were also heavily influenced by Victorian era standards and views. The era of Queen Victoria's rule, from 1837 until 1901, has been widely discussed as a period marked with sexual repression and sexual purification.[20] As historian Vertrees Malherbe argues:

Victoria's sixty-four-year incumbency would see the elevation of "moral regulation" as a social policy in Britain and its (erratic) emulation at the Cape of Good Hope. From its foundation by the Dutch East India Company as a place of European occupation and, soon afterwards, settlement in 1652, Cape Town experienced spasms of official outrage against the sexual transgressions.[21]

Nonetheless, the discourses around sex work at the time do not necessarily highlight the sexual repressiveness of the Victorian era; they demonstrate the desire to police "deviant" sexualities.[22] Michel Foucault describes these sexual deviants as the "other Victorians."[23] These "other Victorians" expressed sexuality outside the confines of the traditional Victorian standards, which limited sexual activities to the marital relationship, and they included those who engaged in sexual discourses with psychiatrists as well as with prostitutes. This included sex workers and those who frequented them.[24] By highlighting the conduct of sex workers, this discourse contributed to the social marginalization of sex workers and was an act of regulation in and of itself.[25]

Social norms of this era treated male and female sexualities differently. Women were expected to remain pure bastions of chastity that required protection from the male sexual appetite. This approach to sexuality encouraged women to suppress their sexual desires and, in some situations, even encouraged women to be asexual.[26] By contrast, although men were encouraged to remain sexually chaste, it was entirely expected for them to have larger sexual appetites than women.[27] They were the more primal and sexual of the sexes, and thus sexual inequality was assumed.[28]

Consequently, it was hardly unusual, and even encouraged, for men to turn to "less moral" women or sex workers to meet their unfulfilled sexual needs. Turning to sex workers was viewed as a necessary aspect of the social order. Men were expected to have unsavory sexual desires that were abhorrent to the tastes of respectable ladies.[29] Sex workers were viewed as an acceptable release for these desires that would otherwise go unmet by men's wives. This tolerance of sex work in Victorian society also protected wives from the unsavory desires of their husbands. The *Cape Argus*, a prominent liberal newspaper in the Cape Colony, warned its readership of the necessity of sex work:

> Harlotry, as an institution, with all its fearful evils to mind and body, is of
> so ancient an origin, that we can hardly now hope to put it down entirely;
> and perhaps, too, it is not quite desirable, while society is constituted as
> it is, that it should be driven into secret places; for experience teaches us
> that even where it is not openly allowed by law, as in the Roman states,
> its evil effects are aggravated. In a measure it must, perhaps, be regarded
> almost as an institution necessarily attendant on the present state of soci-
> ety; as, in a degree, a safety-valve for public morality, and as some protec-
> tion to the chastity and purity of our virgins and matrons, guarding them
> partially from temptations only too seductive![30]

Accordingly, sex work became a brand of immorality for lower-class women
while remaining a tool for protecting the morality of "respectable" women.[31]
The sex workers themselves were merely incidental participants in the preservation of the purity of respectable women. This approach to sex work emphasized sex work as a necessity to protect respectable women from the in-
satiable male sexual appetite that could only be satisfied through encounters
with deviant prostitutes.

Nevertheless, some people protested the license this inequality offered to
men. Although there was very little formal policing of sex work at the time,
civil society began to morally police sex work, particularly the conduct of
"immoral men." During the Victorian era, women's groups launched wide-
reaching campaigns against male sexual immorality. These groups dispar-
aged sex work as a form of this male sexual immorality, while portraying
sex workers as victims of circumstance. The men who engaged sex workers
were portrayed as opportunistic, immoral actors violating the proper moral
order.[32] The groups organized protests against the prevalence of brothels and
visible street prostitution. However, this morality discourse was unable to
motivate formal state action against sex work and, at times, even provided
the rationalization for the inevitability of sex work.

It was only the emergence of public health discourses that eventually trig-
gered the widespread regulation of the sex worker body. Efforts to suppress
sex work were bolstered by a syphilis pandemic that resulted in the deaths of
thousands of people in Britain and its colonies[33] and created paranoia around
the treatment of venereal diseases.[34] Within this social context, sex workers
were quickly constructed as carriers of contagion and largely blamed for the

spread of venereal diseases. They were perceived as outcasts in society and made easy targets.[35] As Trotter has observed, "polite society now worried that their laundry women and domestic servants might be moonlighting as prostitutes, polluting their hearths with diseases."[36]

Doctors and medical professionals blamed sex workers for infecting respectable wives with disease by sleeping with their husbands. Sex workers' bodies represented a threat to other women's quality of life and basic hygiene. This gave rise to an urgent need to regulate sex workers more thoroughly to prevent the spread of contagion.[37] Meanwhile, sex work clients, who were often other women's husbands, were not similarly viewed as carriers of disease. In the public health discourse, proper society treated men as accidental victims, coerced by the temptations presented by sex workers.[38] The sex worker embodied fears about female sexuality, a sexuality that was primarily exploited for the benefit of female commercial empowerment during the act of sex work. Accordingly, the morality discourse became increasingly connected with the public health discourse, as they reinforced and intersected with each other. This allowed the moral regulation of women's bodies and sexuality while maintaining a public health rationale.

THE CONTAGIOUS DISEASES ACTS

The spread of venereal diseases in Britain and the colonies created a fervor to regulate the sex worker body, a perceived site of contagion,[39] and resulted in the passage of the first of the Contagious Diseases Acts in Britain in 1864. The preamble to this Act states that "the peculiar conditions of the naval and military services, and the *temptations to which the men are exposed*, justif[y] *special precautions for the protection of their health* and their maintenance in a state of physical efficiency" (emphasis added). This preamble explicitly treated men as accidental victims of the contagion-carrying sex worker. It set the tone for treating sex workers as accessories to the protection of male sexual health. Sex work was permissible as a necessity for men, but sex workers themselves were viewed with suspicion.

A similar Act was adopted in India in 1868, followed by other British colonies, including Malta, Hong Kong, Australia, and Gibraltar. Historian Philippa Levine has discussed the passage of the Contagious Diseases Act by colonial governments throughout the British Empire: "Enacted principally in the 1860s, at the same time as the British acts, almost every British colony

acquired regulations governing the behavior of prostitute women as a measure against the threat of syphilis and gonorrhea."[40] Most versions of the Act
had language nearly identical to that of the English Act, treating sex workers
as temptresses who preyed on male sexual desire.

The Cape Colony

In South Africa, the first Contagious Diseases Act was enacted in 1868 in
the Cape Colony. This Act mandated regulation of sex workers as "common prostitutes": "A common prostitute was described as maladjusted, an
unbalanced personality and a menace to society. Included in the category
of common prostitute were also latent homosexuals, women who cheat on
their husbands and gold diggers."[41] The Act also required the registration of
women suspected of being "common prostitutes,"[42] and made them subject
to routine examinations for venereal diseases. Sex workers found to be infected with venereal disease were confined to facilities known as *Lock hospitals* and subjected to involuntary treatment and examinations.[43]

The Act blatantly discriminated against sex workers, citing the need to
protect seamen from the "temptation" of the sex worker in its very preamble,
and treating the sex worker, but not the client, as the vector of disease. Only
sex workers, and not their clients, were subjected to mandatory, invasive
physical examinations.[44] This injustice gave rise to a movement to repeal the
Act both in England and in those colonies where the legislation had been
adopted.[45] In England, women's groups in particular opposed the Act as it
exposed sex workers to physical invasions and tolerated male sexual immorality.[46] As English feminist Josephine Butler famously stated:

> I never myself viewed this question as fundamentally any more a woman's
> question than it is a man's. The Legislation we opposed secured the en-
> slavement of women and the increased immorality of men; and history
> and experience alike teach us that these two results are never separated.[47]

Butler and others argued against the unfairness of an Act that focused only
on the sex worker, whom they viewed as a victim of her circumstances.
Moreover, efforts to repeal the Act coalesced well with campaigns to police male sexuality. Women's groups were strictly opposed to sex work and
challenged the morality of men engaging in sexual transactions outside
their marriages.

In the Cape Colony, sex workers themselves became involved in campaigns against the Act. They rioted against the Act[48] and refused to comply with required examinations, and generally protested its requirement of invasive vaginal examinations for syphilis using a speculum.[49] In addition, police officers' role in enforcing the Act, as first-line responders, created tensions in their relationship with sex workers.[50] However, established, White, middle-class men, rather than women's groups, took the lead in campaigning against the Act. In particular, the proprietor of the *Cape Argus*, Saul Solomon, published reports in his newspaper of "a series of incidents towards the end of 1870 involving illegal police action against prostitutes."[51] The Act was repealed in the Cape Colony in 1872, owing to these efforts in response to the police actions. For thirteen years after that, sex workers could engage in their activities without the interference of the law. Eventually, another version of the Act was passed in the Cape in 1885, but it required lay inspectors rather than police inspectors, to avoid the harassment that occurred when police were involved.[52]

Britain's Contagious Diseases Act was successfully repealed in England in 1886.[53] Efforts to repeal the Cape Colony's 1885 version of the Act were not as effective: "Members of the Women's Christian Temperance Union were roused to campaign against 'the indignity done to women' by the Contagious Diseases Act of 1885 but they failed to sway the lawmakers: the offending Act was only repealed in 1919."[54] The language in the Acts and the focus on protecting men from the sex worker as a site of contagion reflects a social order that reproduced the ideology of male sexual dominance. The purpose of the Act was, in effect, to protect male sexual expression while simultaneously disempowering commercialized female sexual expression.

The Colony of Natal

The territory of Natal, which includes Durban and Pietermaritzburg, was proclaimed a British colony on May 4, 1843. Despite the general unpopularity of the Contagious Diseases Act globally, there were efforts to enact a similar act in the Natal Colony from 1885 on. Medical professionals were the dominant voice in advocating for the Act. The social conditions of the Natal Colony fed into the fear surrounding the spread of contagion. Sex work was an everyday feature of Natal town life.[55] But in the absence of overarching legislation, approaches to regulating sex work in the Natal differed. In

Pietermaritzburg, the superintendent was flexible in his policing of sex workers, recognizing sex work as unavoidable, whereas the Durban superintendent took a more hardline approach to sex work.[56]

Despite these variations, the policing of sex work was driven by the medical community, which sought legislation to require the registration of sex workers and force medical treatment for venereal diseases. Medical professionals warned of the dire repercussions that would ensue if immediate measures were not adopted to regulate the health of sex workers, thus galvanizing the state into action. They warned that syphilis would reach epidemic levels in Natal without this legislation, and in 1885, the Pietermaritzburg medical officer persuaded the governor of the need for the Act in Natal. Despite the overwhelming support of the medical community, this impending Act was met with tremendous opposition, as it was proposed during the height of the controversies surrounding existing versions of Act in England and its colonies.[57]

Echoing the experience of the Cape Colony, a group of sixty-five prominent male citizens argued against the gender inequality represented in the Natal version of the Act, suggesting that it would allow "unscrupulous persons . . . to cause injury, shame and indignity to poor but respectable females." Opponents also alleged that the Act would be largely ineffective because it focused only on sex workers and ignored the conduct of their clients. In 1886, the Natal version of the Act failed to pass in light of the overwhelming pressure against it. Medical professionals nonetheless persisted in their claims that the Contagious Diseases Act was necessary for the public health of the colony.[58]

It was only when the public debate then shifted from gender to race that their proposals gained any traction. Black men were dominant features of the domestic domain in Natal, where a large number of Black male servants, called "houseboys," worked in White households. Paranoia around the presence of these houseboys fueled a second campaign for the Contagious Diseases Act, based on an increasing fear about what was described as "innocent infection" of syphilis. Medical professionals at the time mistakenly believed that syphilis and other venereal diseases could be spread "innocently" through casual touch. Thus, having Black houseboys who might engage in morally corrupt behaviors, such as frequenting brothels, posed a direct threat to the White family's health. Although a houseboy might have

no malicious intent to spread the disease, he could nevertheless be the car-
rier. By gently grazing a child's forehead or holding hands with a toddler, he
was believed to be an undeniable threat to the household if he had syphilis.
This version of the public health discourse in Natal exploited racial anxieties
to expand the medical community's power over the sex worker's body.[59]

As a result, the Contagious Diseases Act was passed by the Natal legislature with little opposition in 1890. It was primarily the result of strong
lobbying by the medical community and increasing fears around the spread
of contagion by sex workers and houseboys.[60] However, when the legislation was forwarded to Lord Knutsford, secretary of state for the colonies, he
admonished the colonial authorities for "practically [leading] . . . the official
members of the Legislature to vote for a measure which in other Colonies
gentlemen holding similar positions had been directed by the Secretary of
State to oppose." He blocked the law in light of the global political pressure to
repeal similar legislation in England and its colonies.[61]

Accordingly, sex work was never regulated through the Contagious Diseases Act in the Natal Colony. In general, sex work was treated as a public
nuisance violation and was punishable where there was a public annoyance,
as it had been in the Cape Colony.[62] These public health discourses did, however, empower the medical community as arbiters of morality and protectors
of both health and civility. As Foucault argues, this power emanated from
the very engagement in discourse. Although the Natal medical community
failed to get the Contagious Diseases Act into law, it managed to galvanize
the legislature on several separate occasions to create legislation that would
be explicitly harmful and discriminatory toward sex workers. The public
health discourse was particularly effective when coupled with morality discourses about racial hierarchies and female sexuality, and it reified the conception of the sex worker as a threat to public welfare.

From Contagion to Public Nuisance

The attempts to police the sex worker's body as a site of contagion in both the
Cape and Natal Colonies evince a form of biopower. Scholar Vanessa Munro
defines biopower as, "a peculiarly effective mechanism for normalization
that focuses upon the human body as the centrepiece of important struggles
between various different power formations. This claim that the body is the
locus of important power struggles has also been dominant throughout the

history of feminist theorizing." The sex worker's body was a site for the exercise of biopower and sexual normalization during public health discourses because it embodied a threat to heterosexual norms that viewed marriage as the sole site for sexual expression and sex.[63] The attempts to regulate sex workers illustrate the desire to manage women who threaten dominant sexual norms by expressing female sexuality outside of marital relationships. This regulation was a form of nationalistic self-preservative. These women's bodies threatened the body politic as vectors of disease. In this way, the regulation of sex work is linked to the regulation of all female sexuality. Sex work was still tolerated as necessary for male desire, but it could only be expressed in manners that did not upset the public. Soon, public nuisance regulations became a formal part of its regulation. These public nuisance ordinances were intrusions on the sex worker's body and prioritized conceptions of public decency and nuisance as central concerns in the regulation of the sex worker.

Although sex work was still generally treated as a necessary evil, it was now penalized where a public nuisance was present. For instance, starting in 1882, the Police Offences Act penalized any "prostitute who loiters or is in any public place for purposes of solicitation or prostitution to the annoyance of the public" as guilty of an offence.[64] The original punishment was a fine of £2, with the alternative of 30 days' imprisonment with hard labor, but by 1898, the fine had increased to £5. As was typical of the time, the legislation penalized only the public nuisance aspect of sex work. Sex work was tolerable as long as it did not disturb the public, a theme that would continue throughout South African history.

The Transvaal and the Mineral Gold Rush

The South African Republic, also commonly referred to as the Transvaal, or the ZAR (the Dutch acronym for South African Republic), was an independent country, under White Afrikaner rule, in southern Africa from 1852 to 1902. It occupied the area that is currently home to four provinces of South Africa (Gauteng, Limpopo, Mpumalanga, and North West). After the Anglo-Boer War, it became a colony of the British Empire—the Transvaal Colony—from 1902 until the founding of the Union of South Africa in 1910.

In 1886, gold was discovered in the Witwatersrand area of the Transvaal, attracting mining companies and workers. During the ten years following that discovery, there was very little regulation of sex work in the Witwatersrand.[65]

The city of Johannesburg grew at the center of the 50-mile stretch of gold mines. The population of the Witwatersrand (later "Johannesburg") was 80 percent male and two-thirds single, and made up primarily of young adults between the ages of 20 and 40 years.[66] Black men migrated there to work in the gold mines and also as domestic workers in White households. At that time, Black women were considered too unreliable and immoral to be domestic workers.[67] Consequently, Black women had limited economic options and frequently engaged in sex work and in selling liquor to the Black mine workers to economically sustain themselves. Historian Charles van Onselen argues that these economic choices reinforced negative views of Whites toward Black women.[68] The disproportionate number of men, mostly single and young, contributed to the persistence of sex work in the Transvaal,[69] which quickly earned a reputation for prostitution, an illicit liquor trade, and crime.[70]

At the same time, the face of sex work was beginning to whiten, owing to an increase in European sex workers.[71] During the Anglo-Boer War, between 1899 and 1902, there was an influx of European women into the Transvaal and the coastal regions for organized sex work, as crime cartels also took root.[72] This influx of European sex workers coincided with the rise of brothels, primarily featuring European women. Many of these sex workers were lower-income women, looking to capitalize on the higher incomes that would become available to them in the colonies.[73] Initially, these European women had catered to Cape settlers and Black patrons, and when they eventually migrated to the Transvaal, they similarly had Black clients.[74] These interracial relations contradicted the colonial agenda that was, in part, premised on the essentialization of race and the presumed supremacy of the White race.

At this time, there were also reports of police corruption, as the South African Republic Police colluded with prostitution syndicates.[75] Van Onselen provides a detailed account of the collusion between organized prostitution rings and the Morality Squad of the Transvaal Town Police. Police corruption was pervasive, as the officers sought to benefit from the substantial revenues of sex work. The police often worked cooperatively with sex workers, even though the official policy opposed all organized vice.[76]

Officially, the administration was implacably opposed to "organized vice" and, more especially, to large and visible brothels controlled by gangsters and pimps. Unofficially, this publicly-stated policy would be implemented only after due consideration had been given to "local conditions" that permitted individual prostitutes—practising their craft in private, with some discretion—to offer sexual relief to "single" working men.[77]

This inconsistent approach to policing sex work reflects the tensions in the conflicting discourses about it. On the one hand, sex work was viewed as a moral vice. On the other hand, it was treated as a necessary evil.

Because of the prevalence of sex work, mining companies grew wary of the absenteeism that the flexible laws and easy access to sex workers and liquor presumably encouraged.[78] This was addressed in two ways. First, the mining companies pressured the local government to pass strict laws restricting the movement of Blacks and promoting racial segregation. Second, these companies advocated for regulation of liquor and sex work. They prohibited the sale of liquor within the mines,[79] and supported additional regulations to police sex work more generally. This took the form of laws that penalized the activities of males involved in prostitution and indirectly targeted the criminal syndicates around sex workers. In 1903, Transvaal legislation stated that "every *male person* who (a) knowingly lives wholly or in part on the earnings of prostitution . . . shall be guilty of an offence."[80]

MORALITY ACTS, WHITE ANXIETIES, AND THE UNION

This targeting of "pimps" and syndicates involved in sex work was also found in the corresponding pre-Union legislation in the Cape, Orange Free State, and Natal Colonies. The Natal legislation was not limited to "every male person" but also included females.[81] However, this legislation also contained a new approach to sex work, one that saw an increasing focus on interracial sex and the moral panics that were beginning to accompany this focus. In the early 1900s, a racialized morality agenda became more dominant, as anxieties about maintaining the state of white supremacy manifested themselves in a growing "hysteria" and series of panics over the perceived threat of Black male sexuality to both White women and White masculinity. Much of this hysteria is reflected in the increased censure and regulation of sex work, as sex workers were particularly visible participants in the interracial sex that was seen to be disrupting the dominant racial order. A point of comparison is the similar focus on sex and marriage as a site for racialized morality in

the United States. Most states in the United States prohibited interracial marriages at some point, and this "historical prohibition of interracial relationships exemplifies the state's regulation of intimate life. Anti-miscegenation
laws prohibiting interracial sex and marriage predate the Declaration of Independence by more than a century. At one time or other 41 of the 50 states
have enacted such legislation."[82]

Timothy Keegan suggests that such sexual anxieties in South Africa
emerged "in the context of the perceived crumbling of racial boundaries"
and the threat to White racial dominance.[83] Sex between White sex workers
and Black men threatened White male masculinity by seemingly dispossess-
ing White men of their sexual ownership of White female sexuality and by
suggesting that Black men were sexual competitors. As such, sexual relationships between White people and Black people were considered to be immoral by many White inhabitants of the colonies, even where consensual.

New Moral Regulation and Race

Transactions between European sex workers and Black mine workers threatened the racial order, and led to Morality Act 36 of 1902, the Betting Houses,
Gaming Houses and Brothels Suppression Act, which criminalized relationships between African Black males and White female sex workers in the Cape
Colony. Similar legislation was also passed in the three remaining colonies,
and in 1910 the four colonies united to form the Union of South Africa.[84]

The moral panics rising from the perceived ever-present threat of the
Black man's sexuality and his presumed attraction to the virtuous White
woman, led to the creation of several "black peril" committees and task
forces.[85] "Black peril" refers to a hysterical fear among various groups that
Black men were a direct threat to White female sexual purity. Indeed, Black
men were frequently viewed as threatening perpetrators, unable to resist
their savage urges to ravish White women. As a result, rape perpetrated by
Black men against White women was punishable by death.[86] This was excep-
tionally clear from reports at the time.[87]

Timothy Keegan has argued that "in white imaginations, respectable
white women were bound to become the sacrificial prey of the black beast
unleashed by the breaching of racial boundaries."[88] In fact, White women
were prominent voices in the discourse regarding the black peril. Keith Shear
describes the panic that ensued among women's groups:

A white women's movement coalesced in these years around opportunities to mobilize against the "black peril." Not only did Leagues for the Protection of Women and Children emerge specifically in response to urban racial scares, but "black peril" issues attracted the range of existing women's societies into alliances such as Johannesburg's Standing Committee of Women's Organizations, which brought nineteen associations together "first of all as a Black Peril Committee" early in 1911.[89]

A White Afrikaans woman wrote in 1912 to a local newspaper, responding to charges that South African country girls ("veld girls") were submitting to their "passions" toward Black men:

> [T]he veld girls know exactly where is the place of a black brute. They do not allow a Kaffir any further in their houses than in the kitchen. To their modest minds it is the greatest disgrace to allow a Kaffir to enter their bedrooms to bring in early coffee or to attend to the tidying up of their houses inside. If they haven't a black woman to do it, they do it themselves. Neither would they dream of carrying on a conversation with a Kaffir.[90]

The Black man was viewed as a moral threat to the White woman vis-à-vis his presumed ability to corrupt her delicate sensibilities, but this account suggests that veld girls knew how to put the "black brute" in his place.

These fears about Black male sexuality reflected a general anxiety about interracial sex. Interracial sexual liaisons were treated as morally repugnant and a threat to the purity of the White race. Because of this, the thought of White female sex workers who willfully engaged with Black male clients further fueled the moral outrage.[91] Accordingly, the threat of Black male sexuality came to focus on White sex workers, and the 1913 Commission on Assaults on Women shared that fear:

> [F]oreign professional prostitutes allowed, and indeed often invited, intercourse between themselves and natives. Amongst their companions such natives gloried in the fact of having had intercourse with white women, and on their return home the fact was repeated and spread abroad. So desire was stimulated in minds previously innocent of such an idea, and individuals unable to discriminate between one class of women and

another were inclined to gauge the standard of morality of white women by the examples presented under such circumstances, and to fancy that they need only make advances to be accepted by white women generally.[92]

There were reports of taverns where Black men socialized with White sex workers, subverting the dominant social rules that relied upon racial essentialization and separation.[93] This phenomenon was doubly troubling because White women's willingness to engage with Black clientele was perceived to be a form of resistance against the dominant White male patriarchal order. Sex workers were already using their bodies for their personal benefit, with little regard for the dominant ethos regarding respectability and morality. On top of this subversion, they were openly entertaining men of a race deemed to be inferior. This was the ultimate violation of the prevailing sexual mores. In some senses, this subversion defied the possibility of future redemption or compliance within White male hegemony. Consequently, the black peril was also a moral panic spurred by the threat that Black male sexuality posed to the free exercise of White male masculinity, which presumably included exclusive ownership over the White woman's body. White women were rejecting the dominant racial norms and rejecting White male dominion over their bodies in these transactions. The attempts to regulate the transactions between White female sex workers and Black male clients was an exercise of biopower over the White woman's body and an exercise of White male masculinity by allowing for the regulation of White women's sexual partners. White women who chose to resist racialized morality discourses were rejecting White male sexuality and were thus a threat to White men's masculinity. The moral panic was not simply the fear of the Black man's sexuality—it was hysteria about the White woman's free exercise of her own sexuality. These sexual acts further threatened White male sexuality by treating Black men as potential sexual partners. In this way, the moral panics reflected the general anxiety of White men in the postcolonial state.

At the same time as the "black peril" became an issue, women's groups began to launch broad-reaching campaigns in the interests of promoting "social purity." Sex work was targeted as a form of male sexual immorality, and sex workers were portrayed as victims of circumstance. Women's groups such as the Cape Women's Christian Temperance Union in Cape Town aimed to save sex workers from a "damned" life while also ensuring that men would stop seeking sex workers to meet their sexual desires. "The WCTU," says Shear, "had been particularly concerned with issues of 'Social Purity' and the enforcement of local 'Morality' legislation regarding prostitution and inter-racial sex," and it was representative of the many middle-class White women's reformist organizations that actively participated in producing the post-1910 anxiety over South Africa's urban social environment. Central to all were concerns about racial purity and separation, expressed in campaigns to rescue destitute White children, monitor interracial sexual contact, and combat prostitution and liquor consumption.[94]

This paranoia around the risk of the contamination of the White race eventually led to the promulgation of strict anti-miscegenation laws in the newly formed union. Several legislative measures were adopted to address the issue of non-discriminate sex work. In an effort to curtail the migration of European women for the purposes of sex work, Union Bill 350, No. 553 of 1913, prohibited the immigration of "any prostitute, or any person, male or female, who lives or has lived on . . . any part of the earnings of prostitution or who procures or has procured women for immoral purposes." But the dynamic forces around race and gender that shaped the passing of such laws had been put in place at a very early stage in the colonial state.

As historian Jeremy Martens has observed, "'particular standards of behaviour were as important as physical appearance' in defining race and nationhood, and . . . poverty and 'moral malaise' in the white population threatened to breach racial boundaries and undermine racial hierarchy, respect and dominance."[95] The regulation of sex work during the 1910s was very much been intertwined with understandings of race, gender, and patriarchy. These moral panics represent a convergence of several of these issues, manifesting in a singular movement. Miscegenation was considered to be the ultimate violation of the social order, and thus, even the most casual interracial relationships were met with suspicion.[96] The panics were a reproduction of racial anxiety: the anxiety of White men about their masculinity, the anxiety of White men about the sexuality of White women, the anxiety of White women about the sexuality of White women, and the anxiety of the colonial state in the maintenance of a social order that respects an essentialized racial social order. The discourses that allowed for the moral regulation of sex work now focused on a racialized morality that was terrified by the possibility of White sex workers engaging in transactions with Black men. They also reproduced a subjective hierarchy of sex workers by prioritizing the protection of White female sex workers against the Black male, while at times ignoring transactions between White men and Black female sex workers.

SEX WORKERS: THE UNRELIABLE PUBLIC NUISANCE

The discourses on public health, racial essentialization, public nuisance, and morality intersected with each other, and, at times, reinforced each other. Where there was no racial element, sex work was problematic only to the extent it posed a public nuisance. However, sex workers themselves were generally perceived with suspicion and treated as unreliable characters by the legal system. This is reflected in several court judgments. In 1913, in *Rex v Weinberg*, the Orange Free State Provincial Division court (OPD) noted that "[e]very Court that tries this kind of case ought to be very careful not to convict a man upon the uncorroborated evidence of a prostitute." In 1917, the same court further held, in *Rex v Christo*, that "before the Court accepts testimony of this kind [by a prostitute] it must be amply corroborated." This finding was later affirmed in 1948, in *Rex v Dikant*. These legal decisions deemed the sex worker to be inherently unreliable, encouraging the marginalization of sex workers in public discourses. The law both constituted and reinforced discourses pertaining to the sex worker as untrustworthy and unreliable.

In 1915, Cape Town women formed volunteer patrols "to save foolish women and silly girls from moral danger, to lessen the social evils of [the] streets and other public places and to raise the moral tone of the community, particularly the female portion of it."[97] Johannesburg women attempted to enact a similar program in the Witwatersrand (modern Johannesburg) but failed, and the Cape Town program was disbanded in 1919. The Union Public Health Act of 1919 repealed the Cape Colony's Contagious Diseases Act,[98] and established a uniform method for regulating sex workers' bodies throughout the newly created South African union.

Black migration from rural areas to urban mines continued in the 1920s and 1930s, which contributed to an increase of sex work in these areas. Historians Peter Delius and Clive Glaser discuss this phenomenon in depth:

During the 1920s and 1930s, as conditions deteriorated in many rural areas and male migrants increasingly "disappeared," black women flooded into the cities. A large portion were involved in domestic beer brewing and many turned to prostitution in order to survive. Most eventually attached themselves to urban men and, with sex ratios beginning to approach normality, the black urban population gradually stabilized. Urban administrators and welfare workers became alarmed by what they perceived to be a high rate of promiscuity among urban women.[99]

In 1927, "carnal relationships" between all African Blacks and Whites, including relationships between Black women and White men, were completely prohibited by the Immorality Act 5 of 1927. Thus, racial anxieties also came to affect White men who engaged Black sex workers. During the debate on the Act, in 1926, the member of parliament for Barberton, South Africa, of the Afrikaner Party, W. H. Rood, argued that when a White man openly slept with a Black woman, the state should "take away the vote from the man who makes himself guilty of such things." He reasoned that if the White man wants "to become a native, then give him the same rights as the natives in the Transvaal."[100] Despite the influx of women into urban spaces, sex workers were subject only to civil penalties under Section 27 of South African Act No. 31 of 1928, which provided that "loitering or being in any street or public place for the purpose of prostitution or solicitation *to the annoyance* of the inhabitants or passengers" was an offence punishable by fine (emphasis added). However, anyone running a brothel was subject to six months of hard labor. Again, sex work was policed only where a public nuisance occurred.

The public health of sex workers remained a curiosity. A University of Pretoria research report on European sex workers in Johannesburg, conducted from 1939 to 1941, found that "[t]he great majority of all prostitutes in Johannesburg are infected with one or other of the venereal diseases." In explaining the political economy of sex work for White women in Johannesburg, the report stated:

> 71.4 per cent of convicted prostitutes originate from the rural areas. The economic retrogression of many rural towns and areas . . . due largely to depressed agricultural conditions, and the continuous industrial development in cities like Johannesburg . . . [means that the] problem of

prostitution in Johannesburg cannot be dissociated from the modern phenomenon of industrialization and urbanization.[101]

As was the norm, the sex worker as a vessel of contagion was highlighted:

> Prostitutes are the principal disseminator of venereal disease in the community. The percentage of infected men in Johannesburg who contract their venereal infection from prostitutes is approximately 64.6 per cent. Over the 19-year period, 1920–1939, approximately 30,000 men in Johannesburg contracted one or other of the venereal diseases.[102]

This report also strongly favored decriminalization, highlighting that even in the years of increasingly authoritarian rule, there were those advocating for a lenient approach to policing sex work. However, the discourse continued to treat the sex worker as a host for contagion.

APARTHEID

In 1948, the National Party won the election, beginning the apartheid regime in South Africa. This deepened the existing system of racial segregation in political, economic, and social life, and imposed an even more conservative racial and sexual morality on South African society. During this period, sex regulation focused on the provisions of the Immorality Act, which were largely concerned with a racialized and gendered policing of sexual activity, sexuality, and sexual morality. Apartheid legislation strictly prohibited sex between persons of different races and contributed to the discourse of sex workers as suspicious and unreliable. This prioritization of regulating the racial aspects of sex work is reflected in the criminal penalties of the Sexual Offences Act of 1957, which looks back to the racialized morality discourse of the earlier black peril moral panic.

Deepening the Gendered and Racialized Censure of Sex in Law

During apartheid, the courts began to question the legal discrepancies in the regulation of sex work, noting that clients should not be treated more harshly than sex workers. In the 1951 decision *Rex v V*, the Eastern Districts Local Division court noted that South African law should not be lenient in its treatment of sex workers when compared to that of the clients:

[A] prostitute herself whose act in soliciting is not less immoral than that
of the accused, and who makes money out of immorality in the ordinary
course, is only liable to the £5 fine and not even that if the soliciting by
her occurred in a quiet public street where no member of the public is
annoyed. That . . . seems a glaring injustice.

The court therefore reversed the conviction of a man who had solicited a
Colored sex worker, arguing that the solicitation law was intended to regulate
the actions of "pimps" and "touts."

The Immorality Act of 1950 repealed the 1927 Immorality Act and was
the dominant law that regulated South African sex lives during the apartheid
era.[103] In a 1957 revision, this Act was renamed the Sexual Offences Act, although often still referred to generically in documents as the Immorality Act.
This Act prohibited all forms of sex between all races, all aspects of sex work,
"indecent" sexual acts, and the creation and management of brothels. It was
a great interference into the sex lives of South Africans and represented a
brand of morality that was consistent with the beliefs of the Dutch Reformed
Church.[104] This brand of morality in many respects perceived women as the
property of men and less culpable in the sexual act. For example, the penalties for "sexual deviance" varied between men and women in the Sexual
Offences Act of 1957, with women receiving four years of imprisonment and
men five years. This reflects sexual norms that presumed women's sexual
innocence and ignored women's ability to be sexually culpable beings. The
Prohibition of Mixed Marriages Amendment Act, No. 21 of 1949, outlawed
all mixed-race marriages and marked the first time interracial marriage was
statutorily prohibited in all of South Africa.[105]

In fact, even during apartheid, sex work was a priority for the state only
when it defied the racialized and gendered social order mandated by apartheid, as reflected by the penalties attached to the Sexual Offences Act of 1957.
Section 10 of that Act criminalized the actions of brothel keepers,[106] while Section 19 targeted the client and criminalized the actions of a person who "entices,
solicits, or importunes in any public place for immoral purposes."[107] Section 20
of the Act criminalized the activities of persons living off the proceeds of sex
work.[108] Section 22 provided penalties for these crimes and stated that those
convicted of living off the proceeds of sex work (presumably mostly female)

were subject to "imprisonment with compulsory labour for a period not exceeding three years." Those who attempted to procure prostitutes (presumably mostly men) were subject to "compulsory labour for a period not exceeding two years" and a whipping not exceeding ten strokes. However, regardless of gender, "where it is proved that the person convicted kept a brothel and that unlawful carnal intercourse took place in such brothel to his knowledge between a white female and a coloured male or between a coloured female and a white male," the person will be imprisoned "for a period not exceeding seven years." This highlights the shift toward imposing stricter penalties, especially where there was a racial element in the alleged sexual deviance.

Legal actors continued to view sex workers with suspicion. In recognizing that there were instances when the uncorroborated testimony of a sex worker may be relied upon, the Appellate Division, ironically, further marginalized sex workers in its dicta in *R v Sibande* 1958:

> Rape upon a prostitute, for example, though it is the crime of rape, would not ordinarily call for a penalty of equal severity to that imposed for rape upon a woman of refinement and good character. *Prostitutes are not respected members of the community and, generally speaking, one does not expect them to be truthful.* But that is not to say that no prostitute ever speaks the truth; and the question you have to decide here is, was this woman speaking the truth? . . . If you are dealing with a reputable person, that person's evidence is something which you will more readily accept as being that of a truthful witness than if you are dealing with a disreputable person. *Prostitutes are disreputable people, undeniably.* (Emphasis added.)

This court decision normalized the view that sex workers were disreputable and should be viewed with suspicion by the legal system. It further normalized rape against sex workers in its flippant remarks that the rape of a prostitute is somehow less problematic than that of "a woman of refinement." This is a continuation of the discourse of sex workers as unreliable, reflecting social practices that contributed to their continued marginalization.

Resisting the Immorality/Sexual Offences Act

Despite this legal activity, previous reports had suggested that criminalization might not be the best mode for regulating sex work. As previously mentioned, a 1948 study found that "the penal measures operated by our Criminal Law in respect of both adult and juvenile prostitutes have not reduced the volume of prostitution in the progress of time, nor have they, in the majority of instances, served as a deterrent to prostitutes with previous convictions."[109] There were even reports of open defiance of sex work regulations aimed at barring interracial transactions:

> [I]n the 1950s, anthropologist Sheila Patterson noted that, "visiting ships" crews were said to frequent night-clubs and dives in the more unsavoury streets of the Coloured "District Six" in the centre of Cape Town. So the authorities tried to dissuade the seamen from such "immorality" by handing out notices to the officers of incoming ships which warned: Premises, particularly in the Coloured and Indian quarters of this city, to which contact men, pimps or taxi-drivers, hansom-cabs and rickshas may take you for liquor or women are to be avoided; you are liable to be drugged, assaulted and robbed in these places. SEXUAL INTERCOURSE between white and non-whites is a serious criminal offence in South Africa. MARRIAGE between whites and non-whites is prohibited by law.[110]

Even with the provisions of the Immorality Act that prohibited interracial sex and legal decisions that encouraged societal views that sex workers were suspicious, unreliable characters, there were still reports of White men engaging Black female sex workers during apartheid. One newspaper account details this:

> Hundreds of prostitutes are in action in Johannesburg day and night. On the streets, the ladies of pleasure are almost exclusively black . . . and their customers almost totally white. . . . A doctor with consulting rooms in Hillbrow and Berea said, "Nearly all my patients who come to me for treatment for venereal disease have contracted the illness from crossing the sexual colour line."[111]

This report both exoticized and medicalized sex with Black sex workers: it was against the racial hegemony and exposed one to a host of diseases. Some of the acts of racial defiance were quite open, as demonstrated by dockside clubs in Cape Town where Black and White patrons would intermingle.

There was continued and open sexual integration between seamen and sex workers in Cape Town docks and nightclubs during apartheid.[112]

These incidents highlight that there has always been some degree of resistance against the sexual hegemony, even during the apartheid era. In fact, there were even efforts to work toward the decriminalization of sex work. In 1975, the Transvaal Provincial Division began to poke holes in the Sexual Offences Act of 1957, holding, in the 1975 case of *State v F*, that the Act did not apply to the acts of sex workers themselves:

> The prostitute who earns money from the man with whom she has had intercourse in the brothel, or the woman who accepts money from the man upon whom she has performed some lewd or indecent act, such as pelvic massage, does not receive "moneys taken in a brothel" in the sense contemplated [by the Immorality Act].

In 1977, the Cape Town medical officer of health, Reg Coogan, the city's top health official at the time, supported the decriminalization of sex work for public health reasons, stating: "Prostitution will always be with us. If it is legalized it will be brought into the open, and allow the authorities to more effectively combat not only the occurrence and spread of VD [venereal disease], but other associated evils like pimping and blackmail."[113] In the same year, Professor Hilton Watts, head of the University of Natal's Department of Sociology, argued, "No advanced society has managed to stamp out prostitution and it is unrealistic to pretend it does not exist."[114]

In 1988, there was a parliamentary debate concerning the decriminalization of sex work. D. J. Dalling, a member of parliament for the Progressive Federal Party, argued in favor of this, largely for public health reasons:

> When one talks of immorality, of sex, of soliciting, of prostitution and the like, apart from everyone pricking their ears up there is always the argument that the law should not be tightened up at all, but that it should be relaxed, if not abolished completely. This view is bolstered by the fact that worldwide, over a period of hundreds and hundreds of years, no laws have ever succeeded in stamping out prostitution. This argument maintains, therefore, that the unequal struggle should be abandoned. It maintains that prostitution, far from being criminalized, should be legalized

and controlled, thus at least ensuring standards of health and so helping the fight against venereal diseases and against AIDS.[115]

In *State v Horn*, South Africa's highest court at the time, the Appellate Division, held that the "proper interpretation of sec 20(1)(a) [of the Sexual Offences Act confirms that it] was not intended that criminal liability should attach to the prostitute involved." This 1988 decision thereby confirmed that the activities of sex workers were not to be treated as criminal under the Sexual Offences Act, the only moment in South Africa's most recent history when sex work was unambiguously, fully decriminalized. Despite what appeared to be a wave of support toward decriminalization, the legislature responded to the Appellate Division decision with the Immorality Amendment Act of 1988, in order to clearly criminalize the actions of sex workers and any person who "has unlawful carnal intercourse, or commits an act of indecency, with any other person for reward." Thus, the practice of sex work was only firmly criminalized in South Africa by the inclusion, through this amendment, of Section 20(1)(aA) in the Sexual Offences Act in 1988.

The discourses around sex work during apartheid era were focused on its moral regulation in a racialized social order. The sex worker was most threatening where she deviated from the racialized moral order in apartheid. The penalties were harsher where there was an interracial element in the sex work relationship. This encouraged a discourse that exoticized interactions between Black female sex workers and White men and reflected subjective and racialized understandings about hygiene and bodily capital, as illustrated in the previously mentioned newspaper account about White male patrons with Black sex workers.

As I will demonstrate throughout the book, the contents of many of the discourses discussed in this chapter are very much the same. Both radical feminists who pioneer against the false consciousness of sex workers, as discussed in the final chapters, and well-intentioned public health officials who focus on sex workers as hosts for disease while ignoring the sex workers' clients, reproduce a value system that essentializes sex, treats male and female sexuality asymmetrically, and subjectively evaluates the female body. These discourses also inform the way that the members of the police organization interpret their role as protectors of human rights and enforcers of popular norms in contemporary society. This discourse-driven "policing" of sex workers, which goes beyond the mandates of the black-letter law, impacts how individual police officers interact with sex workers today. In this way officers embody legal norms as well as the discourses that influence both legal and societal norms.

POLICING SOUTH AFRICA

The South African Police Service has an extensive history of violence as the enforcement arm of the colonial and apartheid regimes: "From the start of European settlement in 1652, the country's history has been marked by a brutal, violent, struggle over land, with forcible dispossession of the indigenous population . . . [and after apartheid a] well-developed state security apparatus."[116] The colonial police forces retained a highly militarized approach because they protected "a social order and enforced a system of law based, not on the will of the indigenous population, but on that of an alien power."[117] The colonial forces tortured, coerced witnesses, and routinely used lethal force. The ad hoc colonial police forces amalgamated into the national South African Police in 1913; however, the paramilitary culture of the colonial police forces persisted following this amalgamation. The police maintained a similar command structure and relied upon many of the same abusive practices.[118] The primary goal of the police was social control. It was not a police force concerned with regulating ordinary crimes or police investigative work. This resulted in an organization ill-equipped to handle tasks thought essential to basic police work but well-charged to maintain control through paramilitary measures.[119]

With the rise of the National Party in 1948, the South African Police became the main enforcement arm of the apartheid government, and it "has been described as the 'medium through which apartheid was experienced.'" The South African Police was notoriously brutal: "Once in custody, confessions were often obtained through coercion, and torture was not uncommon."[120] These abusive practices delegitimized the police force in the eyes of many Black South Africans, and "[b]y the early 1990s, (all) the police in South Africa had acquired a reputation for brutality, corruption and ineptitude."[121] The South African Truth and Reconciliation Commission, established in 1996, reported 33,713 instances of gross human rights violations between 1960 and 1994, and noted 5,002 instances of torture (most of which appear to be connected to "non-political" crimes) during this period, attributed largely to the South African Police.[122] Many prisoners were detained and incarcerated for political reasons, and very few legal processes were used in the disposition of such prisoners.[123] It is suspected that the majority of torture victims were ordinary criminals who were incarcerated or detained by the police.[124] The remainder of this section explores how (and if) this history influences the current police organization and the challenges that organization faces in policing competently.

Despite this history of violence, the current police organization, the South African Police Service (SAPS), is today charged with enforcing the human rights laws that are part of South Africa's modern legal system. SAPS members must solve crimes with limited resources, creating order in an increasingly disorderly world, while upholding the numerous human rights standards enumerated in the Constitution of 1996. The police have an obligation to protect people's human rights while responding to the people's demands for increased violence in responding to crime. These demands for increased severity and the desire to maintain order affect how police respond to sex workers and the policing task more generally. Their own perceptions about their compensation and social status following apartheid also impact how they police sex workers. Human rights norms further influence the policing of sex workers, and also affect the police response to domestic disputes.

THE "GOOD OLD APARTHEID DAYS"

Before my interviews with individual police officers, given the brutality of apartheid-style policing, I had expected the officers to distance themselves from apartheid and make proclamations about the value of human rights. I assumed that while speaking with a Black American woman researcher, they would engage in a disingenuous, albeit necessary, performance to validate the legitimacy of police authority[125] in South Africa. But ethnographic fieldwork often defies the expectations of the researcher. Imagine my surprise when several Black police officers informed me that they missed how empowered police were during apartheid. This nostalgia toward apartheid was a reflection of their current frustrations with contemporary policing. The officers I interacted with seemed to believe that the contemporary laws, which focus on respect of human rights, interfere with their ability to police effectively. By contrast, the police power was nearly absolute during apartheid, and everyone was expected to obey the law as enforced by the police.[126] Officers frequently told me that apartheid was a "good time to be police." Police were treated with more respect then and provided with fairer compensation and benefits, according to several police officers:

> DANNY (HILLBROW POLICE OFFICER): Human rights affected policing, I will say um . . . definitely very bad because as the police . . . police hasn't got rights.
>
> INDIA: How has human rights impacted policing?
>
> SIBELA (HILLBROW POLICE OFFICER): Right now, I think it has to be balanced. Right now the police cannot do their work. I think the police are more restricted now. Without taking into account the responsibilities of a policeman. Right now, it seems the system favors the community . . . the perpetrators of crime, then the police. It is hampering their job, without thinking these people will take me to [court]. If we can balance those two: you can do this, you have the right to suppress. Now, that's my opinion. *The criminals are more protected now.* If they can relax some of the laws, there would be less crime. (Emphasis added.)

Similar sentiments were echoed by several of the police whom I interviewed. In addition, officers complained that they were not included in conversations regarding the incorporation of human rights into policing and indicated that SAPS was being managed by "comrades," or African National Congress (ANC) loyalists:

> SIBELA: I think that before apartheid ended things were better. Now things are getting worse. I got 10 years. I never got promotion. That's why the morale of the people is always done. I think the system is collapsing. For instance in the *good old days* no one would have to wait [at] one rank more than 10 years to get promoted. In the *good old days*, it was not like this. The management, we do not know what they are doing if you are not a trained policeman. The management is flooded by comrades who [are] there on

the top. They have never been policemen. The current policemen are . . . the comrades have killed the police. The management is flooded with incompetent people. At the moment because of lack of management and diminished current prospects, the morale is very down. (Emphasis added.)

Even some community members have suggested that police were more legitimate during apartheid. In a study of apartheid nostalgia in Soweto, one township resident recognized the following:

COMMUNITY MEMBER 1: The police tortured people badly. Boers hated black people. They oppressed them. . . . The apartheid police were bad but there was order and the law was obeyed. The SAP [South African Police] ensured that people were protected.

COMMUNITY MEMBER 2: The police were effective in fighting crime. Our lives were better [in] that time period than now. . . . I miss the apartheid period because we were safe at the time and when you had left your possessions they would still be there when you came back, but today, forget about it.[127]

These observations, although not necessarily representative of the opinions of all of South Africans, indicate that pockets of society believe that the apartheid police were more legitimate than their contemporary counterparts.[128] The police were respected then, by the public and by the police organization itself. Both young police officers and older police officers alike expressed nostalgia for apartheid policing.

Table 1.1 shows the perceptions of the interview participants, members of the Hillbrow and Rosebank Police Departments, on the improvement of policing since apartheid. As observed, more than half of the nineteen participants at Hillbrow perceived that policing was much better during apartheid, two perceived that the policing is the same now as then, and two perceived that the policing is much better now. At Rosebank, three of the five participants perceived that policing was much better before democracy, whereas two perceived that policing is much better now.

This fondness toward apartheid felt by the predominantly Black police officers I interviewed reflects their dilemma as the enforcers of the law in a

TABLE 1.1. Perceptions among Hillbrow and Rosebank police interviewees of improvement in policing since apartheid.

	MUCH BETTER THEN		SAME		MUCH BETTER NOW		NONE STATED		TOTAL	
	n	*(%)*	*n*	*(%)*	*n*	*(%)*	*n*	*(%)*	*n*	*(%)*
Hillbrow	11	(57.9)	2	(10.5)	2	(10.5)	4	(21.1)	19	(100)
Rosebank	3	(60.0)	0	(0.0)	2	(40.0)	0	(0.0)	5	(100)

world they perceived to be increasingly disorganized and full of terror. These police officers appeared to view apartheid with fondness because they believed that the contemporary human rights agenda was an obstacle to effective policing. During apartheid, heavy-handedness was rewarded and often expected. Now, human rights require that even criminals be afforded due process and protection of their human rights. Several of these officers indicated that they felt the human rights agenda was thrust upon them, and they blamed it for their problems:

> APRIL (HILLBROW POLICE OFFICER): You see the criminal has got the power to kill. The police don't have the power to kill the criminal. When they are arrested, they have killed a person; they have got the right to a lawyer. They have got the right to everything. . . . How does the rights come into someone who took someone's life? There must be a right there. You know, you have got limitation of using the firearm; we don't use them because every time you use it, they charge you, and therefore it limits us. Every time you are at a crime scene or you are confronting a suspect, you will think twice when you have to shoot that suspect. You will think, if I can shoot him then I will be arrested.
>
> INDIA: What are some of the challenges that have occurred since the end of apartheid with regard to policing?
>
> APRIL: What I can say is that the law that they are bringing to the police, we don't get consulted; even if we've got unions, it seems the union and the government are doing the same thing together. Excluding us, because whatever happens, they just inform us.

Current police officers indicated that during apartheid, police were able to effectuate their task with absolute public compliance. However, apartheid police were under great threat and frequently faced an antagonistic public. This nostalgia for apartheid was more a commentary on the present challenges in policing than a recollection of the past reality of what it meant to be a police officer, particularly a Black police officer, during apartheid.[129] According to the current officers, community members are now disrespectful and unwilling to understand the challenges associated with policing. "They have rights now," one officer stated while reminiscing about apartheid.

Furthermore, dissatisfaction among the police regarding their salaries, benefits, and opportunities for further education, while policing what they perceive as increasing disorder, is also relevant in understanding why corruption, brutality, and poor service occur during the policing of sex workers and why the police I spoke with appeared to genuinely miss apartheid. They argued that during apartheid, police earned living wages and were treated with respect. However, this belief may be based more on a mythology of what it meant to be a member of the police during apartheid than on reality.[130] Table 1.2 presents the perceptions of police officers on whether they deserve a higher salary. Almost all the interview participants perceived that they deserved a higher salary; only one officer, from the Hillbrow police station, did not think a higher salary was deserved.

Police officers were paid adequately during apartheid and therefore, the interview participants argued, were less likely to be tempted to engage in corrupt practices and exploit sex work clients and sex workers for bribes. However, current police salaries are similar to those of teachers, nurses, and firefighters.[131] Police officers are clearly within the ranks of the middle class in South Africa. But becoming a member of the police during apartheid, especially for Black officers, was associated with a middle-class lifestyle that would not otherwise be available to them. Black police officers may now see the lifestyles that Black businessmen and Black doctors enjoy, and may feel a sense of

TABLE 1.2. Responses of Hillbrow and Rosebank police interviewees to the question: Do you feel you deserve a higher salary?

	VERY MUCH		NOT AT ALL		TOTAL	
	n	*(%)*	*n*	*(%)*	*n*	*(%)*
Hillbrow	18	(94.7)	1	(5.3)	19	(100)
Rosebank	5	(100.0)	0	(0.0)	5	(100)

lack. In Johannesburg, there is an open culture of consumption and an "aesthetic of plentitude"[132] that may foster this feeling of lack in these officers. Police would discuss their cars and houses with me, complaining how expensive it was to maintain their BMWs. They were in the trap of keeping up with their peers and associated their feelings of lack with the changes brought about by democracy. This fondness toward apartheid necessitates some reflection on the evolution of the South African policing organization in and of itself.

REFORMING THE POLICE ORGANIZATION

The apartheid police were notorious for their excessive use of force during public demonstrations, and "the brutality and violence with which the SAP fulfilled its mandate—supplemented by the work of the homelands police forces—was notorious."[133] Women were particularly exposed to gendered violence during apartheid. Domestic violence was viewed as an incident of the private realm and more of a family matter than an issue for the police to address. Women were subjected to specialized forms of gender violence and torture at the hands of the apartheid police. For example, during a public Truth and Reconciliation Commission hearing, Zanele Zingxindo testified that she had experienced sexual torture during a police interrogation.[134]

During the political negotiations of the early 1990s, there was a conscious effort to eliminate the police's legacy of violence, which was part of the fabric of the SAP.[135] There was a new policy mandate to shift the police force from an organization rooted in authoritarianism to a democratic organization that respected human rights. It was a change from absolutist control to service-oriented police delivery. Janine Rauch describes these efforts to reform the police organization, following Nelson Mandela's release from prison:

> At the time of Nelson Mandela's release from prison in 1990, there were 11 police forces in South Africa, each constituted under its own piece of legislation, and operating within its own jurisdiction. The largest of these was the South African Police (SAP) with approximately 112 000 members, the other 10 were the "homeland" police forces. Among these, the most significant group was the police agencies of the four "independent homelands"—Transkei, Bophuthatswana, Venda and Ciskei.[136]

By 1991, SAP was amalgamating into one large police force and had adopted a new strategic plan. The 1991 SAP Strategic Plan had six main foci:

- depoliticization of the police force
- increased community accountability
- more visible policing
- establishment of improved and effective management practices
- reform of the police training system (including some racial integration)
- restructuring of the police force.[137]

It was also around this time that the name of the police force was changed to the South African Police Service (SAPS), to demonstrate that this force would now serve the people. Various human rights documents and norms were adopted to transform the police institution into one that would protect and respect human rights. There was great optimism about the changes being made to the police organization.[138] The Minister of Safety and Security, Fholisani Sydney Mufamadi, acknowledged that the police had made great strides in reforming the organization.[139] As Piers Pigou notes:

> With the new political dispensation there has been a clear development of policy towards ensuring that policing in South Africa is conducted in a manner consistent with human rights and democratic values. This process has been multi-faceted in nature and has been underpinned by the adoption of a Bill of Rights, the establishment of a South African Police Service (SAPS) in 1995 and the implementation of a human rights training curriculum in basic police training. A civilian-controlled monitoring and investigative body known as the Independent Complaints Directorate (ICD), tasked with investigating allegations of police abuse, was also established. In addition, and largely in response to ongoing allegations of abuse, the SAPS introduced a "Prevention of Torture" policy . . . in 1998/99.[140]

The police organization appeared to be evolving (at least on a formal level) into a more diverse organization with leadership reflecting the racial and ethnic background of the population.[141]

But this soon changed following the next round of democratic elections, in 1999. During the transitional years, South Africa faced a high crime rate, which was denounced by the media and by a public growing impatient with the police response to crime.[142] The apartheid police force had actually been quite small and incompetent at policing ordinary crime, a legacy that continued through the transition to democracy.[143] The task of expanding that relatively small police force into one that could manage South Africa's high crime rate proved challenging.[144] Moreover, the public demanded that the police be more forceful in managing crime, while the police were simultaneously reforming into an organization that aimed to use less force. As policing scholar Julia Hornberger has observed:

> [A]s the law is shaped by popular desire, influences directed against its formal nature come to inhabit it from within. As South African desires for a forceful state materialise in the rise of more forceful policing, this kind of policing disproportionately targets the very people whose insecurity has led them to be invested in much more immediate forms of violence.[145]

The perception of increased crime encouraged the adoption of practices that deviated from the models centered on human rights policing from the transitional era. Consequently, the police organization resorted to the use of torture, corruption, and excessive force in response to these contemporary demands.[146] There is a theater of policing that occurs in the imagination of the public, and which plays out in the media, sensationalizing (in)justice. It creates the perception of increasing disorder. Jean and John Comaroff recognized that "the specter of illegality [appeared to be] captivating popular imaginations" shortly after the turn to democracy.[147] The South African population began demanding that more heavy-handed policing tactics be adopted.[148] These demands have been complicated by the changing power relations that the human rights era has brought.

POLICING POWER

Police officers were frustrated by their compensation. They were also frustrated by their limited ability to advance within the police organization. Although they were largely content with being police officers, they felt intense pressure to earn additional income to support their families. This pressure was likely spurred by their perceptions of how they should be living and expectations of a middle-class lifestyle.[149] These police officers' frustrations about contemporary policing can be understood through the shifting power relations occurring in the democratic era. Foucault argues that "power must be understood . . . as the multiplicity of force relations immanent in the sphere in which they [police] operate and which constitute their own organization." Assertions of power may resist particular norms or adopt them superficially.[150] Foucault also establishes the omnipresence of power, writing that "power is everywhere; not because it embraces everything, but because it comes from everywhere. . . . Power is not an institution, and not a structure; neither is it a certain strength we are endowed with; it is the name that one attributes to a complex strategical situation in a particular society."[151]

Facially, human rights appear to strip the police of much of their power by placing limitations on police conduct. However, human rights also empower police by rendering them enforcers of human rights and, therefore, guardians of human rights. As Julia Hornberger comments: "These shifts have altered the relationship of the police to human rights, especially in the area of the positive duty of the state. They meant, first, that policing had to be transformed through human rights and, second, that policing would now have a central role to play in transforming society."[152] The human rights discourse aims to create a particular social order with preservation and enforcement of certain rights. However, police may adopt the human rights lexicon without fully embracing its norms, creating a "frontstage" where human rights norms are performed, and a "backstage" where human rights constraints are ignored.[153] "[T]he engagement with human rights discourse [therefore] transforms the subjects and their possibilities for a particular kind of meaningful practice at the same time that the subjects reshape the discourse and the field of practice."[154] Human rights therefore become a strategy for police to exercise their power, particularly when embracing human rights terminology while continuing to engage in conduct that violates human rights norms. The police organization has retained its power through its "complex strategical position"[155] in society and ability to adopt the prevailing vocabulary of human rights without wholly altering its own practices and strategies.

This superficial embrace of human rights does not require that the police enforce human rights norms in their entirety. To the contrary, as Monique Marks has recognized, "police organizational change" is difficult.[156] Thus, the rules may appear to change, but the practical significance of such change is undermined by practices that violate human rights norms. In Hornberger's words, "Human rights thus can best be described as technologies of the self and knowledge practices about law rather than a legal practice per se."[157] The contemporary police can perform human rights by acknowledging them and adopting their vernacular, but can also hybridize them by selectively enforcing them,[158] ensuring that police power remains constant even when it appears to be limited by the adoption of human rights.

This form of human rights policing, which does not fully embrace human rights norms in practice, may be understood through the history of policing in South Africa. As discussed earlier, heavy-handedness and violence, though ultimately rejected, were part of the very nature of policing. "Violence became a currency" through which undesirable conduct was punished.[159] Society in general consequently holds its own views about the extent to which violence can be used by the police, views undoubtedly connected to conditioning to practices of the past. The bar against which what is normal for policing is measured is fraught with violence.[160] The police are faced with the unique challenge of enforcing and respecting human rights while struggling to reduce excessively high rates of violent crime.[161] During the course of my fieldwork, I witnessed how frustrations toward crime and limited resources manifest in excessive police practices.[162]

I observed frustrated community members demanding that the police respond aggressively to those who had wronged them, and police as they walked the fine line of legal physical force against arrestees. For example, on February 14, 2014, while waiting to join a police patrol at the Hillbrow police station, I idly watched as police officers tortured an arrestee by using his handcuffs to cut off his circulation. The arrestee had a thick Nigerian accent and was a physically fit man in his late 20s to early 30s. I watched this adult man squirm on the Hillbrow police station floor, crying for officers to release him. I watched as he cried for his God as his hands slowly changed from a red color to blue and then purple. His accusers stood behind at the service counters, apparently pleased by this scene. They spoke in Zulu and English to the officer who was taking their complaint. During the course of providing the details for their complaint, they pointed to the arrestee in disgust and righteous indignation. I watched this scene, pretending to be unaffected, for approximately twenty minutes; after which time, the officers dragged the arrestee to a separate area because he was crying too loudly. Several officers walked past the arrestee nonchalantly during this time and behaved as if this were a routine occurrence. Even the best-intentioned human rights documents were unable to fully penetrate the halls of this police station. This act of police violence against the arrestee, as repugnant as it was, was arguably being used to maintain order and to instill confidence in the complainants that they could trust the police would dole out justice as necessary. In a sense, police were exercising their power to enforce the victims' human rights through this act of violence. Although they rejected human rights in practice in this instance, they were able to claim that they were enforcing human rights through their act of violence. They were doling out justice on behalf of victims, albeit extrajudicially.

Violence is inherent to the process of governing, and police violence is hardly unusual. As Walter Benjamin has stated, "law-making is power-making, assumption of power, and to that extent an immediate manifestation of violence."[163] Police violence can thus be seen as a form of law-preserving violence in its quashing of social disorder. The violence carried forth by members of the police reinforces the law and strengthens the existing regime. Violence is a means for asserting and reaffirming the existing power structures and is not in and of itself a violation of law; it is rather an expression of the law. Understood as such, police violence is rational.[164] Incidents of police violence after apartheid are not contrary to the democratic order; they seek to strengthen it. Faced with excessive crime and few resources, police often turn to violence to preserve order and law. The law-preserving function of police violence is both a violation of human rights norms and a preserver of human rights as state law. This tension is most explicit when human rights become state law as they have in South Africa.

By their very mandate, police are called upon to maintain law, and the exercise of violence in that task is, by definition, law preserving.[165] However, this conceptualization of law preservation is frustrated within a human rights regime. The act of (unjustified) police violence in some ways perverts the law that it seeks to protect. Human rights law places limitations on police acts and creates competing legal interests—the interest in preserving social order through the law and the interest in protecting individual rights entitlements.[166] Police violence becomes both law-preserving and law-perverting under a human rights framework. With this in mind, it is hardly surprising that police would view apartheid with some nostalgia. The explicitly law-sanctioned violence of apartheid empowered police and allowed them to carry out their task with no interference from human rights mandates. Apartheid police violence was solely law-preserving. In a human rights regime, this law-preserving violence becomes complicated by the competing requirement to respect the integrity of the individual. Human rights have in many ways, in this respect, prevented police from effectively policing.

The issue then becomes whether the imperatives of human rights should trump the police interests of preserving law. The concept of human rights presupposes the existence of rights that transcend the law. While human rights may dictate and create legal standards, their very essence, it is argued by natural law scholars, predates law and is inherent to the human being. In this regard, human rights cannot be curtailed by the state because the state does not allocate such rights and therefore has no authority over them.[167] In a society that accepts this understanding of human rights, certain rights cannot be violated even when doing so would carry forth the mandates of the existing law. The law is limited by the existence of these rights. Accordingly, police violence becomes a law-breaking exercise that serves to frustrate rights that have their origin outside the that law.[168] This is particularly so within a human rights regime because it violates human rights to life, dignity of person, and integrity of body. In this way, police violence both breaks the law and preserves it. This tension becomes clear when considering the different manners in which sex workers are policed and how rules around public decency influence police attempts to respect sex workers' human rights. On the one hand, the law indicates that sex work is illegal conduct. Yet on the other hand, police are required to protect sex workers' human rights. This is further complicated by police leadership statements in some police stations that have been interpreted as decriminalizing sex work, as well as competing with, and at times contradicting, discourses that shape police officers' understandings around how sex workers should be policed, in the broad sense of that word. The police justify their approach by vernacularizing human rights to fit into the police context and particular police understandings of human rights mandates.

HUMAN RIGHTS: LEGAL AND POLICY FRAMEWORK

A full understanding of the human rights element of policing in South Africa requires also understanding the international and domestic human rights framework.[169] The Constitution of the Republic of South Africa, established in 1996, is the supreme law of the country, and it sets out several principles intended to restrict the state's ability to infringe upon everyone's rights.[170] While the Constitution is the supreme law, there is also an explicit recognition of the relevance of international law in South Africa. South African courts may turn to the law of other countries, making use of comparative law, where that might help in interpreting the provisions of the Constitution.[171] Consequently, both domestic constitutional and international legal standards determine how state institutions *should* behave in a paradigm that supports human rights.

South Africa must prevent discrimination on the basis of sex, as required by Article 2 of the Convention on the Elimination of All Forms of Discrimination against Women (CEDAW) and by Article 2 of the Protocol to the African Charter on Human and Peoples' Rights on the Rights of Women in Africa. CEDAW requires governments to repeal "all national penal provisions which constitute discrimination against women." These provisions provide guidance in understanding how the police as an institution should relate to women. The International Convention on the Elimination of All Forms of Racial Discrimination (ICERD) is also instructive in its guideline that states: "Take effective measures to review governmental, national and local policies, and to amend, rescind or nullify any laws and regulations which have the effect of creating or perpetuating racial discrimination wherever it exists."[172] These two conventions read together could be further read as instructing states to especially protect women of color, who may be exposed to both racial and gender discrimination.

ICERD is generally not discussed in the context sex workers' rights. However, the sex workers in Johannesburg are overwhelmingly Black women, many of whom are migrants. Their intersectional identities expose them to additional risks, and they should receive protections that keep this in mind. For example, I discuss in chapter 4 how the spatial organization of sex workers within geographical areas is reflected in material expectations of their beauty, which are in turn tied to perceptions of their ethnic identities. This spatial organization at times has led to further marginalization for certain sex workers. Furthermore, foreign-born migrant sex workers may be subject to additional vulnerabilities through xenophobic attitudes that further marginalize them. The policing of these women should theoretically ensure that they are free from discrimination and able to enforce their human rights by calling upon the police for assistance. Amnesty International has issued international guidance stating that a human rights approach to sex work requires that it be decriminalized.[173] This guidance adopts an intersectional analysis that recognizes the unique positionalities of multiple sex workers in calling for sex work decriminalization.[174]

In addition to the stipulations of international conventions, the Constitution of South Africa requires that sex workers not encounter sex or gender discrimination. Chapter 2 (the Bill of Rights), Section 9, prohibits discrimination owing to "race, gender, sex, pregnancy, marital status, ethnic or social origin." The Constitutional Court has expanded the gender component of this provision, stating that "[s]exual violence and the threat of sexual violence goes to the core of women's subordination in society. It is the single greatest threat to the self-determination of women."[175] Section 9 consequently pertains to the direct discrimination that women may face because of their sex as well as from non-action by the state when it fails to reasonably respond to crimes that have a sexual violence component. Section 9 thus requires police to refrain from discriminating against sex workers not only because of their gender identity and expressions but also because of their race and ethnic origin. It further requires police to act when sex workers may be facing a threat of violence because of gender. This is especially important, because sex workers may rely upon police for assistance when they face client violence. Accordingly, police should respect sex workers' human dignity, refrain from arbitrarily detaining sex workers and sex work clients, and protect sex workers against gender discrimination and violence.

Police are also required to protect sex workers' right to dignity. The state's obligation to respect everyone's "right to dignity" is enshrined in Chapter 2, Section 10, of the Constitution. This section is intended to ensure that the state does not violate the core of an individual's humanity and that it shows a basic respect for human beings.[176] In the context of policing sex workers, police are expected to not only embrace this right but also protect sex workers against violations of their right to dignity. The right to dignity is especially relevant to the policing of sex workers, in that sex workers have long been treated as unreliable and unhygienic, as discussed earlier in this chapter and as reflected in the various discourses about sex workers. This has contributed to deeply ingrained values that question whether sex workers can be viewed as dignified or otherwise worthy of dignity. The inclusion of this right in the Constitution indicates that everyone is entitled to dignity. However, there is tension in understanding what it means for police to respect and enforce sex workers' right to dignity when the police, as individuals, may view sex workers as unhygienic and undignified.

Chapter 2, Section 12, of the Constitution requires state institutions to respect individuals' right to freedom and security of person.[177] This right prohibits state actors from unlawfully detaining individuals or otherwise depriving them of liberty. It requires police to ensure that sex workers are not "deprived of freedom arbitrarily," are "not to be tortured in any way," and are "free from all forms of violence." It is particularly relevant in considering how SAPS has used detention as a form of coercion and as a tool of punishment against sex workers. This section explicitly prohibits police from using arrests as a tool for arbitrarily detaining sex workers, and affirmatively requires that the police protect sex workers' bodily security from torture and violence. It has motivated police to stop the wholesale detention of sex workers, in order to respect sex workers' human rights.[178] Statutory provisions concerning the use of force further limit the police. The Criminal Procedure Act of 1977 contains several provisions that dictate how police should effect arrests, treat detainees, and interact with civilians. Section 49 of the Criminal Procedure Act outlines the manner in which police officers may use force to effect an arrest against a person suspected of committing a crime. Police may use force that is "reasonably necessary and proportional in the circumstances to overcome the resistance or to prevent the suspect from fleeing," but instances that fall outside this provision are extra-legal and considered to be police brutality. Thus police are limited in how they use force against sex workers as well sex work clients. The South African Police Service Act also regulates police action. Section 13 of this Act states: "Where a member who performs an official duty is authorized by law to use force, he or she may use only the minimum force which is reasonable in the circumstances." Common law principles also limit police conduct. The common law prohibits assault, assault with grievous bodily harm, and rape. Police officers who engage in these activities are acting outside the scope of their duties and may be prosecuted for engaging in criminal activity.

These legal reforms were intended to radically reform South African institutions by means of incorporating human rights norms through constitutionally established rights and statutory restrictions. Many of these reforms were instituted with a specific eye toward the police institution, given its history of human rights abuses and apartheid enforcement.[179] SAPS has, further, adopted a human rights training manual, "to provide information and training on how to police in line with International Human Rights principles and the South African Constitution."[180] This addition to police training has presumably influenced how police view their role of policing in a democracy and may explain why several officers complained that human rights limited their ability to police effectively. SAPS has a policy against torture that states: "No member may torture any person, permit anyone else to do so, or tolerate the torture of another by anyone."[181] These legal norms are intended to radically reform the police and create an institution with a culture that embraces human rights.

However, legal reforms are often inadequate when it comes to changing existing attitudes, culture, and the manner in which policing actually occurs.[182] More importantly, it must be in the interests and capacity of the police to carry forth their tasks while adopting these new norms. Although the police may embrace human rights in form, practicing human rights is very different. These policies have in many ways changed the human rights discourse among police and enabled them to adopt a rights-based terminology even in the exercise of rights violations. As Julia Hornberger says: "In South Africa, this has taken the form of using human rights as a shield that works by deflecting criticism and hiding behind it a much more violent and *bricolage* kind of practice."[183] As I detail in later chapters, police frequently adopt human rights terminology to explain their own conduct when it is decidedly outside the parameters of the law. Adopting such language appears to be a mechanism for legitimizing their conduct within a human rights regime. Embracing human rights language without fully embracing the underlying principles allows practices that are inconsistent with human rights principles to persist. It creates a fundamental disconnect between what is said and what is done.

POLICING SEXUALIZED VIOLENCE

The policing of sex workers is a particularly gendered form of policing. Following the new political dispensation, there was a move toward increased enforcement of horizontal rights. In general, governmental actors are barred from barring the constitutional rights of private parties. Horizontality refers to the application of constitutional rights when a private party violates the constitutional rights of another private party.[184] The shift toward horizontal application of constitutional norms provided a passageway for police to regulate private relationships. Police were increasingly required to protect the people from themselves. The police play an integral role in this form of rights enforcement because they have an affirmative duty to protect the public and a particular duty to protect women from violence. Section 12(1)(c) of the Constitution provides everyone with the right to be free from violence in his or her private and public relationships. This constitutional norm provided the foundation for jurisprudence outlining the police obligation to protect women from private violence, as well as for the 1998 enactment of the Domestic Violence Act (DVA). This requirement that police enforce rights horizontally should influence how police respond to sex worker complaints concerning client abuse. It creates an affirmative obligation to protect sex workers in such circumstances and is an entry point for mediating what may be thought of as a domestic relationship in a private space.

The DVA came into operation on December 15, 1999. The Preamble of this Act states that "there is a high incidence of domestic violence within South African society; that victims of domestic violence are amongst the most vulnerable members of society; that domestic violence takes on many forms; that acts of domestic violence may be committed in a wide range of domestic relationships." During the transition from apartheid to democracy, serious lapses were found in officer training on domestic violence law. A Natal survey found that only 60 percent of station commanders knew about the Prevention of Family Violence Act, the predecessor of the DVA.[185] A key innovation of the DVA was its conception of police as social workers. The DVA places an obligation on police to inform complainants that the police are there to provide any assistance that may be necessary, including finding a shelter for the complainant and/or other social services.[186] The police must inform the complainant of his or her right to a protection order and then provide a notice to the complainant. The SAPS national commissioner must submit a report to Parliament detailing complaints of police failure to comply with the mandates of the Act. Police failure to uphold the Act or its regulations must also be reported to the Independent Complaints

Directorate, a civilian oversight body. As Michelle Govender has observed: "previously, where women were beaten by their non-marital partners police were hesitant to intrude because of the wall between the public and private spheres."[187] Indeed, the police were previously viewed as major impediments to the prevention of domestic violence overall.[188] The new safeguards were intended to ensure that police would not treat instances of domestic violence as matters to be resolved privately. This approach is relevant because understandings about private and public shape how the police approach sex work.[189] Requiring police intervention in private spaces strengthens the role of the police in mediating the relationship between sex workers and their clients.

In a series of cases, modern courts have recognized that the police have an affirmative duty to protect women against violence.[190] The case law indicates that police are now expected to play a more hands-on role in the protection of women's rights in domestic disputes. Accordingly, police are expected to assist sex workers when they have domestic disputes, including disputes that involve clients.[191] As police become more involved in the intimate and private sphere, they bring their own interpretations of the ways in which social relations should occur in this space. As will be illuminated in this book, police officers' interpretations of what is appropriate in private spaces contribute to how those police treat sex workers.

CONTEMPORARY POLICING OF SEX WORK

The policing of sex workers is a peculiar and particular type of gendered policing that is further influenced by additional norms around gender and sexuality. Following the new political dispensation in 1994, there were significant efforts to decriminalize sex work, and the discourse around sex work also focused on the question of decriminalization. Nonetheless, sex work still remains criminalized in South Africa under the 1957 Sexual Offences Act, through the 1988 Immorality Amendment Act, Section 12A(1). This legislation criminalizes the act of both the sex worker and the client[192] who employs him or her. However, because the Sexual Offences Act is rather difficult to enforce, sex workers are rarely prosecuted under this Act. Rather, sex workers are more frequently prosecuted under various municipal ordinances and legislation, such as loitering and public disturbance regulations. Police also use loitering regulations and other highly discretionary public disorder ordinances to detain sex workers. This practice is consistent with the way sex work has historically been policed in South Africa—as a public nuisance violation.[193] The Sexual Offences Act may nonetheless legitimize the regulation of sex workers by providing police officers with a moral bargaining chip, a way of explaining why this population should be subject to special surveillance. In this way, even where legislation is unable to directly achieve its aims by leading to more instances of a particular type of prosecution, it is still able to do so indirectly by providing moral currency through delegitimizing the activities of a particular group.

In Gauteng, the province where Johannesburg is located, there have been many false starts in the movement to decriminalize sex work. In 1997, Gauteng adopted a proposal to begin discussions about decriminalizing sex work.[194] Provincial Safety and Security Minister Jesse Duarte had commissioned a report, which was then recommended to the province. He noted that "[t]here is considerable consensus among non-governmental organizations in Gauteng that we should begin to talk about decriminalizing prostitution."[195] The proposal met resistance, however. The House Group, a women's nongovernmental organization (NGO) based in Hillbrow, vehemently opposed any proposal that would decriminalize sex work, stating, "It is our assumption that both 'problems' [prostitution and sex trafficking] arise from unwillingness to protect the citizens of this country from the depravity of a small number"—an argument relying on a morality-based discourse to oppose decriminalization.[196] Gauteng government officials hoped the Gauteng proposal would influence the national government in reforming the Sexual Offences Act. However, sex work remained criminalized by legislation even after the adoption of this provincial proposal.

The South African Law Reform Commission began examining reforms to the Sexual Offences Act in 1999.[197] A 2002 Law Commission issue paper explored the possibilities for reforming the treatment of sex work and whether the policing of that work should change. It ultimately called for revisions of the Sexual Offences Act and included the possibility of decriminalization or legalization of sex work.[198] Despite this and several other efforts to decriminalize sex work in South Africa, none has yet resulted in the repeal of the relevant provisions of the Sexual Offences Act.[199] Nonetheless, the more recent political climate of openly discussing the possibility of

decriminalizing sex work has in some manner resulted in de facto decriminalization. As discussed in the Introduction, the regulation of sex work does
not appear to be a police priority. The Office of the State Attorney issued
the following statement concerning the criminalization of sex work in South
Africa in 1997:

> [T]he Department of Justice has presently not announced policy with
> regard to the decriminalization of prostitution or sex work. What has be-
> come clear, however is a general move towards the decriminalization of
> less serious offences. If one looks at the attorneys-general, it is clear that
> the decriminalisation of acts around sex work has already started.[200]

During the early period following democracy, some courts displayed flexibility in considering how sex work should be policed. In 2002, the Supreme
Court of Appeal rejected the government's attempt to prosecute a brothel
under the Sexual Offences Act, stating, in *National Director of Public Prosecutions v R. O. Cook Properties (Pty) Ltd.*, that there was a lack of evidence.[201]
The alleged brothel owner stated that any acts of indecency that occurred
on the property were acts of private indecency, and the court commented,
"We in contemporary South Africa do not seek windows into other persons'
souls," implicitly recognizing the importance of allowing privacy within the
private sphere, even where sex work is involved. In *State v Jordan*, the con-
stitutionality of the Sexual Offences Act was challenged. The Constitutional
Court of South Africa rejected the challenge to the legislation, reasoning that
the legislature was within its powers in criminalizing the act of prostitution
because prostitution was associated with social ills, such as violence, child
trafficking, and drug abuse.[202] An amendment to the Act was subsequently
passed to explicitly criminalize the actions of the sex workers' clients. The
Court further questioned whether sex work was compatible with the right
to dignity, providing a morality-based judgment on the legitimacy of sex for
work. This case illustrates how courts have become the primary arbiters of
morality in the constitutional era, taking it upon themselves to assess the
social evils of sex work.

Courts have also been critical in ensuring that sex workers' rights are
protected despite the illegality of their work. In 2008, the Supreme Court of
Appeal confirmed a brothel owner's conviction for the rape of sex workers

working under his employ, rejecting the argument that a sex worker's "willingness to dress in lingerie and take part in training was proof of her consent for him to have sexual intercourse with her."[203] The court further noted that even though the sex workers "voluntarily went to the [brothel], this did not mean that this was a license for their dignity and integrity to be violated at will by the appellant."[204] This decision illustrates that despite the illegality of sex work, employers must respect sex workers' rights.

In *Kylie v Commission for Conciliation, Mediation, and Arbitration*, the Labour Appeal Court of South Africa held that the Labour Relations Act applies to sex workers. The court reasoned:

> The fact that prostitution is rendered illegal does not, for the reasons advanced in this judgment, destroy all the constitutional protection which may be enjoyed by someone as appellant, were they not to be a sex worker. . . . By extension from section 23(1), the LRA [Labor Relations Act] ensures that an employer respects these rights within the context of an employment relationship. Expressed differently, public policy based on the foundational values of the Constitution does not deem it necessary that these rights be taken away from appellant for the purposes of the Act to be properly implemented.[205]

Nonetheless, the contemporary policing of sex workers in South Africa is, in some respects, very individualized and particular, with some police stations forgoing the policing of sex work entirely, while others continue to police it strictly.

Some courts have adopted a more conservative analysis when evaluating the enforcement of the Sexual Offences Act. In *National Director of Public Prosecutions v Lorna M. B.*, a Durban court forfeited property that was used as a brothel. The prosecution coaxed a sex worker into accepting money from a detective posing as a client and then used the presence of condoms as proof of sex work.[206] The court proclaimed: "I hope that the message will go out to other brothel keepers and also to the respondent, that their conduct would not be tolerated by courts."[207] In 2008, the High Court in Pretoria confirmed the government's request to forfeit property determined to be a brothel, proclaiming the court's views on brothel keeping and prostitution in *National Director of Public Prosecution v Geyser:*

And there can be little doubt, to my mind, that brothel-keeping would be seen by a majority in society, if not society as a whole, as morally more reprehensible than operating unregistered gaming machines. Brothel-keepers, as mentioned, commit their own offence and aid in the commission of the prostitutes' offence. In doing so, they themselves earn an income from prostitution.[208]

In these decisions, the judges have acted as the moral arbiters of contemporary times, asserting as fact the morally reprehensible nature of sex work. Even the Constitutional Court, in its decision in *State v Jordan*, appeared to assume that the current dangers in the working conditions for some sex workers are inherent in the nature of sex work itself. This conflict between the questioned morality of sex work (inherent victimization and the righteousness of it) and the desire to promote human rights (preventing rights violations and respecting individual agency) appears to be at the heart of current debates on sex work. This tension has resulted in unevenness in the manner in which sex work is policed. Sex work is primarily treated as a public nuisance violation, which, as mentioned earlier, has generally always been the case in South Africa.

Recently, there has been a renewed emphasis on the decriminalization of sex work in South Africa. In May of 2013, the South African Commission for Gender Equality called for the decriminalization of sex work, stating, "We believe it is the only viable approach to promoting and protecting the dignity and rights of sex workers."[209] On November 14, 2014, the Gauteng legislature hosted a Provincial Commercial Sex Workers Dialogue to open a conversation with sex workers.[210] There have been additional calls from NGOs such as SWEAT (Sex Workers Education and Advocacy Taskforce) and Sonke Gender Justice for decriminalization, as well as from advocacy organizations working on HIV/AIDS.[211] Despite this, both the South African Law Reform Commission (SALRC) and the South African government appear to be reluctant to take a decision and move forward. The official law reform process started in the SALRC in the 1990s; however, in a long-awaited report, the SALRC supported the continued criminalization of sex work in 2017.[212] In 2019, Human Rights Watch and SWEAT published a report advocating for the decriminalization of sex work in South Africa, and the activism to decriminalize sex work persists.[213]

While sex work remains criminal despite these various attempts to decriminalize it, these discourses about decriminalization have contributed to de facto decriminalization in many parts of Johannesburg. This current tolerance of sex work has a continuity with the colonial treatment of sex work that tolerated it, so long as there was no public nuisance involved. However, the public health and contagious diseases discourses continue to emerge during police encounters when police question the cleanliness and hygiene of sex work. The police must implement legal norms that require that they enter the domestic sphere to ensure that sex workers' human rights are protected. Yet, given the violent past of the police and the explicit nostalgia concerning how this past has emboldened the police, there are contradictions in how human rights law is embodied in the policing of sex workers in Johannesburg. The following ethnographic chapters reveal how de facto decriminalization complicates the relationship between police and sex workers.

2 | MAPPING THE POLICING OF SEX WORK

THE POLICING OF sex work in Johannesburg appears to be highly localized, creating a complex sex work geography shaped by informal and formal police directives. Former Deputy Minister of Police Makhotso Magdeline Sotyu has stated: "[A]s Police Leadership, we will not tolerate police that continue to harass and abuse sex workers. Failure to rebuke violation of human rights will surely send a confusing message to police that police brutality will continue to go unpunished."[1] Such statements have encouraged several police station commanders to adopt a discretionary policy of decriminalizing sex work in their areas. The sex work geography in Johannesburg includes the members of the SAPS, the members of the Johannesburg Metropolitan Police Department ("Metro police"),[2] private security services personnel, female sex workers, transgender sex workers, South African-born and migrant workers, and clients running the economic gamut.

In general, sex work appears to be tolerated in Johannesburg, so long as it occurs on the police's terms. This is not inherently problematic, but it becomes problematic where the police fail to exercise restraint in creating the terms of these implied contracts with sex workers. The geography of sex work is socially produced and dialogic with understandings of the policing of public and private spaces. As Teela Sanders argues, "the space in which prostitution is advertised, negotiated and administered is an integral part of why and how prostitution happens in certain streets of cities and towns. [That space] is not a haphazard or neutral locale in the urban landscape."[3] The criminalization of sex work, and the corresponding policing of that criminalized work, has a tremendous impact on the spatial patterns and migration of sex workers.[4] Critical geographer Philip Howell argues that the policing of sex workers has often included deliberate efforts to "remove women as far as possible from the public streets and to enclose them in specified spaces of sexual exchange. The intention was to domesticate prostitutional activity, to privatize its geography at the same time as it brought it under public regulation."[5] Howell describes the resulting sex work geography as a "coherent system of spatial organization,"[6] dictated by understandings of public and private. This spatial organization is, in part, driven by a police force's expectations of the public and the private and the forms of sexuality that can be appropriately expressed in this continuum of spaces.[7] In many respects, policing sex work is a fool's errand: despite countless efforts to curtail sex work through the centuries, sex work has never been successfully eradicated,[8] yet, as discussed in chapter 1, it has consistently remained the object of direct morality-driven policing. As Phil Hubbard recognizes, space "is constantly produced and remade within complex relations of culture, power and difference,"[9] including ideas of appropriate sexual behavior. The shift toward increased horizontality and policing of private relationships[10] directly places police in the center of even the most private of relationships. The police in South Africa have always been involved in the regulation of sex work to some extent.[11] However, the move to further include police in traditionally private spaces through the enactment of the Domestic Violence Act and the horizontal application of constitutional rights provides them with additional legitimacy to police sex workers.

Although Lisa Sanchez argues that the "separation of public and private spheres is largely a product of the liberal imagination and its subordinating practices,"[12] whether real or imagined, conceptions of the private versus the public dictate how police treat sex workers, sex work, and the bodily capital and hygiene of sex workers. The *Oxford English Dictionary* defines *public* as "done, perceived, or existing in open view." *Private* is defined as "involving only a particular person or group, and often dealing with matters that are not to be disclosed to others." Sex work frustrates this public-private dichotomy by making the presumably private act of sex into a public transaction. Sex work occurs in spaces marked by their private and public tensions. On the one hand, although the sale of sex occurs in private areas, the procurement of strangers for sexual activity is necessarily a somewhat public act. For there to be an efficient market for sex, there must be public or quasi-public spaces where strangers can purchase sex.

This tension can also be understood as existing between secrecy and visibility.[13] The various levels of visibility and secrecy associated with sex work allow different levels of extraction and protection. The police and hotel-brothel owners become figures of authority in these spaces. The more transparent forms of sex work are subject to higher police scrutiny, while the sex work that is clouded by greater (yet open) secrecy remains in the domain of hotel-brothel owners. These figures of authority reproduce a patriarchal order in the sex work industry. Although sex workers who operated in hotel-brothels indicated to me that they were independent contractors, they were still bound by the social expectations of their operating establishments. The patriarchal figures of the police and of the hotel-brothel owners and managers negotiate informal rules and understandings with the sex workers within their jurisdictional space.

In Johannesburg, sex work is concentrated in several red-light districts throughout the city, each with a distinct character, depending on the locale. Rosebank and Illovo are located in Johannesburg's northern suburbs, and much of the sex work there is considered to be higher end. Sex work hot spots are on and near Oxford Road, a main thoroughfare in the area (see figure 2.1). The market for Rosebank-Illovo sex work is street based and concentrated into several areas. The sex workers cater to clients from the surrounding suburbs, including Rosebank, Melrose, and Houghton, which are some of the wealthiest suburbs in Johannesburg. One sex worker, Maria, explained to me that although she lives in Hillbrow, she comes to Rosebank to work because the clients are high income and tend to make frequent visits. Almost all of her clients are married, and they enjoy the discreet convenience of purchasing sex near their homes. Several sex workers repeated similar experiences to me.

Sex work is marketed in public spaces in Rosebank; nevertheless, on most evenings the sex workers hide themselves on dark street corners and

FIGURE 2.1. Street adjacent to one of the hot spot corners for sex work at night.

maintain a certain level of discretion. By contrast, in central Johannesburg, sex work, although also street based, is highly visible (Map 2.1). Whereas a busy night in Rosebank involved at least seventy-eight sex workers outside in the darker public spaces, one particularly busy night in central Johannesburg easily involved more than three hundred sex workers lined up on a brightly lit street in various states of undress. This form of sex work occupies a very public space and is highly visible.

In Hillbrow, street-based sex work is not tolerated at all, and sex work takes place in various hotels, clubs, and private residences. This geography of sex work involving a public but discreet form in Rosebank, a highly visible form in central Johannesburg, and a completely indoor form in Hillbrow is socially driven by police practices, client preferences, sex worker preferences, and sex worker bodily capital. As Phil Hubbard describes it:

[T]he city is a map of the hierarchy of desire, from the valorized to the stigmatized. It is divided into zones dictated by the way its citizens value or denigrate their needs. Separating the city into areas of specialism

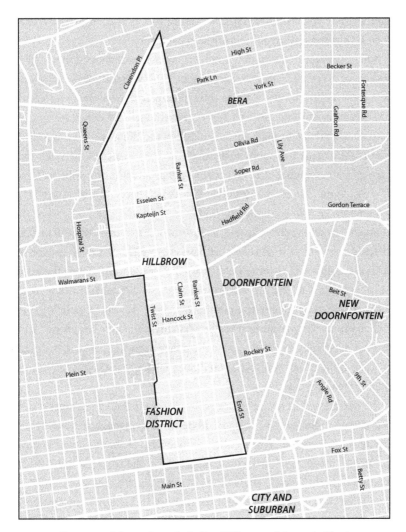

MAP 2.1. Downtown Johannesburg, including Hillbrow and the central business district.

makes it possible to meet some needs more efficiently; it is also an attempt to reduce conflict between opposing sets of desires and the roles people adapt to try and fulfil those desires.[14]

The distinct nature of the sex work in the different neighborhoods allows for a diverse clientele, easily able to participate in a market that meets their preferences. It creates a geography of desire that is shaped by preferences informed by ethnicity, wealth, desire, and convenience.

Where sex work occurs on the streets, as in Rosebank or inner-city Johannesburg, its public aspect is more visible.[15] This visibility allows for greater direct intervention by the state as the police patrol the streets and are the embodiment of the state in that space. Nonetheless, the actual transaction is necessarily private in that it occurs between the client and sex worker and is not readily made for public consumption. The distinction between public and private influences the approaches police adopt in the policing of sex work. Sex work that occurs in public spaces is viewed with great suspicion and generally disdained, although it is frequently tolerated.[16] Sex work that is marketed in semi-private spaces, such as brothels, is heavily regulated and subject to a system of legal rules that have evolved from current gaps in the law. The visibility of the more public forms of sex work provides the police with direct access to the sex worker. Space in the city takes on new meaning as sex workers problematize notions of private and public policing.[17] The problematization of private and public sexuality ultimately has created a policing sex geography dictated by how the police negotiate between maintaining order in the urban landscape and domesticizing expressions of feminine sexuality (see Map 2.2).

The key players in my sex work research sites included sex workers, sex work clients, hotel-brothel owners, hotel-brothel managers, hotel-brothel security, and the police. During the course of this study, no direct controllers, or intermediaries,[18] or "pimps," appeared at the research sites. All the sex workers, including the sex workers who worked from hotel-brothels, indicated that they were independent contractors and retained the entirety of any income earned for services rendered. The market was driven, in part, by client demand. However, sex workers would also dictate the prevalence of supply by favoring warm-weather conditions, missing work on religious holidays, and taking frequent absences as needed.

Figure 2.2 illustrates the interconnecting relationships among the various players in the Johannesburg sex work arena. Sex workers in Johannesburg are generally independent contractors. Sex workers who operate from hotel-brothels pay rent to the brothel owners and expect space to work and live in return for these payments. The hotel owners often have subjective

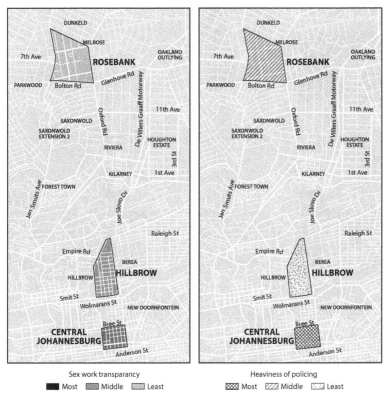

MAP 2.2. Side-by-side maps of Hillbrow, Rosebank, and Central Johannesburg, displaying visibility of sex work (left) and heavily policed areas (right).

expectations about how the sex workers operating from their brothels should appear and express these expectations to the sex workers, regulating how sex workers organize themselves in the market.

Police are expected to assist sex workers with complaints about client abuse and often interact with sex workers to enforce public nuisance regulations in response to community complaints. Police also regularly act as mediators for sex worker–client disputes about payment. Police interact with sex work clients by soliciting these clients for bribes. The clients have a direct relationship with sex workers as patrons and expect the sex workers to fulfill their material and sexual desires. These clients are at times a member of the police, who may enter a patronage relationship with sex workers in which the

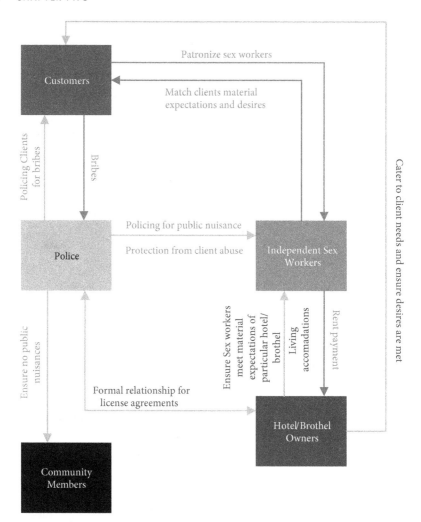

FIGURE 2.2. Relationships among sex work participants.

sex workers are available for transactions during the police officer's shifts and the officer provides the sex workers with additional police protection for this convenience. These interconnecting relationships create dynamic market conditions, where each of the independent components influences the others. Such interconnected relationships are important because they highlight how upsetting one aspect or participant in a relationship may have indirect or direct effects on others.

SEX WORK IN HILLBROW

During my patrols with the Hillbrow police, it quickly became apparent that this group of police officers adopts a hard-line approach against sex work with an overtly public nature. Very few sex workers operate outdoors in Hillbrow because there is a policy of ensuring that such sex workers are promptly removed from the streets. The policing of sex work in Hillbrow is conducted primarily through the negotiating of licenses between police and indoor establishments. Street-based sex workers had previously operated near Golden Ceresta or Lilly and Johnston Streets before the policy of eliminating street-based sex work was implemented.

Table 2.1 presents the demographic characteristics of the research participants from Hillbrow police station in terms of age and tenure in the police department. The Hillbrow police station participants were fourteen (73.3%) males and four (21.1%) females, and one participant failed to provide a gender. Their age ranged from 25 to 53 years, and they had worked at the police station for one to thirty-six years (one participant was unable to provide the number of years served).

In the following section, an entry from my field notes captures the everyday reality of patrolling with the Hillbrow police as they monitored Hillbrow hotel-brothels.

Entry from Field Notes: Hillbrow Patrol

After a couple of attempts at joining the Hillbrow police for patrols, I finally joined an officer patrol on 1 October 2013. I met with Colonel Bongani,[19] and we were discussing my research aims in her office at around 5:30 p.m. Colonel Bongani is a Black woman in her mid-30s to mid-40s. She is a colonel for the Hillbrow police station. She has coordinated the work of other researchers and is quite familiar with the process. Her office is located on the first floor of the police station and is an average-sized office with a sterile feeling

TABLE 2.1. Age and tenure of Hillbrow police station interviewees.

	Minimum no. of years	Maximum no. of years	Mean	SD	No. of participants
Age	25	53	39.79	8.90	19
Police department tenure	1	36	18.81	10.89	18

about it, although there are minor touches of her personal decor in it, including a polyester pillow and photos of her family.

After we discussed my research objectives for a few minutes, she contacted the captain on duty that evening and attempted to arrange a patrol for me to join. Last week, when she attempted to do the same, I was instructed to come back in a few days because there were no patrols for me to join. I was hopeful that I would have a different outcome. After making appropriate arrangements, I went to the ground floor to join officers who are beginning their patrols. The shifts began at 6:00 p.m. and end at 6:00 a.m. There was always a general hustle and bustle in the Hillbrow police station around this time. There were community members waiting in line to file complaints and get documents certified near the seating area. Behind the desk were approximately six police officers handling various community members at the police station. There were a few offices behind the front desk, where officers sign in and submit relevant paperwork before beginning their shifts in one of these offices.

I waited quietly as Colonel Bongani informed the officers about my research and organized my patrol. Colonel Bongani began speaking to several officers in Zulu, and the officers seemed a bit reticent about having me accompany them. Because I do not understand the language, I was a bit confused by the interactions. After waiting for around an hour, I finally joined two officers for a patrol. The officers were at first a bit confused by my research but eventually agreed to have me join their patrol after Colonel Bongani had provided a full explanation of my study. I joined the patrol of officers Sam and Thulo in a four-door police sedan, sitting in the back of the police vehicle. They were both Black officers in their 40s, and each has been with the force for approximately twelve years. They interacted with each other in Zulu, but Officer Sam soon began to interact with me in English. He asked me what I would like to do this evening, and I explained that I would just like to see their ordinary patrol. He suggested that we visit a few of brothels, and I agreed to this.

The first brothel we passed was the Maxime, and we did a simple drive-by of this nondescript hotel that blends into Hillbrow. He insisted that there are "no prostitutes" in Hillbrow and appeared to have equated street-based sex work with "real prostitution," highlighting the importance of public versus private displays of sex work and what constitutes a disturbance that requires additional policing. When I asked about street-based sex workers, Officer Sam stated, "We don't have a problem with them [prostitutes]. There are only hotels." Indoor forms of sex work are tolerated, and the venues where sex workers operate are treated as mere hotels. He stated that the average price for a service at the Maxime is R150. He quickly changed his terminology to recognize that this form of sex work does not even warrant the distinction of "prostitution," and he instead refers to these workers as "working ladies," a more respectable term. As we passed the Maxime, I was told that the owner of the Maxime is "some Mozambican guy." He is apparently quite the entrepreneur and owns several such establishments in Hillbrow.

The next stop was Razzmataza. The officers informed me that it is a bar and that working ladies just hang around and solicit clients, but again, "it is not a brothel"—or rather, it is not a formal brothel, although there are many prostitutes there. It is "just a club." It is most active on Friday and Saturday nights and is a large venue with a parking lot directly adjacent to it and a graffiti-sprayed green fence.

We patrolled around Hillbrow for some time while the officers spoke to each other in Zulu and interjected with a bit of English every now and then to keep me engaged. They asked me about my family, where I'm from, and how far I was in my studies. I could tell that they were trying to socially place me and to interpret where I fit into their understanding of the world. After some time patrolling, we continued our sex tourism excursion, landing outside the infamous Summit Club. Officer Sam informed me that the Summit Club is pricier than the other two clubs, and the women are "real professionals." The women at Summit have a reputation for being "beautiful," and "they know what they are doing." It is an upscale club with a naked woman in bright lights posted on its exterior. It appears to be a strip club from the exterior, and there is a huge banner advertising the club as one crosses the Nelson Mandela Bridge in Newtown.

After leaving the bright lights of the flashy Summit Club, we headed to the Royal Park Hotel. I was told that the Royal Park is another brothel that is quite pricey. It looks like a mid-range hotel from its exterior, with bright Royal Park Hotel signage in red lights. It is an extremely large venue located in a well-kept building on a city street block corner. Several luxury vehicles are parked outside the hotel. We considered entering the club, but the officers informed me that Royal Park does not allow women to enter. We went to the reception and asked to speak to a manager, who arrived a few minutes later. He was a White man in his mid-30s who informed me that Royal Park is merely a hotel and that management cannot control what the men do with the women whom they find while patronizing the hotel. I decided to return to the venue on a different day, without the police escort, because the manager was a bit hesitant to speak in front of the police.

Our next patrol stop was the Ambassador Hotel. We quickly passed it, and it appears to be similar to the Maxime because it is also a nondescript building that blends into the general inner-city landscape. The average price for intercourse at this hotel is R150. After patrolling the Ambassador, we passed by Safari, where sex workers also charge R150 for intercourse. Finally, we passed by the Hillbrow Inn, which also charges R150 for intercourse and was described as being in the same class of service as the Maxime and the Ambassador. After passing these clubs, we continued with the patrol for the evening.

Patrolling Hillbrow

These types of sex work patrols quickly became typical of my nighttime visits with Hillbrow police officers, which began to morph into tours, during which the officers would serve as my dutiful guides, providing me with all their insights about the various brothels, sex workers, and the industry in general. Sex work was hidden and marginal, yet the police officers were all well-versed on how to identify these margins. Initially, I assumed that their knowledge of the Hillbrow sex industry was a natural consequence of police work. However, it quite quickly became clear to me that many of these officers were quite intimately aware of the brothels. In fact, it was clear that a good number of them frequented the brothels as customers. Brothel managers and hotel-brothel sex workers, who confirmed that plain clothes police officers frequented these establishments, verified my suspicions. Although I grew close to several of the police officers, I never felt comfortable in my semi-structured interviews with asking them directly whether they were brothel customers. However, they did indirectly confirm that they frequented these hotels by recounting good times they had had at the establishments or their perceptions of these places.

Officer Sam once informed me that sex work was not a priority for the police. The Hillbrow police were no longer concerned with the sex work and left the hotels and clubs alone. The policy had changed about two years before I entered the field, around 2011. The officers indicated that now the police raid only brothels that do not have "licenses." I was frequently told, "If a brothel has a license, it is operating fine." During a focus group discussion, several commanding officers confirmed that the brothels are policed only to ensure compliance with liquor licenses. Compliance checks happen routinely and are led by the head of liquor compliance checks at the Hillbrow police station. During these enforcement raids, police verify that the clubs are operating according to the terms of their liquor licenses. These attempts to produce social order and legitimatize the conduct of the police through enforcement of licensing agreements that protect brothels are largely theatrical. As Malcolm Young notes, "policing everywhere relies on 'well-directed social productions' to maintain the mythic divide between good and evil."[20] These raids were productions to reify police legitimacy and enforce hotel-brothel licensing schemes. When I questioned officers about the nature of liquor licenses during a focus group discussion, they informed me:

> There is a liquor license and hotel license [obtained] through the liquor board. [Police] enforce the law and must apply [the] terms of the Liquor Act. If the license says that they must close at a certain time, we must check that they are complying with the requirements of the license. They must display the license outside in the front of the club and be clear. The police are ensuring that they don't sell alcohol at certain times and that they are meeting the requirements of the license.

One sex worker claimed that compared to street-based sex work, there was virtually no police presence in the high-end Hillbrow hotels and clubs, noting in particular that "[t]ere is no real police presence at Summit Club. It is a registered place and brothels have licenses. Brothels pay license fees." These liquor licenses, however, did not make the sale of sex legal. In truth, the establishments were allowed to sell liquor and had specified closing times pursuant to the licenses. However, curiously, several officers interpreted the procurement of these licenses as legal entitlement to operate a hotel-brothel. Some officers were insistent in informing me that certain clubs were completely legal. There are two possible explanations for this. Firstly, these officers were conflating the establishments' legal right to sell alcohol with a legal right to sell sex. Alternatively, these officers were alluding to additional "license" agreements that certain brothels entered into with upper-level members of the police force and that allowed these brothels to operate. I believe the latter may well be the case. Although I was unable to obtain direct confirmation of my suspicions, several brothel owners did speak of an arrangement, or an "understanding," they had with the police. In a country where routine traffic stops frequently include bribes that serve as informal "understandings" with the police, this interpretation is not far-fetched.

One club manager informed me that the police and club owners routinely meet during community forum meetings. This practice began around 2011 and radically changed how the clubs were policed. The relationship became more cooperative, with club owners able to communicate regularly with the police. Another brothel manager, by the name of Steve, explained that the hotel-brothel owners had routine meetings with police and had been establishing a positive relationship with police. The police had become less inclined to penalize compliant brothels and even frequented the establishments as customers. These licensing agreements appeared to promote a positive relationship between police and brothel managers and owners and seemed mutually beneficial.

Although many officers mentioned licenses and stated that certain brothels were "legal" because they had the proper licensure, no informant provided specific details about these licensing agreements. It became apparent that these arrangements, if they in fact involved more than the customary liquor licenses, were negotiated fairly far up the police's organizational structure and involved high-ranking officials who had created certain terms that likely included paying licensing fees to obtain cooperation with the police. These agreements would then allow the Hillbrow police to treat the brothels as semi-legal entities operating within their jurisdiction. Police routinely patrol Hillbrow brothels at closing to ensure that liquor is not sold after a certain time and to ensure compliance with the terms of the liquor licensing agreement. Captain Mugabi, one of the officers with whom I met and patrolled, initially indicated that there was no real police presence at Summit Club, that it was a "registered place," and that brothels have "licenses." There thus appears to be a blurring between the liquor license and an actual license to operate brothels. This is reflective of the policing of sex work in general, which displays a constant blurring of lines between the legal and illegal and also some mutability of legalities.

This understanding of licensing also appeared to encourage indoor-based sex workers to request police assistance, without fear of marginalization. The sex workers I encountered in Hillbrow ranged in age from 21 to 45 years, and these sex workers routinely called the police for assistance. Several officers recounted their experiences with sex workers at the police station, and some indicated that such scenarios occur several times a week. The biggest complaints sex workers reported involved domestic violence and street robbery. Sex workers frequently came to the police regarding disputes arising from clients' failure to compensate the sex workers for services rendered. At times, the sex workers claimed that the clients had raped them. The police indicated that they follow up with rape allegations; however, after facilitating negotiations between the sex worker and client, the police often learned that the issue was actually a transactional dispute, and they would instruct the client to compensate the sex worker for services rendered. Here's an example from one of my interviews with a Hillbrow police officer about whether police officers render assistance to sex workers:

INDIA: How do police and prostitutes interact with each other?

APRIL (HILLBROW POLICE OFFICER): Not much, just when they need help they come to the police.

INDIA: When do they ask police for help?

APRIL: When they are in trouble.

INDIA: What type of trouble do they get into?

APRIL: When one of the clients does not want to pay. One of the clients abused or raped them, that type of situation.

INDIA: And how do you resolve the situation where the client doesn't want to pay?

APRIL: Most of the time when the client, when [the prostitute brings the client to] the police, the clients make payment because they don't want to be arrested because they know that their wives are going to find out.

The situation described here again illustrates the blending between the formal and the informal. Officer Sipho, another one of the police officers I interviewed, verified that the police do not make a concerted effort to arrest sex workers for their work in the hotel-brothels; rather, police arrest sex workers for malicious damage of property or theft, after there has been an argument with a client, or if the sex workers are operating from the streets. This function of the police as mediators in private relationships is consistent with the role provided to the police through the DVA. The police officer charged with processing domestic violence complaints at Hillbrow informed me that she frequently resolved monetary disputes between sex workers and clients through her office. Her general approach was to serve as a mediator, and she usually instructed the client to pay the sex worker for any services rendered. However, one police officer indicated that, at times, rape charges were used by sex workers to force a client to pay for services after a payment dispute:

THEMBA (HILLBROW POLICE OFFICER): Sometimes they come and lie, and sometimes [when] we open cases we will, like this one, this one is lying but we know that. When he comes for rape we cannot turn away, anyone away. When someone says, "I've been raped," because with them most of the time they [don't] only come and say, "This person was not, was supposed to pay me this amount," they come and say, "Here, I've got the condom with me, this person raped me," and then we open a case of rape and then that is how we help them.

INDIA: OK.

THEMBA: You get what I'm saying?

INDIA: Yeah. Do they only come if there's, for rape; do they ever come if someone took their money or anything like that?

THEMBA: No.

INDIA: OK.

THEMBA: It's rape, that one is rape.

INDIA: Have you ever responded to prostitutes who have come in regarding rape?

THEMBA: Yes, many.

INDIA: OK.

THEMBA: Many a times. In fact here in Hillbrow many rape incidents, I'm not saying all of them, many of them, when you interview a

person you can see that this rape is not really a rape, but you cannot turn this person away . . . it goes to court and it's proven in
court that this was not rape. You hear what I'm saying? So my duty
as a police officer is just to do my part and open the gates . . .

INDIA: Why do you think they come in and ask, and say that they've
been raped?

THEMBA: I think it's because the person who promised to pay them,
for example that amount of money is not given, the money, because there are cases like that.

This exchange was problematic in that it revealed that officers do in fact view
sex workers' claims of rape with a bit of suspicion. This is consistent with
earlier court judgments that viewed sex workers as unreliable, such the court
decision in *R v Sibande* where the court stated: "Prostitutes are not respected
members of the community and, generally speaking, one does not expect
them to be truthful." However, the Hillbrow officers acknowledged their obligation to treat each claim fairly despite any personal perceptions about a
claim's veracity, reflecting the influences of a human rights perspective and a
type of vernacularization of human rights.[21] In the opaque and "legal" spaces
where sex work is regulated, there have been incidents in which police protect sex workers. In Hillbrow, where sex work is taken away from the public
eye and does not disrupt the public moral order, police allow themselves to
consider their role of protector under the Domestic Violence Act.

Hillbrow Licensing Scheme

The licensing scheme in Hillbrow provides an alternative legal approach for
regulating sex work, one that operates on the fringes of the law by adopting legal terminology to create de facto sex work legalization. In Hillbrow,
although street-based sex work is strictly prohibited and sex workers operating from the streets are promptly arrested, sex work in the various hotel-
brothels operates pursuant to liquor licensing agreements with the Hillbrow
police. These licenses are clearly operating on the fringes of the formal law
in that brothels are expressly illegal. The licenses create a quasi-legal regime
for resolving the operation of sex work in Hillbrow. The establishment of a
licensing scheme for conduct that is explicitly illegal is an exercise of power,

in that it results from the police force's "complex strategical situation in a particular society."[22] The police are adopting a language that provides them with
legitimacy in the Weberian sense, in that it attempts to demonstrate actual
legitimacy as given to them by the people.[23] However, the licensing scheme is
actually an exercise of policing in the Foucauldian sense in that it is a power
that is not necessarily derived from a contract with the populace but rather
an exercise of a discursive technology to give the appearance of legitimacy.
The licensing scheme highlights the manners in which the formal legal regime is being marginalized. Hillbrow police have adopted these rules that
respect "private" space in response to an approach that calls for unofficial
decriminalization. Moreover, among the nineteen Hillbrow police officers
that I interviewed, fifteen favored sex work decriminalization (as discussed
in chapter 5). Their primary concern was understanding how they should approach sex work policing, and whether additional measures (or fewer measures) were required to do the task justice.

During a focus group with members of the Hillbrow police, the officers
informed me that part of the rationale for allowing brothels while forbidding
street-based sex work is the quasi-private nature of brothel-based sex work,
which occurs in private establishments that entertain the public. They explained that the hotel-brothels are private in the sense that their activities are
not readily apparent to passersby on the streets. This theme of privacy was
a constant during my participant observation. Hillbrow hotel-brothels are
less visible and therefore do not require the type of direct state intervention
that street-based forms of sex work require. However, several of the Hillbrow hotel-brothels feature signage that prominently features scantily clad
women, and several of them have strip shows that occur in the public areas of their buildings. Thus, they are open secrets. These establishments also
have more private areas, where business transactions occur. In this sense, the
actual act of sex work occurs only in a very private space within the quasi-
private building, which is also quasi-public.

Licensing and registration appear to immunize the Hillbrow hotel-
brothels from intense policing, and the police frequently describe these venues as "legal," even though sex work is clearly criminalized within the Sexual
Offences Act. Prabha Kotiswaran has similarly observed in Sonagachi, a red-
light district in Kolkata, India, the "multiple illegalities [that] do or do not

incite into action, the lived coexistence of legality and illegality, the negotiations of private disputes in the shadow of illegality, the state's role in fostering illegal markets and its toleration of certain forms of illegality more than others."[24] In Hillbrow, the illegality of certain brothel activities peacefully coexists with the legality of the brothels' registration and licensing as enforced by the police. This legalization of sex work in Hillbrow brothels harkens back to the close cooperation between early Johannesburg area police and the syndicates that operated the sex work industry during the mining boom of the early 1900s.[25] Again, police were working informally to create a sex work paradigm that was mutually beneficial for police and sex work operators in the mining region, suggesting that contemporary expressions of policing reflect some continuity from past practices. There is also continuity in how public nuisance is still strictly policed, and sex workers are completely barred from Hillbrow public spaces. The sex workers continue to be viewed as threats to hygiene and as potential vectors of venereal diseases that must be restricted to these secret spaces. Sex work is permissible in private spaces because these spaces allow for convenient satisfaction of male desire without public expression of female sexuality. The Hillbrow police have demonstrated a form of Black, urban South African male masculinity[26] that allows the expression of female sexuality at the convenience of the male sexual appetite but completely bars it where it violates social mores about what is suitable in public spaces. Thus, street-based sex work is completely barred, whereas regulated sex work in hotel-brothels is permitted.

SEX WORK IN CENTRAL JOHANNESBURG

The quasi-legalized policing of sex work is not consistent throughout Johannesburg. In fact, how sex work is policed is highly context specific. My patrols with Hillbrow police revealed that the policing of sex work in central Johannesburg is radically different from that in Hillbrow, where sex work is highly organized and restricted to private spaces. On January 17, 2014, I met Captain Mugabi at the Hillbrow police station for our nightly patrol. During a previous patrol, we had agreed to go out to central Johannesburg, where I could interview some of the street-based sex workers. After I waited for about twenty minutes on the ground floor of the police station, where patrons were waiting to lodge complaints, Captain Mugabi joined me near the main entrance. Captain Mugabi is Bapedi and originally from South Africa's Limpopo province.

As we drove to central Johannesburg, he informed me that the most dangerous area of Johannesburg is Jeppestown, explaining that it has a high rate of robberies and car hijackings. He suggested that this may be a result of the Zulu influence in the area. He commented that Zulus are very aggressive and combative, resulting in a higher crime rate, thus highlighting the ways that perceptions of ethnicity and race infuse policing. Captain Mugabi and I chatted a bit, and he confirmed my findings that there are no street-based sex workers in Hillbrow. He explained that the police immediately arrest street-based sex workers there and that the only sex workers in Hillbrow work in the brothels and strip clubs. Lisa Sanchez has discussed the displacement of street-based sex workers:

> The law displaces these [street-based] women spatially. This displacement occurs not just through the criminalization of specific acts of prostitution, but through laws that criminalize conduct prior to any actual sexual interactions (e.g., solicitation, procurement, and loitering). In essence, these laws are like status offences, making it illegal to be identified as a 'prostitute' and to occupy certain public spaces.[27]

In Hillbrow, informal law-making processes and policies have disrupted the work of street-based sex workers by making their presence on the streets criminal. Those who are unable to create viable incomes in the Hillbrow hotel-brothels, have consequently been displaced to the streets of central Johannesburg.

Central Johannesburg is approximately seven to ten minutes from Hillbrow. During the course of my first patrol there, I intended to interview several sex workers about their interactions with police. Captain Mugabe and I devised a scheme to promote safety while also ensuring that the police vehicle was not obvious, in order to allow the sex workers to speak freely with me without fear of police presence: I would hop out of the patrol *bakkie* (a small pickup truck) while Captain Mugabi followed several meters behind me or circled the block with his lights off. He suggested this approach because the sex workers would be reluctant to speak to me if I approached them in a police vehicle. This would also allow him to continue patrolling the area.

In contrast to the sex work that, in Hillbrow, is relegated to quasi-private spaces in hotel-brothels, sex work in central Johannesburg is highly visible and public in its operation. I was initially startled during my first visit to the area by just how public the sex work there was. It was a hot summer night in 2013, and I visited some streets known to be frequented by sex workers, near the Fashion District in Johannesburg. During the daytime, these streets are filled with the informal traders and taxis typical of the general hustle and bustle of central Johannesburg. In the evenings, however, the streets morph into an area for an overt sex trade bustling with a few hundred partially dressed women. A row of no fewer than eighty scantily clad women lined one small city street block on this particularly busy Friday evening. The street was so packed that there was virtually no room for additional women to stand and advertise their services. I squirmed past and tried to find a place where I could blend in without interfering with the workers' transactions. Clients were in their vehicles and would drive by and pick up women who suited their desires.

Captain Mugabi suggested that whereas the police officers in Hillbrow have been instructed to arrest sex workers who operate from the streets, the police in central Johannesburg likely have an "understanding" or "arrangement" with the sex workers in central Johannesburg. He stated that these arrangements are characterized by mutually beneficial financial understandings in which the police tolerate sex work under certain circumstances. The creation of arrangements for legalizing the illegal is an expression of diffuse power that aims to create order and give the appearance of legitimacy. On the one hand, this arrangement may be viewed as overt police corruption, which necessarily obstructs the rights of sex workers. On the other hand, it may be viewed as a form of efficient corruption that creates rules that are otherwise outside the parameters of the law but nonetheless effective at regulating legal relationships.[28] After all, the alternative may be merely to arrest all sex workers, given the illegality of their work.

The policing of sex workers in central Johannesburg is very much the prerogative of the Metro police[29] rather than of SAPS. The Metro police are the municipal police service charged with enforcing municipal bylaws on such issues as traffic violations and loitering, and they are expected to engage in "visible policing." The Metro police are lower on the hierarchy of official policing organizations than SAPS but are above the private security forces. When I was visiting central Johannesburg, although most of the sex workers said that SAPS officers were quite accommodating and allowed them to engage in their trade, on several occasions sex worker after sex worker complained about the unprompted and consistent abuse they faced at the hands of Metro police officers. For example, a sex worker in her late 20s, who goes by Lydia, told me that the Metro police have been a problem for the sex workers there. She stated that the Metro police beat her and that if she is with a client, "they take money from the client." In general, the police, both Metro and SAPS, try to take around R10 from clients.

The Metro police also seem to exhibit an unexplained cruelty toward sex workers. Three days prior to my initial visit, Metro police had physically beaten and abused the sex workers, although the sex workers had not encountered similar violence from SAPS officers:

> ANNIE (CENTRAL JOHANNESBURG SEX WORKER): Metro police find us in the streets, [and] they are beating us. There is no reason provided for the abuse. They don't want to see us in the streets. . . . [SAPS] Police are not giving us any problems. . . . Every day there is a problem with the Metro police.
>
> JESSICA (CENTRAL JOHANNESBURG SEX WORKER): Metro come and harass us. . . . They want to beat us with a *sjambok*[30] and pepper spray us and say we must go.
>
> SARAH (CENTRAL JOHANNESBURG SEX WORKER): Metro like to chase us around. If you are in a miniskirt, they bother you. They say we make the street dirty.[31] They say that your mates are married. How can you do this type of work?

I was told repeatedly: "The real problem is with the Metros. The Metro police came and beat us with a *sjambok*!" This is in striking contrast to Hillbrow, where members of the SAPS are the primary police enforcers of sex work regulations and where physical violence is not the primary characteristic of policing. This open hostility toward sex workers in central Johannesburg reproduces social norms that view sex workers as unhygienic and thus threats to public health and safety. This is consistent with the historical regulation of sex workers as vectors of disease. While police officers are no longer armed with the Contagious Diseases Act as an impetus for their hostile policing, they do carry weighted perspectives of sex workers that cover those workers in a cloud of suspicion and assume a lack of hygiene. As discussed in chapter 1, this Act's regulation of the sex workers' bodies was an exercise of biopower that was driven by public discourses about hygiene and public health. These ongoing discourses still empower officers to openly tell the sex workers that they are dirty and that they spread disease.[32] I also heard a Hillbrow police officer echoing the sentiment that sex workers should be driven off the streets, again revealing the bias against street-based sex workers:

> ZOLO: On the streets it [prostitution] should be out because especially for Johannesburg Central there are gross ladies sitting there or it must be on the central venue, central area, then the people know that it's this area. . . . They are so pathetic. Not professional. Those ones, no. You know you just see yourself as a female or not a female. You don't know if this person is having a pain or not [from emotional issues and challenges]. No, you don't want to go there. If you are travelling that side, you don't want to check. . . . No. Have you seen them?

The Metro police officers in central Johannesburg were acting as the arbiters of moral society and using violence to beat these sex workers into submissive roles. This open aggression is consistent with a Black African male masculinity that views Black women as property and gives men license to publicly discipline dirty women.[33] These police viewed the sex workers as undignified and were completely unconcerned with the rights that such women might have. As mentioned, these sex workers frequently stated that the Metro police officers would accuse them of spreading disease, thus adopting the public health discourse of sex workers as carriers of contagion to explain their policing of sex workers in the city.

The Metro police officers' approach reflects popular narratives that emphasize the sex worker as both prototypical victim and vector of contagion, particularly in the public health context. The commentary of many scholars is that sex workers require protection; this is the stance of sex work advocates and sex work opponents alike, particularly in the South African context, where scholars are concerned with protecting sex workers' health but at times fail to fully contextualize sex workers beyond their public health

profiles and victim status.[34] Much of the advocacy for decriminalization focuses on protecting the sex workers from the evils of the police and the clients,[35] whereas sex work opponents essentially argue that we must protect
the sex worker from herself.[36] Under this line of reasoning, the sex worker
is always subjecting herself to an act of violence and thus must be protected
from her poor choices.

The various perspectives on whether to criminalize or decriminalize at
times rely upon metanarratives of the singular "sex worker victim," whose
experience is then universalized. Such arguments fail to appreciate the full
complexity of the reality of many sex workers. As Ratna Kapur discusses, the
reliance on the victim subject, especially in the developing world context, has
been the fulcrum of much radical feminist debate:

> The articulation of the victim subject is based on gender essentialism;
> that is, overgeneralized claims about women. . . . [E]ssentialism assumes
> that "women have a coherent group identity within different cultures . . .
> prior to their entry into social relations." Such generalizations are hege-
> monic in that they represent the problems of privileged women, who are
> often (though not exclusively) White, Western, middleclass, heterosexual
> women. These generalizations efface the problems, perspectives, and po-
> litical concerns of women marginalized because of their class, race, reli-
> gion, ethnicity, and/or sexual orientation. The victim subject ultimately
> relies on a universal subject: a subject that resembles the uncomplicated
> subject of liberal discourse. It is a subject that cannot accommodate a
> multi-layered experience.[37]

Such constructions have led to the creation of a monolithic "sex worker," a
concept that fails to appreciate the plurality of sex worker experiences within
the same city, let alone globally.[38] It also fails to engage in the more complicated analysis of appreciating the intersectionality of the discrimination experienced by many sex workers, and blissfully looks to the criminal law as a
savior, whereas many sex workers are already subject to intense surveillance
and generally mistrust interactions with the carceral system.[39]

The victim narrative is reflected in contemporary public health discourses concerned with the sex worker body as a site of contagion. The public health narrative continues a discourse that places the state's gaze upon

the sex worker as a site of contagion. There is no question that sex workers should have access to health and healthcare.[40] However, it is crucial that the discourse around providing rights to sex worker does not inadvertently pathologize sex workers and treat them as carriers of contagion. The 2016 South African National Sex Worker HIV Plan will expand healthcare access to many of South Africa's sex workers. However, it simultaneously adopts a narrative framework that continues the perception that sex workers require public attention to the extent that this attention is in the interest of the public health, similar to the approach adopted in 1868 during the passage of the Contagious Diseases Act in the Cape Colony. The foreword to the report discussing the plan begins with this statement:

> Sex workers have not received the same attention as the general population
> in our country response to HIV, tuberculosis (TB) and Sexually Trans
> mitted Infections (STIs). A number of recent studies have shown that the
> sex worker community is at a substantially elevated risk of HIV and that
> prevalence rates in this community are among the highest in the world.[41]

The report has spurred articles and media coverage with titles such as "72% of Sex Workers in JHB Are HIV Positive"[42] and has continued the discourses around sex workers' health that are largely exercises of biopower. It is important that well-intentioned public health advocates ensure they do not reinforce discourses that portray sex workers as unclean and unhygienic. This focus on the sex workers' public health profile, which has in turn resulted in popular news articles about sex workers and disease, promotes those discourses. The Metro police officers would expressly state that they thought sex workers were dirty while harassing them. They were not policing the sex workers according to their understandings of whether sex work is legal. They were policing them in the belief that sex workers spread disease and were nuisances to the public. Public health discussants must be deliberate in *talking about* sex workers in ways that do not further pathologize them. It is also important to include sex workers' clients, who also require public health services and education, as mutual participants in the conversation to ensure that sex workers are not being treated as singular carriers of contagion inflicting disease upon society *vis-à-vis* the client. Rather, the clients are equally involved and should be included in protecting the public health.

Finally, there is also a third "police" presence in central Johannesburg, in the form of the active engagement of private security forces. After spending several weeks talking with and observing sex workers on the streets of central Johannesburg, I learned that security guards from a nearby ABSA Bank building routinely harassed sex workers. The sex worker named Jessica told me: "Every day, there is a problem with the security guards. If you have no money, they want sex from you." The security guards asked sex workers for monetary bribes on a regular basis. If a sex worker was unable to provide money, the security guards demanded free sex. The sex workers generally just gave the security guards money in the face of these requests. When sex workers were reluctant, the security guards jailed them in cells within ABSA. These private security forces are at the bottom of the police hierarchy and appear to be adopting the public nuisance discourse for their individual benefit.

Contrary to the practice of sex workers in Hillbrow, sex workers in central Johannesburg rarely go to the police for assistance. One sex worker explained: "Clients are beating us sometimes, taking our money [and we can't go to the police because they are] going to say [I'm] selling my body. . . . [I would] feel embarrassed." The women in central Johannesburg appear to be in the most desperate of situations and face the continuous gaze of the corrupt Metro police. One sex worker stated: "I come every day for money. I have children. The hotels are full [so I'm] working in the street."

On a separate occasion, Captain Mugabi explained to me that SAPS officers generally do not interact with the street-based sex workers in central Johannesburg. Because the Metro police focus on enforcing the municipal bylaws about zoning and public nuisance issues, they are more intense in their approach to sex workers.[43] This might explain why the Metro police are so highly involved in the everyday policing of these street-based sex workers and carry it out in a highly brutal and persistent way that appears to have no rational basis beyond the desire to clean the streets. Such policing is consistent with the history of treating sex work as a public nuisance that should be regulated primarily where it affects the public order in some manner. In central Johannesburg, the sex workers appear less empowered and more subject to random police brutality and corruption than the Hillbrow sex workers in hotel-brothels. The relationship between the Metro police and sex workers is not cooperative, and the Metro police appear to barely tolerate sex workers there. The Metro police inform the sex workers that they need to leave the street, that they are dirty, and the ABSA security personnel coerce sex from them.

This focus on municipal public order regulation is quite consistent with the approach that South African police have always adopted toward sex work. Public nuisance violations would still be relevant even if sex work were to be fully decriminalized. This style of policing reveals the limitations of decriminalization. If aggressive public order policing persists, the ordinances driving that policing may also facilitate the aggressive policing of sex work, even where sex work is decriminalized. Although not directly in line with the colonial policing of sex work that focused on the public disorder of it, there appears to be some connection with this form of policing that is concerned with the "public" aspect of sex work and born of discourses regulating how sexuality should be represented. These discourses influence how sex workers are policed in that Metro police claim that sex workers, in exposing themselves on the streets, will corrupt vulnerable children and families. The women are viewed with suspicion because patriarchy demands that women's sexuality be primarily expressed in private spaces and domesticized. In central Johannesburg, where the sex work is very public and visible, the police are thus especially brutal and communicate a general disdain for the activities of the sex workers. They openly question their hygiene and accuse them of spreading diseases. Sex workers who operate in this environment tend to do so out of desperation and their inability to break into other markets for sex work. The presence of the private security personnel establishes differentiated policing, where the presence of the enforcement of horizontal rights is noticeably absent.

3 | INFORMAL POLICING
IN ROSEBANK

SEX WORK ALONG Oxford Road in the Rosebank area—encompassing the suburbs of Rosebank, Illovo, Houghton Estate, and Bramley—lies somewhere between the extremes of sex work practice in Hillbrow and central Johannesburg. Sex workers in the Rosebank area operate primarily from the streets and are independent operators. Despite their outdoor location, they maintain a certain level of secrecy that is lacking in central Johannesburg by remaining in dark corners spread across several distinct streets over the course of several kilometers in these suburbs. One could very easily drive down Oxford Road oblivious to the more than twenty sex workers who might be operating on a slow night.

This relative invisibility encourages an informal system of rules, similar to those in Hillbrow, negotiated between the individual sex workers, police, and clients. The informality, however, also allows for instability, and during the course of my fieldwork, the rules were ever-changing. The traditional public discourses about sex worker hygiene and public nuisance contributed to the terms of these informal rules, similar to the rules described in chapter 2 for Hillbrow and central Johannesburg. While sex workers were able to exercise some power in their negotiations with the police about the nature of sex work in the Rosebank area, the system was quite unstable, preventing lasting security.

I adopt a narrative methodology in this chapter, using storytelling to illustrate how the changes that I observed over time evolved and to demonstrate the variations of police–sex worker relationships within a locale.[1] I fully employ the three dimensions of narrative: the "personal and social (interaction) along one dimension; past, present and future (continuity) along a second dimension; [and] place (situation) along a third dimension."[2] This approach enhances the strengths of ethnography because the depth of time allows the researcher to observe multiple iterations of the same research object and subjects, and because the ability to consider the dichotomy of time and place together leads to a fuller understanding of their impact on how sex work is policed. Finally, adopting a narrative approach "highlights the relational dimension of narrative inquiry. Narrative inquirers cannot bracket themselves out of the inquiry but rather need to find ways to inquire into participants' experiences, their own experiences . . . [and] the co-constructed experiences developed through the relational inquiry process."[3]

PATROLLING IN ROSEBANK

Oxford Road is a site of visible, street-based sex work and provides access to a large number of sex workers across several suburbs. However, the majority of sex work on Oxford Road occurs in Rosebank, and so I patrolled with Rosebank police officers. The sex workers in Rosebank cater to a high-end clientele from Johannesburg's northern suburbs. The site allows for prompt and discreet transactions for individuals looking to purchase sex, for example, after work while their families are waiting for them at home. Rosebank sex workers are well aware of this and charge a premium for their services. As Melissa, a Rosebank sex worker, said: "The streets are good for a quick one and they go back home because they are married."

Oxford Road is a leafy thoroughfare in suburban Johannesburg. Viewed from another suburb, Houghton Estate, the street appears to stretch endlessly into the distance. The street is adorned with many trees, and the area is primarily residential (figure 3.1). Although Rosebank Mall is located toward the center of the portion of the road, where sex work occurs, the street is primarily residential on either side of the mall. This section of Johannesburg's northern suburbs is home to many of the city's liberal elite, who are attracted by the road's tall trees and picturesque Johannesburg surroundings. The

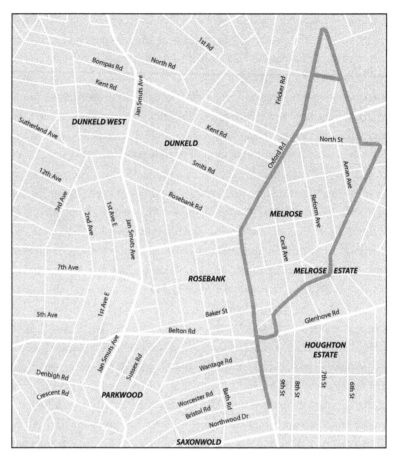

MAP 3.1. Map of Oxford Road starting from Houghton, going through Rosebank, and ending in Illovo.

book *Kaffir Boy* describes Rosebank as "one of Johannesburg's posh Whites-only suburbs," which reflects an apartheid-era description of the area.[4] Now, Rosebank retains much of its historical "poshness" but is also considerably trendy, and the home to several media houses and welcoming to Johannesburg's young, Black elite.[5] Nelson Mandela's estate is within five minutes of Oxford Road, in Houghton Estate. Oxford Road feels and looks like a homey and ideal environment in which to raise children. A preschool stands near one of its main corners, and a bakery is located on another corner. During the daytime, it looks like a typical street in the northern suburbs, with its steady stream of traffic, endless view of trees, and big houses that are only

FIGURE 3.1. A prototypical leafy corner on Oxford Road in Rosebank, adjacent to a preschool.

partially visible behind the tall walls and barbwired gates commonly used in many of Johannesburg's suburbs as barriers against intruders. At night, it retains much of this charm but is also populated with sex workers, who operate from a few distinct corners, hidden under the leaves of the road's tall trees. As Oxford Road approaches Illovo, there are fewer trees and younger residents. Illovo is home to several older apartment blocks that house a young professional class, still considered part of Johannesburg's elite. Many of the residents are childless even though a fair number of young families reside in Illovo. Illovo is livelier than Rosebank and Houghton and is home to several restaurants and after-work bars. Still, there are nightlife options, including several nightclubs and bars, in both Rosebank and Illovo. Both Rosebank and Illovo are surrounded by suburbs that are family-oriented, upper-middle class, and home to Johannesburg's well-to-do. Hyde Park, Atholl, and Houghton Estate, all of which are near Oxford Road, are among the richest areas in the country, with the highest concentrations of multimillionaires.[6]

The Rosebank police station—housed in two small, one-level, connecting buildings around the size of a family home in the area (figure 3.2)—is generally pretty quiet inside, with only a few patrons requesting document certification on any given day. When you enter the building, there is a reception desk where the police officers on duty assist community members. The station is generally most active when officers change over for their twelve-hour shifts, at 6:00 in the evening and 6:00 in the morning.

I joined Rosebank officers for routine patrols beginning in July 2012, during the early stages of my research. During these patrols, we would drive around Rosebank in police vehicles, respond to resident complaints, and engage in visible policing. My first night was July 5, 2012. I went to the Rosebank station around 6:00 p.m., the time when the officers change shifts. There was a bit of activity at the police station, with a couple of community members filling out accident reports and insurance papers. I patiently stood in the line, waiting for my turn, at which point I explained that I was conducting research that evening and would be joining the officers on their patrols. I met a charming young officer by the name of J. R., who informed me that he had been "a cop" for three years. "It's not easy," he told me. "It's not for the faint of heart"—the job has many dangers. J. R. was holding a large semi-automatic

FIGURE 3.2. The Rosebank police station.

gun as he nonchalantly spoke with me. He was incredibly handsome, with smooth mahogany skin, and tall in stature. He appeared to be a bit on the younger side, around 24 to 27 years old. He was very poised and confident in his demeanor. He seemed charmed by me and eager to exploit the opportunity to speak with a researcher about the dangers of police work. He warned me that I would encounter unexpected scenarios and might very well be frightened by the true nature of policing. His bravado added to his charm, but later I would learn things about J. R. that would chip away at this first impression. I continued to wait by the front counter after J.R. called the station commander from the back.

After waiting a few minutes at the front of the customer service line following my initial encounter with J.R., I spoke to the station commander for the evening. I informed him that I would be joining the officers on their patrol that evening, pursuant to an arrangement with Lieutenant Colonel Greggs, the regular station commander, and Captain van der Westhuizen, the head of visible policing. He asked, "Will you be with them for the whole night?" to which I responded yes. He then asked, "How?" and I responded, "With coffee." He chuckled and said he would need to contact Captain van der Westhuizen to confirm my patrol.

After a few minutes, he contacted Captain van der Westhuizen and appeared to plead with the captain about limited space and other concerns that might bar me from joining the officers. Finally, the station commander informed me that the captain had said I could join the officers on one of their trips to the "*prrrossies*"[7] down Oxford Road. I asked whether I could join one of the *bakkies* already on patrol but was told that special officers were being called in for me. Fortunately for me, the special officers did not show up, and I was then assigned instead to one of the *bakkies* on patrol. They were to pick me up when they planned to meet with the sex workers, which would be some time after 7:00 p.m.

One of the on-duty police officers inquired about my family and my home country. He asked whether my family was based in South Africa and appeared to be trying to place me. I informed him that I was from New York, and I just happened to really like South Africa. The on-duty police officers referred to me by the station commander had what seemed to be an intense conversation in Zulu[8] about my joining the patrol. One of them seemed nervous, while the other said there was no problem with the arrangement.

They were arguing with each other, and I heard Captain van der Westhuizen's name mentioned several times over the course of their conversation.

These same officers, who were in their mid- to late 30s, eventually allowed me to join them on their patrol. We entered a sedan vehicle for this patrol. I explained my research study to them as we drove, and provided additional details in the hopes of assuaging their concerns. There was an intense silence in the car following my attempt to make the officers more comfortable.

We drove down Oxford Road and slowly patrolled the streets. The exercise seemed a bit artificial to me, but I realized there was some insight to be gained even from this rudimentary exercise. Through regular patrols like this one, I personally witnessed the fatigue, exhaustion, and ordinary challenges of engaging in police patrol work. After loosening up a bit, a couple of hours into our patrol, the officers informed me that the police no longer police sex workers. They claimed that there was a national directive prohibiting the arrest of sex workers, that sex workers are no longer a police priority, and they insisted that I would not see much during my fieldwork. When I asked them what they think about sex workers, one officer paused and chuckled for a moment. He stated that sex workers are generally women who really need the money and are out on the streets because of necessity. He stated that he knows several of the sex workers in Rosebank and that the police are quite familiar with them. We continued patrolling, and the officers stopped near a few ladies, who seem intimidated by the police vehicle. After driving from Illovo to Norwood a few times, patrolling and watching the sex workers, we headed back to the Rosebank police station and called it a night.

Faced with the officers' sly grins and chuckles, I could, after several months of patrolling, read between the lines. The officers would usually deny frequenting sex workers, as most of them were married, but every now and then, they would slip in a detail about a previous encounter they had had with a sex worker, to indirectly inform me that intimate encounters did occur. Although sex worker advocates might naturally be concerned by these sexual encounters, these encounters seemed to foster positive interactions between police and sex workers. However, the connections were contingent upon the understanding that the police officer was to pay the same rate as any other client. Several sex workers informed me that if they encountered any type of trouble, they could just call their police officer clients for assistance, demonstrating a form of patronage that highlights the fringe benefits that go beyond money in police-sex worker transactions.

The Informal Rules of Rosebank

In Rosebank, a relatively small community of sex workers and police work around the Oxford Road area. Police were familiar with the sex work hot spots and would take me on patrols in these areas. The sex workers know the names of the police officers, and police officers are familiar with the various sex workers. The relationship between sex workers and police proved to be both dynamic and cyclical during the course of my fieldwork in Rosebank. As the months went by, I learned that police officers would negotiate informal rules with individual sex work contractors. Sex workers were, as a general policy in the area, not arrested. Rather, the general policy of the Rosebank, Bramley, and Norwood police was to ignore sex workers. Some officers had solicited "permits" from individual sex workers new to the business or had demanded free services from new sex workers, but despite this, the policy generally was one of tolerance and acceptance of sex work. Such aberrational instances of police misconduct were not in line with the informal policy of ignoring sex workers.

Nonetheless, both police and sex workers reported that in 2011 and 2012 (before I began my fieldwork), police routinely arrested sex workers. Police would also request identification from sex workers and initiate deportation proceedings against sex workers who were unable to furnish identification. I was told that Rosebank police officers had then been charged with corruption and police brutality in connection with the policing of sex workers. This lawsuit had a chilling effect on the arrest of sex workers, and a formal policy prohibiting the arrest of sex workers was adopted. During semi-structured interviews with me, police officers acknowledged that measures were required to protect the human rights of sex workers and prevent their arrest. Adopting this human rights language, they claimed to be tolerating sex workers rather than arresting them or otherwise preventing them from working.

After I had been in the field for several months, between August and November 2013, sex workers confirmed the police officers' accounts to me and repeatedly confirmed that the police were no longer policing them. Several sex workers said that during the prior year, the police would arrest them and harass them on a routine basis. The police were highly problematic but have since reformed. Some of the sex workers were emboldened by this change and had become openly defiant. One evening, several sex workers cursed the police vehicle as we drove past; in general, sex workers boldly ignored the police vehicle, whereas in years past, they would have run from it. During this time period, the relationships between police officers and sex workers were individualistic; their quality depended on the particular sex worker and the particular officer. As one sex worker informed me, police were "like anyone else. You like some and you hate others." Another sex worker stated, "The police are like anyone else. Some are nice, some aren't." As mentioned earlier, sex workers informed me that they felt comfortable going to the police for assistance and would often call upon certain officers, who were usually regular clients. Several sex workers informed me that the Bramley police were particularly helpful, followed by the Rosebank police. One sex worker reported that police officers actually went to the sex workers while they were working outside and directed them to go to the police station if they experienced any police harassment or abuse.

Police officers, including the head of visible policing, acknowledged the illegality of the sex workers' acts but informed me that sex work simply was "not a police priority"; rather, robberies and other serious crimes in Rosebank demanded their attention. The police could no longer devote resources to the issue of sex workers, and so the "ladies of the night"[9] were left alone. I also heard stories from several officers about officers who used to extort money from sex work clients for bribes before the change in policy was effected. This practice was from the "old days" and was no longer prevalent in Rosebank.

SHIFTING MODES OF POLICING: UPSETTING THE SEX WORK MARKET

Up until November 2013, I had been consistently told that sex workers were no longer being harassed or arrested by the police. During one of my nighttime patrols, I did, however, observe an interaction between one of my regular police patrol partners, Sipho, and a sex worker that demonstrated how easily police and sex workers could end up in altercations. One corner near an Illovo gas station generally has a large population of transgender sex workers. As we drove past this corner one evening, Sipho was particularly annoyed by the sex workers and stated that they tended to be a bit disrespectful. One of the sex workers shouted profanities at Sipho, and he became visibly angry, stopped the police vehicle, and began swearing at the sex workers.

He mumbled something about arresting them but then drove off. But this near-confrontation was atypical. I spent my first five months in Rosebank being told that "the situation is fine," and with the exception of a few outliers, the relationship was cooperative and sex workers were comfortable going to police for assistance.

However, following the December holiday period in 2013, the relationship between police and sex workers around Rosebank rapidly deteriorated. Sex workers informed me that the police had shifted their energies toward the clients and had begun to extort clients whom they found soliciting sex workers. This endeavor became so lucrative that patrolling officers would spend time at known sex work hot spots, waiting for clients to finish with sex work transactions so that they could engage in their scheme. I observed police from central Johannesburg patrolling in Rosebank and heard reports of police from Pretoria traveling to Rosebank in hopes of reaping huge returns from the large bribes that were being extracted from Rosebank clients. One officer recounted the practicalities of obtaining a client bribe:

INDIA: What is the situation in terms of dealing with the clients of the prostitutes?

KARABO (ROSEBANK POLICE OFFICER): [The officers] must also arrest them because they are loitering in prostitution so they are accomplices.

INDIA: The police, you see a man who is about to pick up a prostitute, what do you do then? . . .

KARABO: Yes he gets arrested. . . .

INDIA: And then he gets detained in the police station?

KARABO: Yes.

INDIA: How often do you have to make those arrests?

KARABO: Almost every day.

INDIA: How do the clients react?

KARABO: They try to bribe the police because they don't want their family to find out. At the end of the day we end up taking the bribe.

The policing of sex work during this period eventually became entirely motivated by financial rewards. The possibility of supplementing their incomes, which most police officers view as wholly inadequate for supporting a family, became too much to resist. This was a radical shift from the previous strategy of ignoring sex work to focus on more serious crimes. Police also attempted to partner with sex workers to extort their clients, but most sex workers refused such arrangements, as it would compromise their livelihood and thus was not worth the associated risks. As illustrated in the previous chapter (figure 2.2), there are several interconnecting relationships in a sex work transaction. By affecting one component of the interaction, police were also affecting sex workers. Although the police did not return to arresting sex workers during this period of intense client scrutiny, their demands on the sex worker clientele began to severely upset the delicate balance of the market that existed in Rosebank. The male clients who purchased sex in Rosebank were ordinarily married, White, and middle to upper middle class. They frequented Rosebank because the sex workers who operated there were reputed to be "professional" and "beautiful" and because the location was conducive to relative invisibility. Oxford Road is near several of Johannesburg's wealthy northern suburbs and this proximity to their homes allows clients to be stealthy in their purchase of sex. The sex workers in Rosebank were also less visible than those operating in central Johannesburg. They were generally careful to be discreet, to remain hidden under shadows and in dark corners, and repeatedly bragged among themselves that they were "true professionals." Accordingly, Rosebank attracts a wealthy clientele, and police officers were highly sensitive to this fact. As a method of getting extra money and also a perverse method of getting around human rights directives prohibiting the arrest of sex workers, police began targeting sex work clients, creating some devastating consequences.

As this corruption intensified, police began demanding up to R7000 from clients, threatening to report them to their wives. The illegality of sex work had very little impact on the conversation; it was a negotiation whose currency was morality, driven by the clients' fear of exposure to their wives and families. Several sex workers complained to me about the incessant police corruption:

GRACIOUS (ROSEBANK SEX WORKER): Right now they took R1000 from a client. When they [police] get money, they don't share. The client can come back, and the client can be dangerous.

MELISSA (ROSEBANK SEX WORKER): I had a client with a gun, and he was extorted by the police. We went to do business and the police were waiting outside. They ask for bribes and say that you must pay to stand on this corner. You must pay, pay, pay. . . . If it's a White guy, they take so they don't want their wife to be told. If they [police] get 1000, they will give you 20. There were three Chinese guys who paid 1000 each [to the police]. They were driving a nice car. The police gave me 40 bucks. Luckily we did business, 200 each. It was a quick fuck, those guys cum fast.

CHRISTINA (ROSEBANK SEX WORKER): The clients are scared of police and will pay 1000 in bribes. I feel like I'm working for the police. The police have stopped arresting the sex workers and have been engaging these extortion schemes instead. They are targeting the clients.

The police were mostly complying with their newly adopted "human rights approach" to policing sex work, which prohibited the arrest of sex workers. But they were at the same time subverting the law for their individual benefit; they were abusing their authority by making unlawful demands on both clients and sex workers.

Several of the sex workers informed me that the police had been seeking "freebies" and resorting to dropping them several kilometers from their work sites if they refused to provide officers with free sex. "Some of the police just want to pay 50 and some nothing. If you are caught with a client, they will say that you are sleeping in the cells." The sex workers also began to recount instances of police abuse of power, after several months of informing me that the police were "OK":

MELISSA: The Rosebank police ask for sex and if you don't agree they drop you off somewhere far from Rosebank as punishment. It is difficult because you have to take a taxi and sometimes you haven't even made taxi money yet. They drop you near Zoo Lake if you refuse. When they get money from clients, they don't share it. . . . They want us to work for them, but we don't want to work for them. The clients are scared. They are always patrolling us.

HAU (ROSEBANK SEX WORKER): They asked for sex from me just the other day. They really go after the new ladies. They ask for business while in uniform for less than the normal prices. The police used to arrest too. They no longer arrest so they instead go for the money. They threaten to arrest us, but we don't care. However, it is a problem for girls not from here. They do target the girls who are not from here.

This shift toward extorting clients was police officers' way of complying with policies to respect sex workers' human rights by eliminating the practice of frequently arresting them while continuing to police aspects of sex work. Rosebank police indicated that they did not police sex workers. However, this rationale is similar to the Swedish approach to sex work in its focus on client criminalization and sex worker "protection." The police did continue to harass sex workers, however, they frequently stated that their policy was to no longer focus on sex workers and that the new policy was an effort to respect sex workers' human rights. Sex workers did not feel that their rights were being protected:

ALANNA (ROSEBANK SEX WORKER): The police follow the clients. The clients are scared to approach [us] and are sometimes just watching. They take the clients and take money from them. The police are busy taking money from clients. They say we want the number for your wife. We will call her if you don't give us money.

Many of the clients were confused by the new approach to policing sex work. On January 30, 2014, I went on an evening patrol around Rosebank by myself.[10] As I was driving around Oxford Road in Rosebank, I noticed a police officer pull over a BMW whose driver appeared to be cruising for sex workers. I decided to follow the police vehicle to see where the trail would take me. I followed the police from a few meters behind, as they took a roundabout way to the Rosebank police station, using primarily back routes. When I arrived at the police station, one of the officers asked whether he had seen me on Oxford Road, and I confirmed that I did first see the officer and his partner on Oxford Road. I told him that I was doing research with the police and had been visiting the police station for several months already. The police officers took the arrestee to the back of the station to have a chat with him. I waited in the front.

From the front desk, toward the right side of the police station, I could hear conversations that were taking place in the back room. I decided to sit in this corner to hear the conversation between the police officers and the arrestee. During this conversation, one of the officers approached me and seemed flustered and confused. He seemed a bit shocked to see me there at that moment. It became clear to me that I had caught them in the middle of some sort of inappropriate act. The arrestee was apparently Nigerian (he had a Nigerian accent), and fortunately, this meant that the conversation was in English and not in a language native to South Africa that I would have been unable to understand. The arrestee pleaded: "In 2012, they abuse us. I was driving and there was a lady there. You stop because I was talking to a prostitute. We were stationary. Whatever we were doing were between us. So, it's not a crime, *this is still the system.*" The police officers responded, "Back in your country . . . you might talk like this but you are going to get into trouble for nothing." The arrestee initially appeared surprised that the police had arrested him and had assumed that it was related to incidents in 2012 in South Africa of xenophobic attacks on foreigners, which were at times at the behest of the police. His understanding was that sex work transactions were private in nature and thus noncriminal. This was the "the system" that had been place over the past several months.

After hearing this conversation, I was able to confirm that the arrest in process did in fact involve alleged solicitation and that officers were reaching an "understanding" and making "arrangements" to resolve the matter. Soon after, I saw the arrestee place some money into one of the officer's hands. As the police officers and arrestee were exiting the station, the officer was less firm with the arrestee and feigned concern, stating that it was not 2012 anymore. The client appeared so relieved to learn that this shakedown was connected to his involvement in a sex work transaction rather than a xenophobic attack that he seemed nearly elated to pay the bribe. The police officer used a patronizing tone to instruct the arrestee to be careful, as if the arrest were for the arrestee's own educational benefit. As he was about to enter his BMW, I had an informal interview with the arrestee. He confirmed that he had been arrested in connection with sex work but denied giving a bribe for his release, although I had observed the entire transaction.

This focus on clients had devastating effects for sex workers in the Oxford Road area. Clients were directing their anger at the sex workers and had even shot rubber bullets at sex workers standing outside. The clients were hesitant to make arrangements with sex workers and suspected that they were in cahoots with the police. The police had begun demanding larger bribes, and in mid-February, the trickle-down effects of the intense police scrutiny and corruption fell down to me, and I was nearly arrested.

I received a phone call on February 16, 2014, alerting me to go to number 333 in Illovo.[11] I headed to this parking lot on my motor scooter, wearing a black jacket and my bike helmet. I noticed a number of sex workers standing in the parking lot and a parked Metro police vehicle. A private security officer and the Metro police officers allowed me to enter the parking lot after I explained that I was a researcher and that I had been working primarily with SAPS. It was strange to see Metro police in Rosebank, because the Rosebank SAPS usually policed the sex workers in the area, whereas the Metro police were ordinarily based in central Johannesburg in the evenings. This was not an area that Metro should have been policing. A Metro police officer, Officer Langa, informed me that he was concerned because he had seen people he did not know in the parking lot. I asked him whether they were arrested, and he said no. I then asked him why they were being detained in the lot, because I had already learned that they had been detained there for three hours. One of the sex workers who was being detained, Lucy, stated, "I came and the Metro entered in here. They asked what are you doing here." Officer Langa told me, "We still do not know what is going on here. . . . We are still wanting to know what's happening. We are working to see what happened, maybe they have a bad reason to be here." This was a parking lot where sex work transactions often took place because the security officers had a special arrangement with the sex workers there. The Metro police appeared to be aware of this and had waited there to find clients whom they could extort.

After another hour of detention for the sex workers and clients who had been gathering in the parking lot, one sex worker complained to me that she had a child and that "the baby does not even have milk. How will she eat? Last night I was dropped off by a client and the police asked for 500 rands. Today police asked for 500 for each of the sex workers present." The sex workers were also concerned that these clients would not come back after the negative experience. Another sex worker detailed the severity of the situation in Rosebank at that point in time: "One of us is in hospital because of a client. You call the police, and they don't help. They are committing a crime because of the money. After they collect their bribes they don't care about . . . [who] hurts us." She was recounting an incident where a sex worker had called the police for assistance because her client was being abusive to her. The police came to the scene, but instead of providing her with protection, the officers extorted a bribe from the client, and that client in turn became more physically violent with her and sent her to the hospital.

Backup Metro police arrived in the parking lot after another hour, and an officer of Indian descent, Officer Vidz, got out of his vehicle wearing a bulletproof vest. He was in his mid-30s to mid-40s, and he quickly began to interrogate me. I complied with his questioning and provided him with my contact information. After speaking with him, I was ready to leave the site, because the situation was getting tense, and I was concerned that the police officers would become violent. As I pulled up to the gate on my scooter to leave, Officer Lerato told me that I could not leave. He appeared to be posturing, and despite my pleas to be released, I was stuck. In fact, the officers instructed a female officer to handcuff me, but I walked away from the exit and stated that I would not leave of my own accord. I walked down an alley, and the female officer followed me, saying she would use force on me if I did not come closer to the group.

I complied. The officers had now been talking for some time with the large group of detainees. The sex workers continued complaining about their lost income. I remained behind them in a dark alley and slowly crept behind a building near the parking lot. When it seemed clear that no one was following me, I jumped over the fence, cutting my hands and ripping my pants. I then jumped over a second fence as some sex workers watched me from the outside and pleaded for me to be careful. Both of my hands were bleeding by this time. I ran into the Thrupps shopping center, gesturing for the sex workers to keep quiet. I quickly ran through the indoor center, dropped my bike helmet and jacket on the ground in the back of the center's covered parking lot, waved at the center's security guards, and made my way up a set of parking lot stairs and skipped through the rest of the lot. I threw off my black jacket and was now sporting the bright blue sweatshirt that I had been wearing underneath. I walked from the shopping center to my house, casually, so as to avoid looking suspicious. I arrived home, asked my husband for some assistance in retrieving my abandoned scooter. I waited for the Metro police to leave number 333, which I had successfully escaped, before speaking to the security staff at 333 about retrieving the scooter.

I narrowly escaped getting seriously hurt, but this experience forced me to seriously rethink my research methodology. Despite all the dangers of

FIGURE 3.3. Area near the arrest site, in the parking lot to the left.

nighttime patrols in which I visited with sex workers, my biggest danger had become the police, the ones sworn to serve and protect us. Rosebank and Illovo sex workers called me endlessly the following day, each with different reports about Metro and SAPS officers asking clients for large bribes, and clients in turn inflicting violence upon the sex workers. Many women vowed not to return to Rosebank, and for several weeks following this evening, the streets of Rosebank were nearly empty, with very few sex workers operating on any given evening. In early February 2014, I had counted more than one hundred sex workers outside one evening. In the evening of the day following my near-arrest, I could find only two sex workers on the streets, both of whom appeared to be new to Rosebank.

If nothing else, this experience indicates that upsetting the market for sex work can reap devastating consequences. The quasi-private nature of sex work encourages informal rules to be adopted that shape how police deal with sex workers. These rules adopt legal language in their use of licensing and threats of possible arrest, yet they are a perversion of the law. These informally created rules are often motivated by greed, as they allow officers

TABLE 3.1. Timeline of sex work policing and sex worker activity in Rosebank.

Date	Event
July 2013	• Informal decriminalization in effect • Sex workers recovering from prior arrests • Sex workers recovering from prior news coverage by journalists
August 2013	• Informal decriminalization in effect • Tension low
September 2013	• Informal decriminalization in effect • Police and sex workers in agreement • No tension
October 2013	• Informal decriminalization in effect • Police and sex workers in agreement • No tension • Individualized nature of relationship recognized
November 2013	• Informal decriminalization in effect • Isolated incidents of police abuse, but generally, according to sex workers, a police policy of no arrests
December 2013	• Informal decriminalization in effect • Increasing incidents of police targeting sex workers' customers
Late December 2013	• Informal decriminalization in effect • Number of sex workers reduced due to holidays and travel
January 2014	• Partial decriminalization in effect • Heightened police surveillance of sex workers' customers • Extraordinary bribes
February 2014	• Partial decriminalization in effect • Heightened police surveillance of sex workers' customers • Extraordinary bribes • Author arrested
March 2014	• Partial decriminalization in effect • Heightened police surveillance of sex workers' customers • Extraordinary bribes • Drastic decrease of sex workers due to sex workers moving to other locations
April 2014	• Partial decriminalization in effect • Heightened police surveillance of sex workers' customers • Extraordinary bribes • Drastic decrease of sex workers due to sex workers moving to other locations
May 2014	• Partial decriminalization in effect • Heightened police surveillance of sex workers' customers • Extraordinary bribes • Drastic decrease of sex workers due to sex workers moving to other locations

(continues)

TABLE 3.1. (*continued*)

Date	Event
June 2014	• Partial decriminalization in effect • Heightened police surveillance of sex workers' customers • Extraordinary bribes • Occasionally a small number of sex workers
July 2014	• Partial decriminalization in effect • Heightened police surveillance of sex workers' customers • Extraordinary bribes • Occasionally a small number of sex workers
August 2014	• Partial decriminalization in effect • Heightened police surveillance of sex workers' customers • Extraordinary bribes • Occasionally, a small number of sex workers
February 2015	• Partial decriminalization in effect • Heightened police surveillance of sex workers' customers • Extraordinary bribes • Occasionally, a small number of sex workers

to share in the profits to be gained from sex work. There is an explicit focus on police officers' monetary gain, which encourages the policing of the private lives of sex workers and their clients and of the semi-private spaces that sex workers and their clients negotiate. Police officers appear cognizant of the legal mandates and have adapted means of bending them. As discussed in chapter 1, many police officers feel they are owed additional income and believe they were better compensated during apartheid. This belief appears to have fueled the individualistic greed of some officers.

In Rosebank, the police corruption was excessive and deviated from the expectations of "efficient" amounts of corruption. The formal law worked in encouraging police officers to respect sex workers. However, the police found a fail-safe to get around these legal requirements by focusing on the clients and exploiting the conditions of sex work. This can be considered a form of *lawfare*, described by Jean and John Comaroff as "the resort to legal instruments, to the violence inherent in the law, to commit acts of political coercion, even erasure. . . . As a species of political displacement, it becomes most visible when those who 'serve' the state conjure with legalities to act against its citizens."[12] The focus on client activities is just such a conjuring with legalities, an attempt to comply with human rights standards that has led police to remove their attention from the sex workers. Police informed me that they did not police sex workers anymore because sex workers have human rights. They were purposely adopting a policy that did not involve the frequent arrest and direct harassment of sex workers. However, officers did not mention the law when harassing clients. Those actions were about morality and extorting the clients' desires to remain invisible in sex work transactions. In many respects, this looks like the Swedish model of policing sex work that focuses on clients, but this model fails here. This model looks inadequate in its focus on client criminalization because clients can always turn their gaze onto sex workers.[13] Moreover, sex workers need clients to work. If one-half of the transaction is criminal, the sex workers cannot freely work. Sex workers were most concerned about their inability to work. Several of them said that they were the main support for their family and needed sex work to provide for themselves and their children. As one sex worker told me, "I wouldn't be standing here if there was another job. I am the breadwinner for my family. I have kids." The Rosebank officers' conduct was an abuse of the law in its manipulation of legal standards to produce an individual monetary benefit for the officers involved. Here, the police manipulated dominant mores around sexuality and marriage to entice clients to pay bribes. Police were acting as moral arbiters while personally benefiting from their lawfare against clients. The police perceived their conduct as consistent with human rights because they were no longer systematically harassing and abusing sex workers. However, their targeting of clients was indirectly compromising the rights of sex workers and giving the guise of legal compliance to acts that were in fact law breaking. Following this turn to the Swedish approach to sex work, sex workers desperately called me asking for financial assistance to provide formula for their children and food for their extended families because they could no longer work. The Swedish model of targeting the clients succeeded at eliminating sex work, but it also devastated these sex workers' lives. Abolishing sex work did not benefit the women in Rosebank. They needed work. Now. They did not need it in a distant political reality where patriarchy has ceased to exist. What would be the immediate work substitute if sex work were eliminated? Would these women be able to provide for their extended families as they had with sex work?

4 | POLICING BEAUTY

DURING MY PATROLS WITH Hillbrow police station members, officers often spoke about sex workers as being either "professional" or "unprofessional," attributing assorted values to the sex workers depending upon their perceived professionalism. Police officers frequently tied such so-called professionalism to the perceived beauty of the sex worker. The more beautiful sex workers were more professional. They were more "about their business" and knew their jobs well. They were also more desirable. In the officers' words, they "really know" their work. This theme of beauty and professionalism constantly recurred, especially as police officers began to feel more comfortable having casual conversations with me. The perceived beauty of sex workers deeply influenced other perceptions of the sex workers held by the police and also the required approaches toward policing them. Beauty was a form of bodily capital that was reflected in the geography of the various red-light districts and their corresponding policing. These subjective views of beauty reproduced a spatialization of sex work. In other words, a sex worker's particular perceived identity as being of a particular class of sex worker (for example, a "beautiful," South African, female, thin sex worker) was spatially reproduced in the geography of the various brothels. This spatialization is itself a reproduction of a patriarchal hegemony that provides the standards for female beauty. Through this mapping, the body, as expressed through beauty, is written into the fabric of urban life in Johannesburg. At the same time, it is expressed not in the negative language of immorality but in the positive, subjective language of appreciation of beauty.

The subjective experience of desire reflects gendered norms that speak to a particular social order. Women who were perceived as appearing South African or Whiter, with leaner bodies, lighter skin, and straighter hair, were universally lauded. Women who looked foreign catered to narrower, more specific demographics. These perceptions reflected larger social forces that included positionality within a country that struggles with race and xeno-phobia.[1] This subjectivity was reflected in the policing task. The sex workers' "beauty" appeared to be a separate element influencing how they were po-liced. It created a type of subjectivity in the policing of sex workers that was inconsistent and subject to the tastes of the individual police officers. Polic-ing became guided by the desires of the officers rather than by the objective of reducing crime, echoing the public hygiene discourses around sex workers that are part of the legacy of how sex workers have been policed in South Africa.[2] In this way, the pernicious male gaze not only defined the hierarchal status of the sex worker body but also determined the level of police scru-tiny and interaction it must withstand. In general, brothel-based sex work-ers were perceived as more hygienic and professional than street-based sex workers. Both police officers and sex workers acknowledged this distinction:

> MICHAEL (HILLBROW POLICE OFFICER): In the clubs they are pro-fessional because I think they are going to go to the hotel and they are using condoms so they are taking life professionally. By taking care of your life, that is professional. They are clean. Yes, I think that that is more professional.

Likewise, sex workers confirmed that police were frequent patrons at the high-end establishments; as one sex worker noted, "At Summit, there are a lot of police as clients and they are not in uniform; even White guys come to drink."

In those brothels where the sex workers were denounced as less attractive, the police appeared less enthusiastic in their policing. These brothels were also presumed to be bastions of violence and crime. Ironically, the fear of vio-lence in these brothels and clubs kept some officers from entering them. This is precisely what happened during one of my nighttime patrols in Hillbrow, on January 10, 2014. I went to the police station to join one of the routine patrols to which I had become accustomed. As I have been describing, I regularly accompanied Hillbrow police officers during their nighttime patrols, during which they would respond to complaints, patrol clubs, and engage in routine police tasks. The nighttime shifts always began at 6:00 p.m., but given the time needed for the police officers to check in for their shifts, complete the necessary paperwork, and ensure that there was a vehicle large enough to accommodate everyone joining the patrol, we would usually leave around 7:00 or 8:00 p.m. By this time, I had already joined the officers on several patrols of the Hillbrow hotel-brothels and was familiar with several of them.

On this particular evening, I asked whether we could visit the Maxime hotel-brothel, as I had only been driven past it during previous police patrols and was interested in exploring it with the police. I had visited the hotel's club on my own during one of its live sex shows several weeks prior to this patrol and was curious to see how it was policed. Officers John and Jimmy, who were my patrol partners for the evening, quickly protested this suggestion. They informed me that "those ladies" were not professionals and that we could be in imminent danger if we were to enter the club. I was surprised to hear this because the club had not appeared particularly dangerous when I visited it for the sex show. Certainly, it was not an ordinary bar, but it was no dodgier than any of the other clubs in Hillbrow. The officers insisted that we should not go to this club and made offhand comments suggesting that the physical appearance of these sex workers left much to be desired. They also mentioned the lack of cleanliness of the venue and suggested that the sex workers who worked there were a bit "rough around the edges." They further claimed that two police officers had been shot outside the brothel two weeks prior and that it would too dangerous to enter.[3] The mention of the shooting was enough to deter my persistence. The officers were allegedly patrolling outside the club and were purposely struck by two shots from inside the venue. Officers Jimmy and John claimed that the building was incredibly dangerous and that the very sight of a police vehicle would be enough to cause some residents to shoot.

This cautionary tale served as my introduction to the officers' tendency to link perceived sex worker "beauty" with the perceived levels of brothel danger and of the sex workers' professionalism. I was fascinated by these connections, and I had now seen first-hand the fear these officers had at the proposition of entering the Maxime hotel. Interestingly, police officers never had an issue with taking me to the clubs where they proclaimed that the sex workers were professional and beautiful.

That same evening, I entered the Summit Club with officers Jimmy and John and without any hesitation on their part. Jimmy appeared to be good friends with the brothel management. The Summit Club manager was a burly Afrikaans man, who was sweating excessively. There was a slickness about his demeanor, and he appeared completely comfortable with the police officers. I sensed that Jimmy had made many visits to Summit Club, because he was intimately familiar with the staff and the club's layout. The club manager and Jimmy greeted each other by name, and the manager offered us a warm welcome and a drink upon our entering.

The manager gave me a very superficial tour of the bottom levels of the club, where strip shows and teases took place. I peeped into the bar as the officers continued chatting with the management. As we watched the semi-clothed workers walk past us, the officers reiterated that these ladies are professionals and reminded me that they "know what they are doing." I nodded in agreement and decided to browse the lower levels of the club further. This was how a typical night of patrolling these clubs went. I would always look curiously toward the upper levels of the brothels, to which, of course, I never received a managerial escort. The women at the Summit Club were generally relatively thin, and several wore long weaves with Brazilian hair. Both sex workers and their clients had informed me that the sex workers in the Summit are mostly Black South African women and that they cater to men who have a particular desire for upscale sex workers that fit popular subjective norms of beauty, which included women with long hair, thin bodies, and flashy outfits. The manifestation of this desire was not, however, restricted to particular ethnic groups; in fact, the clientele was quite diverse, its precise composition depending on the hour.

During the daytime, old White men salivated at the gyrating bodies on the dance floors. I would visit Summit around noon on Saturdays and would frequently find older White men viewing strip teases on the lower levels. The men appeared to be as old as the mid-80s and seemed to be more infatuated by the attention they received from the workers than by the promise of a sexual escapade. These men left large tips and were surrounded by young women who ordinarily would not give them the time of day. The Summit Club provides a total experience. It is very clean and about as well decorated as a gauche Las Vegas casino might aspire to be. Of course, it serves drinks and meals, but it also has a swimming pool, a full gym, and private rooms on the top levels. The parking lot, filled with Mercedes Benzes and BMWs, is a testament to the caliber of men the club attracts. It is obviously designed to cater to well-to-do businessmen venturing to the notorious Hillbrow enclave to engage in sinful behavior. This club is in many respects the epitome of the Hillbrow brothel. It represents what many of the other clubs aspire toward. It is the gold standard.

After exploring several other Hillbrow clubs, I noted that they each had a distinct reputation with the police, and I began to explore how such perceptions influenced the way each establishment's sex workers were policed. One hypothesis I had was that the more professional the sex worker, the less likely she was to be policed. This did not pan out in my findings, however. The police were more likely to police those sex workers they perceived to be professional and beautiful. Beauty in some way appeared to result in higher scrutiny for the sex worker. This might have been because the police preferred frequenting establishments where they would find women they believed were desirable.

However, focusing on perceptions of beauty is inherently problematic. Beauty is ordinarily viewed as a constraint on womankind. It is a construction created by men that necessarily oppresses women.[4] Feminists are generally suspicious of it, and the notion of spending any serious time evaluating it in academic work seems suspect. Yet I could not turn away from this topic because it is in many ways an inherent means of evaluating sex workers in particular. After all, the clients evaluate sex workers according to the women's perceived beauty. Sex workers compete fiercely for clients, and some women are accused of engaging in *muti*, or African magic, by fellow sex workers who do not understand their strong client demand. Sex workers themselves organize themselves based on their perceptions of their own beauty and their ability to compete with sex workers from a particular locale. My key informant, Erica, explained to me that she left the Summit Club for greener pastures at the Hillbrow Inn because she is heavier set and was unable to find work at Summit, where the women are typically much thinner. Mary, a sex worker who was already relatively thin, recounted a story about the Summit Club manager admonishing her about her weight and instructing her to spend more time in the club's gym. The physical standards of the respective establishments were enforced by the hotel-brothel owners and management.

Beauty is highly subjective and may be difficult to study. However, exploring how perceptions of beauty influence approaches to policing sex workers provides an interesting arena for exploring the intersections of gender, race, sexuality, and policing. In some ways, women who were perceived as higher on the beauty hierarchy had more control over where they could work and their choice of patrons. They also tended to be higher earners. However, they were subject to greater surveillance and regulation by male police officers.

In order to explore police perceptions of sex worker beauty and sex worker professionalism, I focused on six clubs that fell across the spectrum of such clubs in Hillbrow. I visited each of these clubs on five to fifteen separate occasions and spent several hours in each as a patron to get a sense of their clientele, reputation, and energy. I selected the Royal Park Hotel, a high-end hotel with flashing lights and a significant international sex worker population that included Thai and Russian sex workers; the Summit Club, a high-end club that specialized, as Janelle, a sex worker there, said, in "beautiful thin South Africa women Brazilian weaves;" the Maxime, a mid-range hotel with a notorious weekly sex show; the Hillbrow Inn, a lower-mid-range hotel with a significant portion of clients from Zimbabwe, that specialized in "thick women;" the German Club, a lower- to mid-range club that was reputed to have thinner and younger sex workers and was patronized by older White men; and the Kilimanjaro, a low-end, casual establishment that served food and was reputed for its affordability. (See Map 4.1 for club locations.)

For each of the sex worker and club attributes I was exploring, I asked my Hillbrow police interviewees to rate the attribute on a scale from 1 (most or highest) to 6 (least or lowest). After the means of their responses were obtained and ranked, the ranks were then inversed, so that in the final scores shown in the following figures, a higher score means a greater level of the attribute and a lower score means a lower level. Among the six establishments, the Summit Club and Royal Park Hotel tied for the highest ranking of beauty

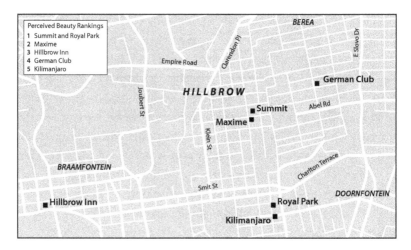

MAP 4.1. Brothels and their beauty rankings.

of sex workers, followed, in descending rank, by the Maxime, Hillbrow Inn, German Club, and Kilimanjaro (figure 4.1). The Royal Park was found to have the highest level of professionalism, followed by the Summit Club, Maxime, Hillbrow Inn, German Club, and Kilimanjaro (figure 4.2). The Summit Club was perceived to have the highest number of foreign sex workers, followed by the Maxime, Royal Park, Kilimanjaro, German Club, and Hillbrow Inn (figure 4.3). And finally, the Royal Park was thought to have been subject to the highest number of raids, followed by the Summit Club, German Club, Maxime, Hillbrow Inn, and Kilimanjaro (figure 4.4).

To determine the relationships between the variables of beauty, professionalism, foreigners, and raids, I conducted pairwise correlation tests (using the inversed scores reported in the figures, meaning that 6 is the highest rating). Because tests for normality showed non-normality of data ($p < .05$), nonparametric tests of correlation (Spearman's tests of correlation), were performed. As displayed in table 4.1, all four variables were statistically significantly correlated ($p < .05$). Beauty of sex workers was positively correlated with professionalism of sex workers ($p < .001$), which indicates that in brothels where police perceived sex workers to be more beautiful, the perception of the professionalism of sex workers was higher as well. Beauty of sex workers was also negatively correlated with foreign sex workers ($p = .026$), which indicates that brothels where police perceived sex workers to be more beautiful

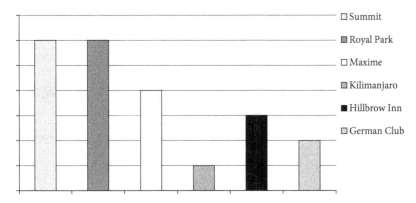

FIGURE 4.1. Ranking of clubs by beauty of sex workers, as perceived by Hillbrow police interviewees.

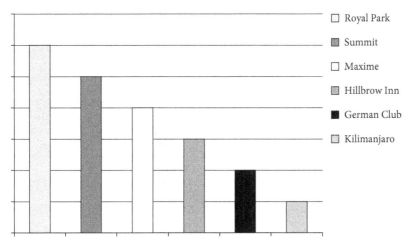

FIGURE 4.2. Ranking of clubs by professionalism of sex workers, as perceived by Hillbrow police interviewees.

were also perceived to have lower numbers of foreign sex workers. And finally, beauty of sex workers was positively correlated with the frequency of raids ($p < .001$). Professionalism was negatively correlated with foreigners ($p = .014$), but positively correlated with raids ($p < .001$). The number of foreign sex workers was negatively correlated with number of raids ($p = .006$). The relationships shown by the correlation tests are illustrated in figures 4.5 through 4.8.

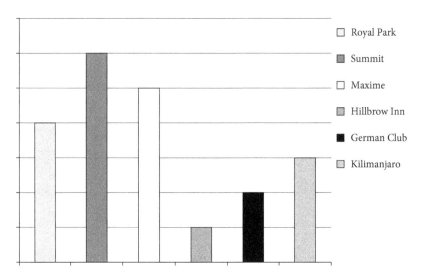

FIGURE 4.3. Ranking of clubs by number of foreigners, as perceived by Hillbrow police interviewees.

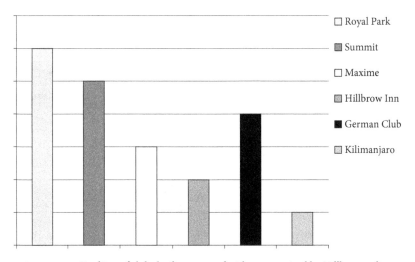

FIGURE 4.4. Ranking of clubs by frequency of raids, as perceived by Hillbrow police interviewees.

TABLE 4.1. Relationships between beauty, professionalism, foreigners, and raids: Spearman's correlation coefficients.

	Beauty	Professionalism	Foreigners	Raids
Beauty	1	.904**	−.253*	.724**
Professionalism		1	−.278*	.721**
Foreigners			1	−.310**
Raids				1

*p < .05; **p < .01.

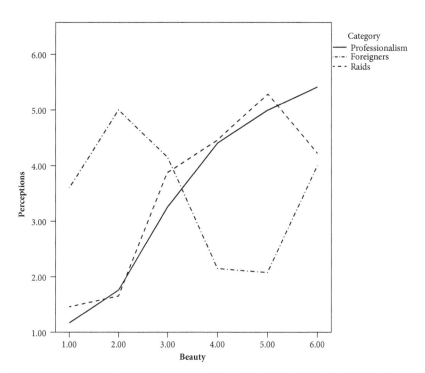

FIGURE 4.5. Relationships between perceptions of beauty (*x*-axis) and professionalism, foreigners, and raids (*y*-axis).

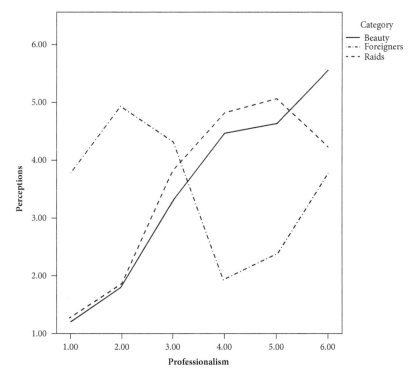

FIGURE 4.6. Relationships between perceptions of professionalism (*x*-axis) and beauty, foreigners, and raids (*y*-axis).

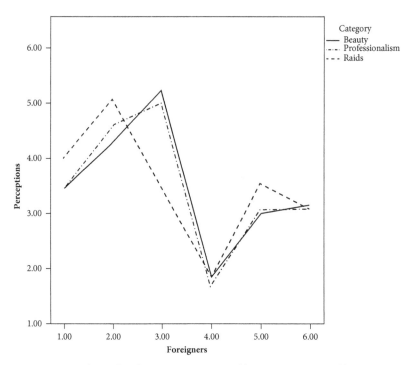

FIGURE 4.7. Relationships between perceptions of foreigners (*x*-axis) and beauty, professionalism, and raids (*y*-axis).

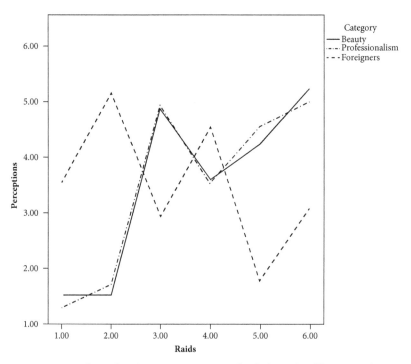

FIGURE 4.8. Relationships between perceptions of raids (*x*-axis) and beauty, professionalism, and foreigners (*y*-axis).

In those brothels where sex workers were perceived to be more beautiful, the police were more likely to believe that the sex workers should be regarded as professionals. In those brothels where the sex workers were perceived to be less beautiful, the sex workers were more likely to be assumed to be foreign. Police were more likely to raid brothels that housed sex workers believed to be beautiful and professional. This finding is surprising if we assume that police engage in police raids to curtail activities likely to occur in less organized environments that are not highly professional. The women in the more professional environments reported that they felt safe and comfortable in their working conditions because they had the protection of these highly organized environments. My visits to the various brothels confirmed that those deemed to be more professional were highly organized and had adopted a tourism approach to the trade, meaning they were customer service driven. As such, one would expect police to investigate the less professional brothels if they were primarily interested in investigating crime.

Thus, one explanation for the inverse relationship between the professionalism of a brothel and its likelihood of experiencing police raids is that police are not motivated by a desire to curtail crime. Rather, brothels that are highly organized and professional are more likely to be raided because police are motivated by other incentives. Police appear to be patrons at the more upscale establishments and tend to return to familiar territory. The policing of these locations is quasi-policing and quasi-socializing. Sex workers did confirm that they had police officer clients during the raids, and some indicated that certain police officers expected to receive discounted services during these encounters, although most paid full price for the services. The police visit these brothels late in the evenings and often partake in beverages. There may also be a greater opportunity for police to extract bribes at highly organized establishments, precisely because of their higher profits, high-profile clientele, and willingness to cooperate with the police.

These policing practices further reveal that sex worker choices concerning an appropriate venue for work are far from accidental. These spaces are socially produced by a sex worker's understandings of her bodily capital, competition, potential clients, and general comfort in various social situations. The perception of the sex worker's body then becomes a mode for reproducing misogyny and exercising power over female sexuality. It becomes an excuse for heightened surveillance and exercise of authority over the sex worker's expression of sexuality. Sex workers at the Hillbrow Inn and German Club were described as "foreign" and were marginalized. Sex workers at the Summit Club and Royal Park Hotel were valorized but simultaneously subject to exploitation at the hands of the police. In this way, assertions about the sex workers' beauty alienate certain sex workers and valorize others, those who are frequently described as domestic to South Africa.

Declaring their hotel-brothel preferences also was a method for police officers to brag to each other and demonstrate their superlative desires and tastes. During a focus group discussion with Hillbrow police members, I saw that officers were proud of their preferred brothels and appeared to judge police officers who had alternative desires. It was a way for officers to brag in the locker room and discuss their "conquests," so to speak. The expression of their subjective desires was a mode for the expression of masculinities that hierarchize female sexualities, reflecting a geography of sexual desire in the urban space.

Moreover, beauty is also a way of thinking about hygiene. The sex worker body has consistently been policed in hygienic terms and subject to regulations based on concerns around hygiene. Here, beauty is treated as synonymous with proper hygiene. Sex workers in indoor locations have generally been considered more professional and, correspondingly, more hygienic; sex workers in the streets were often perceived as "dirty," or less hygienic. The varied policing due to subjective understandings of beauty highlights the continuity with past practices of policing that focused on the hygiene of various sex workers. The logic of the hygiene discourse is that the sex workers considered the dirtiest would receive the most policing. However, my ethnography suggests that at times and counterintuitively, being more hygienic subjects sex workers to more policing. The more hygienic, or beautiful, sex workers in both Hillbrow and Rosebank were more heavily policed. However, the type of policing that the more hygienic sex workers experience is not the crude policing focused on driving them out and making them invisible, as occurred in central Johannesburg. Instead, it is a more benevolent form of policing that is a more direct expression of biopower in its gaze on these sex workers' bodies. It is a more intense gaze, but also more reverent. There is a level of respect associated with it that is not present in the form of policing that relies on brute force and violence to enforce the law.

This extension of biopower to more beautiful sex workers illustrates how desire and biopower can take form in unexpected ways. Patriarchy and hegemony do not reproduce themselves in simple ways. One patriarchal form is not necessarily going to be replaced by another that is its equal. Rather, it may be transformed into different and unexpected forms, and even within these forms, women can express power and resistance.

5 | SEX WORK, FEMINISM, AND POLICY

I STARTED MY RESEARCH ambivalent about the policy and legal choices posed by the question of whether sex work should be criminalized or decriminalized. However, as my research took place at a time in which the legal framework for sex work in South Africa was under review and many advocacy organizations were calling for decriminalization, the theme of criminalization kept emerging, and everyone with whom I spoke seemed to have an opinion on it. I was insistent that determining the appropriate legal or policy choice in relation to criminalization was not the primary subject of my research and that I was interested in the nature of the policing of sex work in a broad sense. The legality of the act was relevant only to the extent that it influenced how the sex workers were policed and perhaps to understanding how they should negotiate their relationships with police officers. I could appreciate arguments made by advocates from various sides of the argument. Although I anticipated that I might lean toward the "pro-sex" stance,[1] I was not completely sold on any particular approach. My research would be undertaken from a neutral position, one that did not necessarily promote any particular advocacy agenda.

However, as I became immersed in my research, spending nights on the streets of inner-city Johannesburg speaking to sex workers, becoming a friend to the many sex workers who operated from the streets of Rosebank, my orientation on this subject rapidly shifted. I put in many hours with po-lice officers—patrolling with them, interviewing them, and just spending time with them—and I heard their views on sex work criminalization. It was impossible for me to be so closely immersed in the reality of sex work, float-ing between the perspectives of the police and the sex workers and constantly shifting my frame of reference, without developing an opinion on criminal-ization myself. I occupied a space of liminality that is common for the eth-nographer but even more so in my situation, as I floated between spaces oc-cupied by presumed rivals. And yet, these rivals appeared to be more in sync than an outsider might presume.

The policing of sex work, I found, was constantly evolving and subject to the variables of passing time, seasonal and political changes, geography, and the observation of religious holidays. There was no singular "policing of sex workers." The policing of sex workers largely occupies a space on the margins of law, sometimes within the law and sometimes outside it. It is a space where rules are constantly renegotiated to satisfy the needs of the po-litical moment. Much of the feminist debate around sex work has focused on the sex worker and issues of consent, coercion, subordination, freedom, and sexual autonomy. Some of these debates proceed as if sex work were static. There often is a blanket recommendation for decriminalization or partial criminalization, without much discussion about how these legal ap-proaches would actually look when practiced. Much of the debate tends to be circular because it avoids the most direct question: How do we, as femi-nists, want to think about sex? Radical feminists have argued that sex should never be a tool to address economic struggles. Scott Anderson notes, "Pro-hibition [of sex work] not only denies individuals the choice to sell sex for money, it also signals that no one should be expected to make choices about sex just to escape economic hardship."[2] Arguments regarding subordination and coercion can easily be transplanted to marriage, yet no contemporary feminist movement is aiming to outlaw the institution of marriage.[3] Some-thing about commercialized sex makes it especially troubling for feminists to grapple with.[4] Although patriarchy exists as a structural force that women experience in South African society, the ways it is expressed and experienced and the ways in which it influences women's lives are not uniform, let alone static, throughout time. In fact, women have power and agency and can exert resistance to defy societal standards and norms. This power to resist lies even with women who are often to be deemed "vulnerable," including sex workers.

THE ROLE OF LAW IN INTERPRETING SEX WORK IN SOUTH AFRICA

When South Africa underwent its lengthy and much delayed law reform process from 2007 to 2017, with guidance from the South African Law Reform Commission, much of the effort around sex work was focused on influencing policy and advancing a particular legal outcome. In the international arena, several feminist approaches to sex work have been taking the form of *governance feminism*, which has been defined as "the incremental but by now quite noticeable installation of feminists and feminist ideas in actual legal-institutional power."[5] Although they adopt different rationales and proposals for sex work, these approaches are aimed at incorporating feminist legal thought into the legal hierarchy. Governance feminism emphasizes the use of law-making to set the feminist agenda;[6] it turns to legal enforcement of feminist ideals, including the use of criminal law. At times, feminism seeks to create a middle ground for the competing approaches to sex work through "[appreciating] the individual as agentic and self-determining in the face of limitations, instead of ascribing a narrow status of victim or agent," and in this way aiming to provide a more nuanced understanding of sex work.[7]

Generally speaking, there are four approaches to the management of sex work: (1) criminalization, (2) partial criminalization with the goal of eventual elimination of sex work, (3) regulation, and (4) decriminalization.[8] In South Africa, sex work is currently managed pursuant to the first approach. Since 2007, sex work has been explicitly criminal for both the sex worker and the sex work client.[9] Partial criminalization relates to the so-called Swedish model, which prohibits the conduct of the sex work client but does not criminalize the conduct of the sex worker. Radical feminists generally support this approach because, theoretically, it protects the sex worker, who is a victim of her[10] occupation, while criminalizing the client, in the hope of eliminating future demand for sex work. Regulation involves the decriminalization of sex work for both the client and sex worker but allows laws and/ or ordinances aimed at regulating aspects of the sex work trade, for example, zoning ordinances specific to brothels.[11] Finally, decriminalization is the total elimination of all criminal sanctions relating to sex work.[12] Under decriminalization, sex work would be treated like any other occupation, and would be subject to the same general laws.[13]

SWEAT and Sisonke, a movement of sex workers led by sex workers, are leading sex work activist organizations in South Africa that have called for the decriminalization of sex work. They argue that sex workers have agency and choice[14] and should be allowed to choose their occupation.[15] Much of the debate has been driven by these two groups, resulting in a distinctly governance-based approach to the sex work question. Their advocacy is concerned with policy and legal reform, and is specifically focused on advocating for decriminalization and on law-making as agenda-setting.[16] Advocates have favored decriminalization as a form of harm reduction for sex workers, while also highlighting the individual autonomy of the sex worker.[17] This approach has garnered widespread support across the women's rights sector in South Africa. For example, in 2013, the South African Commission for Gender Equality released a report calling for decriminalization, outlining the various ways that criminalization violated the human rights of sex workers.[18] Similarly, the commission's 2013 *Position Paper on Sex Work* adopts a liberal rights-based framework in discussing the violations of sex workers' individual rights caused by the environment of criminalization. It highlights sex workers' right to choose their own form of work and occupation.[19] The emphasis here is less about using criminal law to protect sex workers and more about freeing sex workers from the mandates of criminal law through decriminalization.

The ANC Women's League, the women's wing of the African National Congress, has also adopted a rights-based approach in discussing sex work. In 2012, the African National Congress adopted a stance in support of decriminalization of sex work, stating:

> Whatever the ideal approach would be going forward, it is imperative and critical that it embraces the dignity of women, increases job opportunities and decent work for all women; and affords sex workers their human rights, human dignity and access to health care and social justice.[20]

The treasurer for the organization, Hlengiwe Mkhize, confirmed that this statement was a show of support for decriminalization.

THE IDEAL VICTIM IN RADICAL FEMINIST THEORY

The theoretical underpinnings for the various legal approaches to sex work generally rely upon principles advanced on a continuum from radical feminism to liberal theory. Western-based radical feminism is often in conversation with liberal feminism and its ideas of individual choice and sex work as work. Jody Freeman provides an honest account of the radical feminist position:

> Conceiving of sexuality in market terms dehumanizes how we think and act about something extremely important to our conception of self. It would reduce sexuality to just another fungible good because commodification leads to "the domino effect"—the tendency in our society to completely commodify in all respects and for all purposes. . . .[21]

She boldly claims that "we need to reclaim values that affirm and enhance, not demean human beings. Feminism that is unwilling or unable to choose amongst an assortment of behaviours may be tolerant, but to me it is apathetic and apolitical."[22] But the declaration begets the question: Whose values matter?

The sex work victimization paradox is present with the emergence of radical feminism in the 1980s. However, victims are not empowered.[23] They require help and by definition are subject to the authority of those who deem them helpless. Although scholars who engage in sex-worker-as-victim debates presumably aim to help or save the sex worker victim, they are simultaneously depriving sex workers of aspects of their self-determination and ignoring their voices in the debates about what is best for them. "Most simply, sex workers' own understandings of their lives, and the ways of living embedded in those forms of understanding, are themselves part of the phenomenon under investigation."[24] Radical feminism in many ways continues the work of Josephine Butler and the Christian Temperance Union in imagining sex workers as hapless victims of circumstances. For example, Carole Pateman argues that women who sell sex are selling themselves and thus their womanhood.[25] She claims that the social conditions of prostitution are such that, inherently, the women are subordinated. Christine Overall similarly claims that women are subordinated in prostitution.[26] Debra Satz argues that although sex work is not inherently wrong, it is wrong to the extent that it influences men's perceptions of women.[27] Central to the debate is the issue of autonomy: "Radical feminists say that prostitution is not a harmless, 'private' transaction but a powerful means of creating, reinforcing, and perpetuating the objectification of women through sexuality."[28]

Scott Anderson resists the liberal treatment of sex work as another form of labor and argues that it reduces female sexual autonomy. He claims:

> A person's sexuality almost always figures prominently as an aspect of his or her self-conception, status in society, and economic and social prospects. . . . It is because sex plays such a pivotal role in the lives of most adults . . . that it creates its own special . . . realm within which one can be more or less autonomous.[29]

In this way, he argues that sex work reduces sexual autonomy. Radical feminists can be said to implicitly subscribe to the theory of asymmetry: "Those who hold the asymmetry book believe that markets in reproduction and sex are asymmetric to other labor markets."[30] They believe that sex markets cannot be compared to other markets because there is asymmetry between the contracting parties in a sex work relationship. Sex is essentialized and universalized in this worldview. "[I]n the hegemonic Euro-American culture, sexuality and money are thought of as things that cannot, do not, and/or should not mix."[31]

Catharine MacKinnon and other radical feminists argue that sex work is a form of violence against women and that sex workers cannot exhibit agency in a system of male subordination of women.[32] Andrea Dworkin reduces sex work to the male experience: "In the male system, women are sex; sex is the whore. . . . Using her is using pornography. . . . Being her is being pornography."[33] She views sex work as a per se violation on the woman and as an act of violence against women. This perspective suggests that those who engage in all forms of sex work are victims of patriarchy based on the sexual objectification of women. Judith Vega argues that "[f]eminist politics as well as theory have declared the incompatibility of coercion and genuine consent. It is precisely this thinking in opposites . . . that paralyzes feminist thought about sexual violence."[34]

Under radical feminist theory, individual women's choices are given little regard or expression, and it is presumed that women cannot exercise a choice

that involves the giving away of their bodies. This marks a deliberate devia-
tion from traditional liberal theory. Much of "traditional liberal theory . . .
is committed to autonomy, individualism, and minimal state interference in
private choice. Liberal theory is premised on an assumption that individuals
are atomistic, pre-social beings who exist independent of their community."[35]
Radical feminism concerns itself with structural concerns and views the
woman who chooses to engage in sex work as either a victim of circumstance
or a victim of her own false consciousness. Pornography is condemned for
reinforcing the masculinity and patriarchy that demotes women to satisfiers
of male sexual urges.[36] Melissa Farley has declared, "Like slavery, prostitution
is a lucrative form of oppression. And both slavery and prostitution are rife
with every imaginable type of physical and sexual violence."[37] She advocates
for a form of radical feminism that intends to save women from the captivity
of patriarchy. Unfortunately, her logic may serve more to entangle the very
same women whom she intends to save.

In South Africa, sex workers were historically perceived as victims who
should be tolerated so long as they did not create a nuisance to the public.
As a result of her perceived helplessness, the sex worker frequently received
more favorable treatment from the law than her accused client or brothel
owner did. As previously discussed in chapter 1, a judge of the Eastern Districts Local Division court complained about this differential treatment
in *Rex v V*, stating that it "seems a glaring injustice." The portrayal of the
sex worker as victim resulted in her receiving less severe punishment than
brothel keepers or "touts" because she was viewed as a victim of circumstance. She was not treated as harshly because she was, after all, a victim. This
result created a paradox in depriving the sex worker of her sexual autonomy
as an individual,[38] while simultaneously empowering her through more lenient punishment and treatment under the law.

The philosophy underlying the radical feminist approach to sex work,
which treats sex workers as victims and sex work as a universal evil, is influential among many who are concerned with the lives of sex workers. This
perspective underlies much of the work in human trafficking courts, and
was evident in a letter signed by several Hollywood starlets in opposition to
Amnesty International's support for decriminalization, and is the premise of
several movies and documentaries about sex slavery. Radical feminists aim

to abolish sex work but argue that sex workers should not be criminalized for engaging in it. They are concerned with the structural harms of sex work and have formed alliances with groups that oppose sex work due to moralistic philosophies. Like radical feminism, this book considers the systemic harms of sex work and criminalization. However, it arrives at a very different conclusion.

As much as it purports to support subjectivity, the radical feminist position is predicated on its presumed objectivity—on its ability to proclaim universal truths about male and female sexuality. Sex is a topic infused with multiple subjectivities and alternate realities but is treated like an immovable object in some of these discussions. Popular artists have come out against decriminalization of sex work, while they, ironically, portray characters who are decidedly sexually liberal and have the choice to frame their own sexualities.[39] For some reason, these women are enlightened enough to manifest their conceptions of sexual liberation but feel the need to limit whether sex workers can do the same for themselves. Perhaps, only rich White women are allowed to profit from their bodies? But the question remains, if all women are subject to male domination and oppressed by it, then how can any of us define or defy this domination, let alone proclaim to identify uniform parameters for it? And whose version of domination do we accept? Are we to accept that of privileged Western feminists without question because they proclaim to have a higher consciousness than their research subjects do? Are they not similarly blinded by male domination and thus unable to see(k) sexual liberation or provide consent?

Ronald Weitzer has criticized the methodology of the radical feminist approach:

Violating the canons of scientific inquiry, the radical feminist literature on prostitution and other types of sex work is filled with "sloppy definitions, unsupported assertions, and outlandish claims"; such writers select the "worst available examples" of sex work and treat them as representative. Anecdotes are generalized and presented as conclusive evidence, sampling is selective, and counterevidence is routinely ignored. Such research cannot help but produce questionable findings and spurious conclusion.[40]

To destructively declare sex work advocates to be victims of false consciousness while silencing the voices of those sex workers with opposing views is
a form of violence against the sex worker victim whom the radical feminist
presumably aims to protect and save.

Radical feminists have nonetheless captured the imaginations of many,
creating a political movement to ban the scourge of sex trafficking and child
prostitution. As Phil Hubbard notes, "conflicts between different sexualities,
moralities and identities are often orchestrated by the press in a lurid and
sensationalist manner to create national 'moral panics' about particular individuals and groups."[41] Western discourses around sex trafficking and its
conflation with sex work is very much a testament to the power of moral
sensationalism to regulate sexual deviants, even when it purports to protect
them. All women who have traveled afar for sex work become subsumed
under the blanket label of "sex trafficking victim." Through intense advocacy,
the radical feminist movement has managed to pass several anti-prostitution
bills and to garner global support for a movement aimed at preventing sex
trafficking, support that includes the UN Protocol to Prevent, Suppress and
Punish Trafficking in Persons, Especially Women and Children [42] and the
2000 US Victims of Trafficking and Violence Protection Act.[43] In 2013, South
Africa enacted the Prevention and Combating of Trafficking in Persons Act,
to assist in bringing international agreements regarding trafficking into
force.

The monolithic narrative of the sex worker as victim, without appreciation of the nuances of various sex worker life situations and of the variations
between different classes of sex workers, and with disregard for the colonial
or postcolonial contexts of sex workers, serves only to benefit discussants
promulgating a particular moral agenda, colored by their perceptions of appropriate female conduct. It is sexual Puritanism—with a radical edge.

SEX WORK ABOLITIONISM IN SOUTH AFRICA

In South Africa, the sentiments of the sex work abolitionists are reflected
by organizations such as Embrace Dignity, a radical feminist organization,
and the New Life Centre 4 Girls, a rescue organization. "Embrace Dignity
recognizes prostitution as a form of violence against women. In conditions
of gender inequality and deep poverty, it is false to assume that people

involved in prostitution are exercising free choice and agency.["44] The organization is committed to the abolition of sex work in South Africa and does
not support an individual sex worker's choice to engage in sex work. It aims
to preserve these sex workers' dignity. This approach to sex work is consistent with the approach adopted by Catharine MacKinnon and other radical
feminists, but slightly different in its concern with poverty and inequality
as structuring women's choice for sex work. Similarly, the New Life Centre
4 Girls

> rehabilitates children and women who are commercially sexually ex-
> ploited and trafficked in South Africa. It was established in April 2005 as
> a response to the high influx of children and women who are involved or
> at risk of being involved in prostitution due to child sexual abuse, traf-
> ficking, poverty, unemployment, lack of family structure and Orphans.[45]

These organizations embrace a discourse that focuses on the moral regulation of sex work, which finds the nature of sex work as inherently undignified. They are attempting to police the morality of sex work by premising
their work on the notion that sex work is distinct from other forms of work
and inherently so undignified that it would be a rights violation to allow an
individual to choose to engage in it. The South African Christian Lawyers'
Association, a socially conservative organization, has also argued that reform
efforts should be focused on ensuring that sex work is abolished, evincing the
strange bedfellows that radical feminists and conservatives have become in
the fight to abolish sex work.[46]

On March 2, 2016, Embrace Dignity briefed a Parliamentary committee to "support measures to stop the menace of sexual exploitation, to en-
able victims to pursue other purposeful options in life, and to give a proper
voice and protection to sex workers."[47] The organization provided life histories that reiterated the narrative of sex workers who had been victimized,
and its submission was framed as striving to end oppression stemming
from sex work. It focused on the morality of sex work[48] and followed in
the lineage of morality discourses advanced by the Christian Temperance
Union, as discussed in chapter 1, spreading narratives about the inherent
indignity of sex work, albeit in this case with an explicit focus on poverty
and inequality.

INTERSECTIONAL RISK MANAGEMENT

The radical feminist body of feminist scholarship suffers from a critique that has long plagued feminism—it is advancing a Western, middle-class, White female agenda that only superficially considers other experiences, particularly those of women of color or women in postcolonial societies. It is generally lacking in its attention to intersectionality[49] and the unique experiences of women who experience overlapping and intersecting forms of oppression. Even more critically, it is disconnected from classes of the women who live inside this postcolonial world and thus is plagued by assumptions and premises that simply do not apply in certain contexts. In their world of limited opportunities, sex workers in this world manage risks and have made a calculated choice to adopt a profession within their existing economic paradigm. Sex work provides higher economic opportunities for many people within limited economic stations. In this manner, it is empowering and provides the sex worker with a lifestyle that would not otherwise be available. There have been efforts to empirically ground feminist theory and ensure its applicability in various contexts. In this effort, consideration of different contexts and how sex work may at times become a tool for female empowerment, particularly in the Global South, is critical. Martha Nussbaum has argued that feminists should protest the stigmatization of sex work rather than its occurrence.[50] She argues that the problems with sex work are not inherent in its nature but rather are a result of this stigmatization and of working conditions.

Sex workers who are also low-income, or also migrants, or also women, or also Black, may already exist in a paradigm where they have limited choices because that paradigm prioritizes White supremacy, patriarchy, and wealth.[51] Nonetheless, it seems repugnant to suggest that—even under these conditions, and despite experiencing structural barriers—these women do not have some agency. Adopting an intersectional lens makes it clear that one can almost always argue that women, particularly women with multiple identities, are in fact making choices even within a paradigm of structural disadvantage. So we cannot say that these women can never exercise any choice. To do so would silence these women, and in turn make the feminist advocates, who seek to liberate these women from their own false consciousness, the oppressors of these women, some of whom may choose to sex work in light of their choices. This begets the question, who is really empowered in these discourses? The sex worker or the scholars or activists who feel they know better than the sex worker herself? As Foucault has stated, to engage in discourse may be an expression of power in and of itself.[52] Here, the radical feminist advocate or scholar appears to assert her power over and against the sex worker.

The radical feminist interpretation of sex work, as Ratna Kapur says, "produces the fiction of a universal sisterhood, bonded in its experience of victimization and violence. There is no space in this construction for difference or for the articulation of a subject that is empowered."[53] My findings pertain to the situation in the locales I studied. However, I suspect that similar stories are found throughout the world and that taking a position on criminalization does not rest on assuming either agency or victimization and nothing in between. Sex workers are exposed to increased risks. They are often victims. And yet they have nonetheless developed mechanisms for managing these risks and have perhaps chosen to face the risks associated with sex work over those associated with abject poverty. Because sex work is not static, even within my three research sites, it is presumptively changeable and able to adapt to more ideal conditions. More simply put, the reality of sex work cannot be neatly categorized. It is not black or white.

Moreover, there is growing concern about the risks inherent in criminalization itself, which may bring a host of punitive consequences that harm the populations that criminalization aims to protect. Sociologist Elizabeth Bernstein has described the increasingly punitive brand of feminism that addresses social harms through increased policing and punishment as *carceral feminism*. Carceral feminism places

social problems in deviant individuals rather than mainstream institutions . . . [and] seeks social remedies through criminal justice interventions rather than through a redistributive welfare state . . . [advocating] for the beneficence of the privileged rather than the empowerment of the oppressed. As such, this approach leaves intact the social structures that drive low-income women (and many men) into patterns of risky migration and exploitative informal-sector employment, including those relatively rare but very real situations that would rightly qualify as "trafficking" or "slavery."[54]

Policing and criminalization tend to be most harmful to sex workers who deal with intersectional subordination. These women are marginalized not just as women but also as Black women, women with disabilities, or women who are poor. Aya Gruber's book *The Feminist War on Crime* demonstrates how feminist efforts to embrace penal law can be both ineffective at preventing the undesirable conduct and also harmful to the women feminists claim to protect.

Sex workers live in a complicated reality and occupy contradictory spaces. In the areas I researched, they are not mere victims who require saving under any approach that depends heavily on criminalizing or decriminalizing. At times, decriminalization is overemphasized as a saving grace for sex workers when in fact, in the case of South Africa, they already exist under a de facto decriminalization regime. Ellen is a sex worker whose stories highlight some of the complexities of taking a hard-line approach to sex work that lacks nuance. A mutual friend introduced me to Ellen, who is a short Black woman with a "thick" build. She has a short haircut and voluptuous curves. Although she used to work at the Hillbrow Inn, I met her in the Midrand section of Johannesburg, near where she now lives. When she first arrived in South Africa, from Zimbabwe, she had to "squat" with her aunt for some time because she didn't have a place to stay. She eventually began working as a domestic worker. She was being paid very little and earned no more than R1500 each month. At first, she was working for a married man and his wife, who was very suspicious of her husband. The husband told Ellen that she was a "pretty girl" and promised to take care of her. She soon left this employment.

One day, she saw a group of male friends with some "beautiful ladies who worked at Royal Park." The ladies bought all the guys drinks and told Ellen, "You can use your body to do that yourself." Ellen asked the guys she was with where to go, and she soon started working at the Hillbrow Inn. The money she was earning was "too much." Ellen bought a fridge for R4000, earned in one week. She would go to restaurants, like Ocean Basket (similar to the American restaurant Red Lobster) in Eastgate, and was enjoying life in ways she could not have before beginning sex work. She did not want to do this work, but she had to. Ellen has two brothers, a mother, and two kids. She is the breadwinner for them, and she "sacrificed for the family."

As Ellen frequently told me, "It's not about men or sex, just money. . . . It wasn't easy [to do this]. This work can sometimes be humiliating." One client failed to pay her for services rendered. She was very upset because she went to his place for the transaction, and he failed to compensate her. She said to him, "I need my money, and you wasted my time. I can't waste money." She had been with this client for two days. His wife learned of his infidelity and returned home early from a family trip to her mother's house. When the wife arrived, Ellen informed the wife that she was just a friend and that she did not want her husband. Ellen, who is in her early 30s, said that she was just passing through and that both the wife and the husband were younger than her. "Why would your husband want me? I'm old," she said to the wife. However, the husband had not yet paid her for the services she had rendered, and she waited there from 10:00 a.m. to 4:00 p.m. as the husband and wife argued. She finally left, but not before she had an opportunity to take his identification and phone number as insurance of future payment. Once the husband realized he was missing his personal items, Ellen was eventually compensated. Ellen found a strategy for adapting to the uncertainty of future payment for services that had already been rendered.

Ellen recently quit working at Hillbrow Inn and is now a domestic worker again, earning R4000 per month. She was reconsidering her decision to leave the sex industry, however, because she cannot earn as much money as a domestic worker as she did as a sex worker. She missed the companionship, albeit performative, that came during sex work encounters. Ellen's story was echoed by the dozens of sex workers I interviewed during the course of my ethnographic research. Most of them did not want to do sex work, but they enjoyed the financial freedom it provided. Sex work allowed them to provide for their families but also exposed them to certain occupational hazards. Yet these hazards were negotiated by a system of coping mechanisms that allowed sex workers to minimize the risks. Sex workers often recounted working several sex work hot spots before settling on a location where they felt comfortable. They often worked with friends and were able to check out potential clients before entering their cars. Several sex workers had police clients whom they would call if they were having issues with other clients. They found ways to manage the risks of their occupation.

Ellen was not merely a victim. She made choices but nonetheless had to manage real risks and dangers associated with her job as a sex worker. Treating sex workers as victims is an understandably attractive option. After all, victims fit into neat narratives that portray women as needing protection. However, we must question whether, in the denunciation of sex work and the relegation of its workers to victimhood, radical feminism reinforces male sexual hegemony predicated on the assumption that women are helpless and require protection as they are unable to remain emotionally detached during sex. Men are not perceived as victims in sex work transactions because they are presumed to be emotionally detached from the sex, viewing it merely as physical release. Can't the women be similarly detached, viewing sex as a mere physical act for obtaining money? Furthermore, in adopting the typical radical feminist approach, do we not simply strengthen arguments that underlie patriarchy and systems that deny female expressions of open sexuality and women's ability to exploit their sexuality? Several domestic workers in South Africa have confided in me and told me that they feel degraded by their work or would choose other work under more ideal circumstances. Should their form of labor also be criminalized to protect their dignity? Is sex for work really so different from other types of body labor in exchange for income?

There are strong arguments for acknowledging the various contexts in which sex work occurs, particularly where it is used as a survival strategy by marginalized women. Kamala Kempadoo criticizes radical feminists for failing to recognize that "the global sex trade cannot be simply reduced to one monolithic explanation of violence to women":

> The agency of Brown and Black women in prostitution has been avoided or overlooked and the perspectives arising from these experiences marginalized in dominant theoretical discourse on the global sex trade and prostitution. Our insights, knowledges, and understanding of sex work have been largely obscured or dominated by White radical feminist, neo-Marxist or Western socialist feminist inspired analyses that have been either incapable or unwilling to address the complexities of the lives of women of color.[55]

She argues that sex work should be treated as a form of labor, and that the role of race in the engagement of sex work should not be overlooked. She notes that "[t]hrough recognizing sex worker agency it becomes possible to uncover resistances to, and contestations of, oppressive and exploitative structures and regimes as well as the visions and ideologies inscribed in women's practices."[56]

People concerned with the well-being of sex workers should abandon dominant notions of morality rooted in sexual Puritanism and instead strive to fully appreciate the complexities involved in any consideration of sex work. Such moral notions are particularly dangerous when analyzing the agency of sex workers. Partial criminalization (the Swedish model) appears to be an option for many feminists, but in certain contexts, it may place the sex worker at greater risk. Recall that at my Rosebank research site, sex workers reported that police officers began to intensify their policing of sex work by focusing on the activities of clients. The clients were subjected to bribes and arrests. As a result of this policing, several sex workers were abused by clients, with one client going so far as to shoot rubber bullets at a street corner filled with sex workers. The Rosebank sex workers were unable to find alternative forms of work, and some resorted to working in central Johannesburg, where there was more open hostility and violence toward sex workers from the Metro police. In this particular context, partial abolition of criminalization would have been devastating. The presumption behind abolition is that sex workers are harmed by the criminalization of client activity. However, the sex worker–client relationship is far from traditional.

Although sex workers may have a level of familiarity with regular clients, there is also an inherent suspicion in the interaction, given the nature of the work. Sex workers are paid to feign interest in men whom they do not know. Sex work is mutually exploitative. The client takes from the sex worker her sex in exchange for the illusion of a sexual act. The sex worker takes money in exchange for her performance of this illusion.[57] Sex workers are masters of deception, by profession, and the men who frequent them know this. Unlike the scholars who speak about sex workers as weak victims subject to male tyranny, those who interact with them regularly are aware that these women can be cunning, deceptive, and at times manipulative in improving their bottom line.[58] Accordingly, clients can easily become suspicious of sex workers. This dynamic creates a relationship riddled with suspicion, endless bargaining, and shifting power dynamics. Given this inherent volatility, it is hardly surprising that any regulation that upsets the dynamics of the sex worker–client relationship may have disastrous results.

MUTUAL EXPLOITATION: ECONOMIC FREEDOM AS RESISTANCE

It is important to appreciate that even the most exploitative of power relations present complexities. As Foucault has argued, discourses around sexuality and the power relations defining them are not one dimensional. And as Vanessa Munro points out, "Foucault's post-structuralist theory posits the emergence of peculiarly modern forms of power that operate via mechanisms of normalization rather than authority and command."[59] Within these discussions around sexuality, there may be expressions of resistance. South African sex workers have historically been penalized and tolerated, regarded as charlatans and renegades and as sites of contagion and disease, yet treated as necessary evils. Within the complexity of the competing views on reasons for the existence of sex work, sex workers have been both required and disdained. They have nonetheless managed to push the discourse around sexuality and have served as a resisting force against conservative morality around sexuality. The very act of sex work may be perceived as an exertion of sex workers' own power, as resistance to the male patriarchal system that relegates female sexuality to private expressions of domesticity. And the economic aspect of sex work cannot simply be ignored. Money is how men have long controlled women—marriage, which has been a site for the exercise of patriarchy and male dominance,[60] has historically been about money and access to power.[61] Sex workers have frequently benefited from the economic independence that sex work has afforded them.[62]

Sex work advocates have argued that sex workers' sexual autonomy is not compromised because they retain the right to withdraw the contract at will.[63] Peter de Marneffe argues that sex work contracts should be treated in the same way as other labor contracts involving hazardous conditions.[64] Although the law has prohibited contracts that are considered void due to public interest rationales, there may be reasons to be particularly careful about labor contracts, especially in contexts where limited labor options provide similar economic benefits as sex work in developing countries.[65] Sex workers frequently express their experiences as a form of dual consciousness of resistance and choice.[66] Sex work does not fall neatly into a binary of choice or victimhood. There is frequently a contingent choice, which can be explored in Foucauldian terms.[67]

[The] Foucaultian conception of power as a force which bears out its effects on every social agent, rather than as a commodity to be wielded in the interests of the socially privileged to maintain the ongoing derision of the socially subordinate has been welcomed by contemporary feminist theorists who have become increasingly dissatisfied with the more totalitarian arguments of the radical genre.[68]

Accordingly, there is no centralized form of power, and power can be expressed through resistance. Power is diffuse and cannot be attributed singularly to one source. In this way, sex workers are subject to male subordination and patriarchy. Yet, like all women, they still manage to retain some power and may express resistance to their subordination. They are still able to organize and exert power against the subordination through their resistance. The denial of this ability is critical to radical feminist arguments. However, the only thing that separates those feminists from their sex worker "sisters" is that sex workers exert their power through sex rather than scholarship. Is the choice to be a scholar under male patriarchy really much different than the choice to be a sex worker? Why can we exercise our choice and they cannot? The only reasonable answer is that there is something about sex itself that creates a bar to this. But who should decide whether sex should make the difference?

Through its ability to change the economic reality of sex workers, sex work also has the ability to change lives and create greater freedom from male patriarchal structures. The question then becomes whether economics is an accurate measure for assessing freedom. In capitalist societies, it is undoubtedly such a measurement, if not the measurement. Capital affords its holders access to opportunities otherwise unavailable. Still, suggesting that sex work can empower sex workers provides many moral dilemmas. For many, on its face, it is a suggestion that is morally reprehensible and should be avoided at all costs. As Embrace Dignity argues in South Africa, if women must resort to sex work, then we must do more to create economic empowerment and economic freedom. This argument is fine and should be considered; however, it does not preclude sex work as one avenue for seeking such freedom. Various approaches can be adopted to encourage the same outcome. There is nothing to prohibit this from occurring. Yet sex work should not automatically be excluded as a possible approach, especially in a developing country with high unemployment such as South Africa.

It is critical to explore whether discourses around female sexuality and sex work simply reproduce particular modes of power as described by Foucault: "Often the argument is simply a circular appeal to 'sex'"[69] Discourses around sexuality often serve to reinforce the power of those dictating the sexual norms. While openly discussing sexuality and the role of sex workers makes such discussion more robust and transparent, it may also reiterate models of sexuality that strengthen male dominance by presupposing that men sit at the top of the sexual hierarchy. Are we to assume that men are naturally more sexual beings and thus the sole beneficiaries of anything relating to sex? Admittedly, contemporary feminist perspectives are not so black and white. We must question whether sex work is always sex. If we position ourselves in the place of the male client, then sex work is a sexual transaction. However, for some sex workers, sex work is solely work, and not at all sex. It is not necessarily an expression of their sexual prowess, and they are not mere victims in the exchange of their services. They are merely engaged in bodily work. In this sense, discussion around sex work is not merely about sexuality and sexual appetite; sex work is to be considered as a form of labor, as alternative employment for women with limited employment options. While sex is occurring in actuality, in the experience of the sex worker, it is reduced to work in this transactional relationship, and she may in fact only perceive herself as having sex when she is with her domestic partner or spouse. The next question is whether we can separate sexual experiences in this way. I believe we can. Men have been encouraged to think of sex in such an impersonal manner; thus why should women not be allowed to do the same? Some men cheat on their spouses, claiming that the infidelity was "only sex." Men have been lauded for being able to separate sex from emotion, viewing sex as a release or as a transaction. Why should women be deprived of this option where it would allow them to benefit economically? Because such an approach ignores patriarchy? Because such an expression of sex belies our essentialization of the sex experience?

The history of sex work in South Africa reveals that sex work has been used there as a means of economic gain for women since the 1650s. There are reports of female slaves purchasing their freedom using the proceeds of their work as sex workers.[70] While these women were undoubtedly in a position of lesser power than the men around them, this power imbalance does not erase the fact that sex work was a tool for empowerment in their particular circumstance. This raises the question of whether feminist debates around sex work need to consider more thoroughly the pragmatic consequences that flow from the current stances toward it. As a matter of practicality, sex work was the tool that empowered women in this particular historical context to, quite literally, buy their freedom. As Noah Zatz reminds us:

> It is important to acknowledge connections between concepts and phenomena without simply reducing them to each other. In addition to crushing conceptual complexity and cultural variety under the heel of totalising theory, such a move encourages us to forget the variety of meanings that participation in a "single" practice can have for different individuals or groups, even within a single historical moment; there is great evidence to suggest, for instance, that prostitutes experience their profession in widely varying ways and that johns go to prostitutes for similarly various reasons.[71]

Feminist discourses should focus on how to create the ideal conditions for sex workers in practical terms.

Prabha Kotiswaran has suggested a middle ground for feminism that allows consideration of sex workers as agents, without going as far as taking a "sex work advocate" approach.[72] She finds that the majority of feminists are situated somewhere in the middle ground and that there is room for the toleration of sex work as a form of labor. She suggests that *material feminism* provides a mode for understanding the evolution of sex work in its sensitivity to the historical position of gender and to other structures relevant to an understanding of gender. Material feminism recognizes that gender implications are situated within a particular historical context and reflect the political economy of the time.[73] This approach is favorable in its recognition of female social positions as shifting.

Within the particular context of Johannesburg sex workers, all the women with whom I interacted were independent workers. Almost all of them had children, and none of them had skills for work outside domestic work in South Africa. In a country with a 23 percent unemployment rate,[74] it is difficult to fathom outlawing the primary means of work that allows these women to provide a good lifestyle for their families. Teela Sanders finds that "[in] prostitution, the consequences of risk are different across markets because different categories of women have different risk profiles. . . . They have different degrees of control over their exposure to these risks."[75] This was also the case in Johannesburg, where the sex workers were managing their risks within their particular societal context. They were adopting various strategies to protect themselves against the inherent dangers of their profession, but none of them had been coerced into the business. Abolitionist models ignore the economic realities of developing countries and the postcolonial social condition. They are not intersectional, and they ignore how women who experience intersectional subordination are constantly making constrained choices that allow them to survive. Police officers in Hillbrow acknowledged the economic necessity of sex work for many women and also suggested that decriminalization might actually reduce crime against sex workers:

> DENI (HILLBROW POLICE OFFICER): Prostitution is done because of poverty. Poverty is the reason why there is prostitution. . . . Legislation and legalizing might drop rapes.

As Sanders has observed:

> [W]omen use space strategically to avoid physical violence, arrest, criminalisation and harassment. The debates of agency and victimhood within prostitution have set out the complex parameters of whether a woman can consent to sell access to her body parts or whether all forms of prostitution are exploitative. . . . In this sense, the space on which women rely to advertise, negotiate and supply commercial sex is strategically used to their advantage in order to make cash and minimise chances of harm.[76]

The strategic use of space becomes its own form of resistance and enables women to negotiate power within oppressive structures.

THE ROLE OF POLICE IN UNDERSTANDING CRIMINALIZATION
Police may at times be unexpected allies as sex workers manage the risks of their work. Much of South African policy work paints the police and sex

workers as non-cooperative, when in fact their interests frequently align. There is great diversity in the relationships between police and sex workers, despite their being actors with seemingly differential access to power. The police and sex workers are sometimes in sync. Police officers indicated to me that there should be a policy in place that protects sex workers and addresses their concerns:

INDIA: [W]hat are your thoughts on prostitution?

APRIL (HILLBROW POLICE OFFICER): I think there must be a system or a department that deals with it because they are human and they need to be helped so that they can deal with the challenges that they are facing. If need be, they can be put in a very secure place so that they can trade.

Sex workers frequently displayed autonomy and agency in their relationships with the police, evincing dispersed power relations and demonstrating that even those who have been labeled as vulnerable or marginalized retain the power to resist and act upon others.[77] Engagement with the state is complex, and power can be harnessed by various actors, even the seemingly vulnerable. This complexity may not be considered in policy debates advocating for legalistic rights-based reform.

In many instances during the course of my study, police officers abused their authority and failed to protect sex workers, despite their legal mandate to do so. However, the relationship between police and sex workers was complicated. Sex workers often recounted times when they called upon the police for assistance and made it clear that their relationship with police was individualized. Police officers generally expressed a willingness to improve their relationship with sex workers and commented that the current state of affairs was quite poor. In the literature on sex work, police are frequently described as oppressors and abusers of sex workers, and many instances of police mistreating sex workers are recounted. However, sex workers often stated to me that they went to the police for assistance, and police told me about responding to sex workers who needed help, demonstrating the complexity of these relationships. For example, a sex worker told me:

CARY (CENTRAL JOHANNESBURG SEX WORKER): We meet some bad guys on the streets . . . guys were trying to rob us, and they

[SAPS] helped so many times. . . . Metro is full of shit. They chase us way, if you don't run it's a problem.

And a police officer commented:

INDIA: Do prostitutes call police for assistance?

CHRIS (HILLBROW POLICE OFFICER): Yes, they do. When they need help, they do.

INDIA: Have you responded to prostitutes' calls for assistance?

CHRIS: Yes, once. He slept with someone else so the guy didn't pay the lady. So they came to the police station. She wanted to open a case, but it was an argument between two parties. I talked to the guy to give the lady the money that she deserves.

And another officer gave a similar answer:

INDIA: OK. Do prostitutes ever call the police for help?

MIKE (HILLBROW POLICE OFFICER): Usually. Mostly, yes. They only call the police if there are any problems like someone stole their money or broke into their room. They are not segregating themselves.

Some sex workers, however, indicated that the criminalization of sex work prevented them from seeking police assistance:

ANNIE (CENTRAL JOHANNESBURG SEX WORKER): Clients are beating us sometimes, taking our money.

INDIA: Do you feel comfortable going to the police?

ANNIE: No, going to say [I'm] selling my body, they took something. . . . [I would] feel embarrassed.

The continued criminalization of sex workers makes it difficult for sex workers to seek open, civil legal assistance for their client disputes. Advocates frequently argue that sex workers need to access the police for criminal remedies when they experience violence from clients, but little attention has been paid to the civil remedies that would be available to them in a de jure decriminalized system. Formal decriminalization may improve access to justice by encouraging sex workers to enforce contracts they have with others in the sex industry and to be forthcoming about the nature of their disputes when seeking police assistance. Some officers believe that sex workers resort to criminal charges to coerce clients into making outstanding payments:

SAM (ROSEBANK POLICE OFFICER): They [prostitutes] come and say the person didn't pay. And they fabricate stories. The police must go in now, but it becomes a civil matter. Those issues become civil matters. The problem is that this person will be saying that I was robbed. Then as police we must handle the case. But if the guy is prepared to pay then the case settles. Most times the lady will say, he raped me. The guy will be looking so scared that he will just pay the money that he owes her.

Human rights laws have been successful in influencing some aspects of policing. While these human rights laws are not perfectly maintained, a vernacularized version, where police adopt the terminology and implement those aspects that resonate with them, is in place.[78] Police officers acknowledged to me that sex workers have human rights that require protection:

ZOLO (HILLBROW POLICE OFFICER): I think as police, according to the Constitution, we have to treat every person with dignity and respect. We have to be respective [sic] of whoever, of that particular person and how he is dressed and as a client, we just have to respect him and not to discriminate that this one or I heard someone that is no. As a police official, the man who is speaking peace in the country, we have to treat that person all equally irrespective of color or nation, because if that particular person then refers the NGOs and other organizations so we have to [suggesting that the possibility of sex workers reporting police failure to provide assistance to local NGOs promotes police compliance with human rights norms].
THEMBA (HILLBROW POLICE OFFICER): There definitely has to be [respect], there's no way that we can be saying, "Hey you're a prostitute." Those people are mothers, they are sisters to others, they are still human, the right to human dignity.

All the police officers I encountered acknowledged that there were some merits to human rights laws. Some indicated that officers need additional training in interviewing sex workers and hearing their complaints. They expressed a willingness to learn what the policing of sex workers should look like. What are their obligations to the sex workers? How should they operate in this quasi-legal realm?

> INDIA: OK, what is the relationship between police and prostitutes?
> MIKE: It is not that properly. The prostitution is illegal. They are doing it illegally and have no permission to do those things and the police are arresting them without interviewing them before. . . . To improve the relationship between the police and the prostitutes, if the police can give them a chance just to sit and interview them and why they are doing it and they are taking drugs, it would improve the relationship. The police are just arresting the prostitutes.

Formal decriminalization may encourage a less hostile relationship between police and sex workers in Johannesburg. Moreover, police were interested in practical recommendations about how they should police sex workers and complained that they had very little guidance. Most of the police officers I met believed that sex work should be a low priority policing task, and several were able to recount specific situations where they served as mediators for sex workers. Several police officers said they were hesitant to form formal partnerships with sex workers because the sex workers were engaging in unlawful activities:

> THEMBA (HILLBROW POLICE OFFICER): We're going, really, as a police officer, whatever is not legalized in the country there is no way that we can work hand in hand with them. You hear what I'm saying? It's like; it's like it's saying: "I won't be charged," like being a friend of a drug dealer. You cannot say, I'm not saying you should hate them but we are not supposed to have a relationship since it's not legal as yet.
> SIPHO (ROSEBANK POLICE OFFICER): To be honest with you now, being a police officer working in an area where there are some prostitutes it's not easy at all because sometimes they feel like we are after them. So it is not easy at all. So even the prostitutes they don't feel safe where there is the police because what they think of is to get locked up if they do it.

APRIL (HILLBROW POLICE OFFICER): Since their trade is illegal it is hard to deal with them because they are too much. They are human beings and you feel for them, but their kids need some food, so it like you are still a criminal. It doesn't help to prevent it because they are there on the street. If you arrest them it is going to be like it is personal, so we just have to ignore them even though we know it is wrong.

The police called for decriminalization of sex work and clear rules about how sex workers should be policed. They believed that definitions about their roles in policing sex work were necessary:

INDIA: What are your thoughts on prostitution?
SIBELA (HILLBROW POLICE OFFICER): Must be a control mechanism, it is illegal right now. As police, it's useless. You cannot enforce that thing. They must find a way to work with that thing. You won't even see the magistrate. It is only to inconvenience for that evening. I think they must legislate it. We thought it would be a deterrent but it is not a deterrent.
INDIA: How do you think the policing of prostitutes can be improved?
SIBELA: Create red-light districts; these people are operating here. It is illegal only by name.
SIPHO: There should be proper legislation on how they do their operations. The criminalization of prostitution only promotes crime and *creates a gap in how the law operates with regard to prostitutes*. We need more laws that tell us how it should happen and provide us with guidance concerning the regulation of prostitution. The current gap in the law is not helpful to police.
   Prostitution also gives rise to robberies where the transaction goes wrong. Then the client doesn't pay, and then the prostitutes want to come in to report the faulty client. Sometimes they are working with the criminals [and there is organized crime relating to prostitution]. They [organized criminals] are working with the prostitutes. Sometimes they get killed and are caught up in their involvement in these other crimes.

Contrary to what is often claimed, these data indicate that police are not always adversaries to sex worker interests. Many police officers appeared interested in more clearly defining their role in the protection and policing of sex workers. Moreover, a majority of the police I spoke with indicated that they would like sex work to be decriminalized and were frustrated by the inefficiencies associated with continued criminalization. In these police stations, there may already be space to begin defining how the policing of sex workers should be improved, redefining the informal practices that affect policing, as well as developing a discourse that normalizes sex work and thereby reduces the stigmatization of it.

I also asked my police interview participants from Hillbrow and Rosebank whether prostitution should be decriminalized (see table 5.1). Twenty officers, a majority of the participants, responded that prostitution should be decriminalized. Only four officers, all from Hillbrow, responded that prostitution should not be decriminalized.

In addition, I asked the police participants how they felt about sex work (see table 5.2). Twenty officers, a majority from both Hillbrow and Rosebank, felt that sex work was permissible, and four officers, a minority from both Hillbrow and Rosebank, felt that sex work was very immoral.

Finally, participants were asked whether they should get more respect from prostitutes (see table 5.3). Twenty-three of the participants, all but one,

TABLE 5.1. Opinions of Hillbrow and Rosebank police interviewees on decriminalization of sex work.

	YES		NO		TOTAL	
	n	*(%)*	*n*	*(%)*	*n*	*(%)*
Hillbrow	15	(78.9)	4	(21.1)	19	(100)
Rosebank	5	(100.0)	0	(0.0)	5	(100)

TABLE 5.2. Perceptions of Hillbrow and Rosebank police interviewees about sex work.

	VERY IMMORAL		PERMISSIBLE		TOTAL	
	n	*(%)*	*n*	*(%)*	*n*	*(%)*
Hillbrow	3	(15.8)	16	(84.2)	19	(100)
Rosebank	1	(20.0)	4	(80.0)	4	(100)

TABLE 5.3. Perceptions of Hillbrow and Rosebank police interviewees about prostitutes' respect for police.

	MUCH MORE		SOMEWHAT MORE		NOT AT ALL		TOTAL	
	n	(%)	n	(%)	n	(%)	n	(%)
Hillbrow	11	(57.9)	7	(36.8)	1	(5.3)	19	(100)
Rosebank	5	(100.0)	0	(0.0)	0	(0.0)	5	(100)

perceived that they should get much more or somewhat more respect from prostitutes.

Decriminalization may not be the ultimate resolution for sex work everywhere. And even where there is decriminalization (or de facto decriminalization), sex workers may still be marginalized and subject to various forms of social control. Moral policing occurs outside the law and may be an effective method for regulating the activities of clients and upsetting the sex market where sex workers work. Overemphasizing criminalization fetishizes the penal law without critically examining the limitations of this approach and its ability to disempower vulnerable women. Ultimately, any approach to sex work must consider the particular social and economic contexts and the variables that make the various approaches to regulating sex workers suitable or unsuitable. Any chosen approach must also be localized, to recognize the different ways in which sex work manifests itself.

CONCLUSION

PERCEPTIONS OF BEAUTY, hygiene, and female sexuality; expressions of masculinity; race; continuities with historical practices for regulating sex work; the evolution of the police organization; and the expectation that police will play a greater role in regulating private relationships, all influence the policing of sex workers in Johannesburg. Police officers' own perceptions of their role as enforcers of human rights and protectors of the public—a public that questions their power—also play a role in how sex workers are policed in Johannesburg. As the ethnography presented here shows, these factors create a complex geography of sex that reproduces social hierarchies and patriarchy. The multiple approaches to policing sex work that I found illustrate that even within a single city, the policing of sex work is widely varied. There is no static "sex work," as even within each location, practices evolve over time. Mapping sex work in the city reveals how hierarchies and patriarchal structures are reflected in the sex work geography. Rosebank, central Johannesburg, and Hillbrow have distinct expressions of sex work that are strongly influenced by how police understand their role in the policing of domestic disputes and appropriate levels of transparent sexualities.

There are continuities between discourses relating to sex workers' public health and hygiene and the police approach to the policing of sex workers.

South Africa has a long history of both competing and complementary discourses that regulate the sex worker's body and shape public perception of
it. The history of sex work in South Africa also demonstrates how sex work
can be both oppressive and an exercise of resistance, both economically and
socially transformative albeit in a social order that promotes patriarchy and
female social oppression. Sex work once enabled some women slaves to purchase their freedom, and it still enables widows to provide for their families
and enterprising women to earn an income that surpasses that available to
them given their other skills. Although sex work may be viewed as the outcome of a system that is born of inequality and unfair social access, it may
equally be viewed as a form of practical economic adaption. I cannot say it
better than one Hillbrow police officer, who recounted the complex social
conditions that allow sex work to be lucrative for some sex workers:

> JOHN (HILLBROW POLICE OFFICER): We find that the prostitutes,
> some of them do it just to commit crime and others want to do it
> to better their lives. Like I said, some of them do it because they
> want to commit crime, they don't know any other life, but others
> do it to better their life. I know I once interviewed a lady, I think
> in the late nineties, she said she is only going to be here for a little
> while; [at] the time I had arrested her she had been here for about
> eight months if I'm not mistaken and she had already accumu-
> lated 80,000 [that she had deposited] in the bank . . . and I was
> surprised. And she told me she just wanted to give it one more
> year and then she was going to leave it and she is going to get
> herself her degree. So you find people who are forced to do it to
> better their lifestyles. Others want to do it because they don't know
> anything else. It's the only life that they know.

During the Victorian era, the public health of sex workers was a curiosity that spurred the enactment of the Contagious Diseases Act, an exercise of biopower upon the sex worker. The Act permitted state intervention
through the inspection of the sex worker body. Contemporary approaches
to the policing of sex workers are deeply influenced by these historical
discourses. As discussed in chapter 2, Hillbrow police are now less likely
to police those hotel-brothels that they view as less hygienic. In central

Johannesburg, Metro police brutalize sex workers because they view them as unhygienic, yelling expletives at them and calling them dirty, reflecting the historical discourse of the sex worker as a vector of contagious diseases. These perceptions of the sex worker's body as a site for discussions regarding public hygiene are consistent with socially engrained discourses that seek to regulate the female body, and that are also a kind of biopower that guides the application of state force.

Police in all three of the research sites relied upon their understandings of private and public to determine the appropriate method for policing sex work, reflecting historical discourses regarding the sex worker as a public nuisance and female sexuality as a thing to be regulated. In chapter 2, I discussed the exercise of police power through a licensing scheme in Hillbrow and of biopower through the violent policing practices in central Johannesburg. As a general matter, sex work is perceived as an act that should occur in private spaces. However, police officers' interpretation of what was private varied in the different sites. In Hillbrow, sex work was permissible so long as it occurred in private hotel-brothels. A complex system of liquor licensing registrations and other agreements creates a de facto state of decriminalization in Hillbrow. The central Johannesburg Metro police resorted to historical approaches to policing sex work that relied on public nuisance ordinances and maintenance of public order. The police were overtly hostile toward the sex workers there because they perceived them as threats to the public order. As I showed in chapter 3, in Rosebank, the approach to sex work was constantly evolving and varied from being overtly tolerant of sex workers in an attempt to respect human rights to perverting human rights mandates in order to focus on the sex workers' clients to police officers' individual financial benefit. As discussed in chapter 1, dissatisfaction with salaries, as expressed through nostalgia for apartheid-era policing, made any form of security in the relationship between police and sex workers fragile.

The policing of sex work in Johannesburg is informed by understandings of human rights, and the law is often used to rationalize police actions, even when the police act unlawfully. The formal criminalization of sex work was less relevant to the policing of sex workers than police officers' interpretation of sex workers' rights and police attempts to maintain order in the city. Police often coopted human rights and legalistic language to explain conduct that was outside the law. Describing hotel-brothels as having "licenses" became a way of informally legalizing hotel-brothels in Hillbrow. Informal "understandings," or provisional agreements, facilitated street-based sex work in central Johannesburg. In Rosebank, police vernacularized human rights by refraining from the arrest of sex workers while taking bribes from the sex workers' clients. All these sites are in the same city. Yet they illustrate the diverse ways that sex work may be expressed. Even within the same research site, sex work evolved and was not static.

The ethnographic findings illustrate that patriarchy is not expressed in a singular manner, and it can take on surprising forms. In both Rosebank and Hillbrow, the sex workers who were perceived as the most hygienic had more police interactions and were more heavily policed, even though our intuition might suggest the opposite should happen. The type of policing that these sex workers experienced reflected a benevolent police gaze; it is still a type of biopower but relies less on brute force.

The policing of sex work also demonstrates the continuities in the historical policing of sex work and in the exercise of biopower to define the sex work community. The public health of sex workers remains prominent in contemporary discourses about sex work. In fact, much of the contemporary research on sex work focuses on biomedical questions and interrogates how to reduce sex workers' exposure to HIV, as South Africa has a high HIV rate.[1] As discussed in chapter 2, the focus of a significant portion of the local research on sex workers relates to the HIV status of sex workers, sex workers' vulnerabilities, and public health features of the sex worker community. This research is undoubtedly well intentioned, but several of the studies are premised on the notion that sex workers' bodies are inevitably sites of contagion, given a sex work occupation. The 2016 SANAC program has been important in expanding sex workers' access to healthcare and focusing on their social and political rights. However, it also fosters discourses that focus on the sex worker as a site of contagion and reinforces views about the sex worker as being unclean, while ignoring the sex work client's part in the public health agenda. This focus reflects a continuity with the Contagious Diseases Act, which was expressly concerned with protecting public health and exclusively focused on the sex worker's body as a tool for advancing the public health. In fact, this public health discourse is still so powerful that it may be the basis for ultimately decriminalizing sex work in South Africa.[2] Public health discussants should be especially careful in how they talk about sex workers and should deliberately build a narrative that develops the sex worker beyond her public health profile and beyond the issue of how regulating her ends the spread of disease.

It is frequently treated as a foregone conclusion that sex workers are more diseased than the general population. This has promoted certain campaigns that advocate for decriminalization by arguing that it would be in the interest of public health. This is not inherently problematic; however, it continues the tradition of treating the sex worker body as a site for public inspection and investigation—a place for surveillance. The sex worker's interests matter to the extent that they protect the public from her hygienic practices. This assumption is problematic because it reinforces the stigmatization of the sex worker and reinforces the public's imagination of the sex worker as dirty and undignified. However, an increased HIV rate is not a foregone and inevitable occupational hazard for South African sex workers. These public health discourses have the unintended consequence of reinforcing the narrative of the sex worker body as site of contagion.. They unintentionally continue the discourse that enables lawmakers to exert power over the sex worker body by employing a public health rationale, suggesting continuities between past forms of regulation and contemporary forms. And they rarely mention the sex worker's clients or highlight the client's role in advancing the public health.

The question of criminalization is also central to understanding the policing of sex workers. As discussed in chapter 5, the contemporary feminist discourse has in large part focused on the issue of criminalization. Feminists generally agree that sex workers should not be criminalized for engaging in sex work. However, feminists disagree as to whether sex work should ever be viewed as viable work. Radical feminists argue that abolition of sex work is the ultimate goal because sex is never a viable employment option, and they consider the structural harms of patriarchy in assessing how sex work should be treated. They argue that sex work reinforces a structure that supports patriarchy and the availability of women for sex at the disposal of men.

This book has also considered the systemic harms of patriarchy, but it arrives at a very different conclusion from that of the radical feminists.

Abolitionist arguments are problematic because they rely upon the essential-ization of sexuality, womankind, and sex. Radical feminists reify patriarchy by assuming that sex is necessarily harmful to women, without acknowledg-ing circumstances where women are able to exploit the desires of men to their economic benefit. Their views are premised on the notion that sex is necessarily an oppressive act for women and that women are incapable of separating their body work from their personal selves. Their arguments also completely ignore the autonomy of the individual sex worker, subjugating her choices for the betterment of a larger structure, which works against her individual interests. The ethnographic chapters illustrate that eliminating the ability to engage in sex work is at times more harmful to women than engag-ing in sex work itself. And even after considering the structural harms of pa-triarchy and racism, sex workers may be more empowered within these op-pressive structures when their power to resist and survive is acknowledged, rather than erased to serve a singular womankind. Abolitionists frequently argue for the Swedish model for sex work regulation, seeing it as a universally suitable approach. The Rosebank case study highlights just a few of the prob-lems with the Swedish model in the South African context, such as making women who are desperate for work even more desperate as their primary source of income is eliminated.

Other feminists argue that women should be able to make the choice to use sex for employment options. Though clearly sex work is often danger-ous and hazardous, these dangers can be mitigated under decriminaliza-tion. Accordingly, decriminalization seems suitable in most contexts in its recognition of the sex worker's autonomy and liberty. However, a singular model for sex work regulation should not be transposed to all contexts. The treatment of sex work should be localized. As seen during the course of my ethnographic inquiry, there is no singular sex work, even within the same city or the same locality. Sex work is continuously shifting, and its formations are vulnerable to minor geopolitical changes. The appropriate regulation of sex work will vary by location, and different sites may require different solu-tions to accommodate this. In South Africa, stark economic realities make sex work a viable option for some women. Taking away these women's clients does nothing to redress their economic situation and treats them as infants incapable of independent decision making. In this way, a perspective that is decidedly intersectional, that is sensitive to overlapping systems of oppression by considering the sex workers' gender, race, and economic status, allows for a nuanced analysis of the realities of using sex for work. Many women do not view criminalization and policing as sources of protection. Several sex workers, all of whom were Black women with no comparable economic alternatives, complained about the economic realities that brought them to their work, and their words best describe the reality of their options:

> ANNIE (CENTRAL JOHANNESBURG SEX WORKER): I come every day for money. I have children. The hotels are full so I'm working in the street.
>
> CATHI (ROSEBANK SEX WORKER): They are taking our clients. The clients now know about it that in Rosebank that the police take money. This is our money. These Rosebank police must stop; Norwood must stop. Some are from Norwood and Johannesburg Central. Our clients are under threat. We are raising our children and we need this money. . . . All police are involved, men and women.

Although I agree with the sex workers and the police I encountered that sex work should be decriminalized in Johannesburg, I do not think that the question of how sex work should be treated stops there. There has been an overemphasis on legal change and a fetishization of the law. As I have discussed, there are strong reasons why sex work should not be criminalized, but there should be an infrastructure in place that guides police on how to interact with sex workers, circumventing the need for the informal rules that generally dictate the police approach to sex workers in the current state of de facto decriminalization. It is inadequate merely to state that there should be decriminalization without specifying what decriminalization should look like. Furthermore, overemphasizing formal criminalization, even if only of clients, places too much confidence in the penal system to address issues relating to sex work. Policing sex work increases sex workers' contact with the state actors charged with the violent enforcement of the law. Even if this violent enforcement is intended to protect all womankind, the most marginalized women are likely to suffer the most brutal aspects of policing, as was illustrated in the policing of sex workers in central Johannesburg.

The history of the policing of sex work in South Africa reveals that sex work has mostly been policed informally and treated as a public nuisance matter. The overemphasis on pushing for decriminalization or against criminalization fails to appreciate how other discourses indirectly police sex workers' bodies while empowering the discussants rather than the sex workers. The continuing tension between policy and practice indicates that policies have been unsuccessful in responding to the lived reality of sex work. In this sense, broad pronouncements about the decriminalization of sex work require additional nuance that appreciates the historical conditions that inform sex work, as well as localization to address the particular concerns of the relevant community. In fact, activist attempts have reinforced the discourses that police sex workers' bodies, for example in the public health context, even while advocating for decriminalization.

The law is viewed as the solution for sex worker issues, and the thrust of the debate focuses on criminalization. However, the law can be violent and discriminatory, especially toward disenfranchised women. In South Africa especially, it is important to establish a broader regulatory framework that recognizes the realities of sex workers. This framework might deploy messaging and communication manuals and toolkits that educate stakeholders about how to talk about sex workers and advance a narrative that empowers them; partnerships and community forums that center the perspectives and views of sex workers to discuss concerns and problem-solving strategies; the funding of community organizations that can provide emergency services to sex workers; increased sensitivity in the public health research that pertains to sex workers in the choice of language used to speak about sex workers and the inclusion of sex workers' clients in the discussions; and the adoption of non-police strategies to respond to sex workers' security needs and the reduction of police interactions with sex workers. These reforms would create much-needed transparency in the policing of sex workers. Where the negotiation of relationships is explicit and not the result of informal responses, more favorable rules can aim to balance existing power imbalances. This may help to insulate sex workers against negative expressions of masculinities and protect them against discrimination.

The interests of police and sex workers frequently align, even though this relationship is often treated as static, flat, and polarized. There is an assumption that the police enforce sex work regulations against sex workers at a much higher rate than they do against clients. This is no doubt true in certain circumstances, but the reality is most likely more complicated. Police may be targeting clients with alternative motivations, and clients may be able to buy their way out of trouble, creating the perception that only sex workers are being arrested because only they are being booked. In imagining a state where decriminalization exists, it will be important to acknowledge the complexity of the relationship between police and sex workers and to promote strategies for security that look beyond the police.

A Note about Methodology

This book focuses on two questions: (1) how the policing of sex work currently occurs (ethnographic questions about the nature of sex work at the research sites) and (2) how the policing of sex work should occur (normative question).[1] I engaged in the three 'archetypal' methods of qualitative research: (1) reading and relying on existing texts, (2) interviewing participants and engaging in conversation, and (3) observing participants. This study focuses on three geographical locations and thus incorporates a case study method. The case study method is appropriate for exploring a phenomenon within a wider context.[2] This approach allows the researcher to understand how social context impacts behavior.

This research project was concerned with exploring police and sex workers' own understandings of their relationship and with describing the historical policing of sex workers to understand the contemporary policing of this population. The study strives for contextualized knowledge and therefore benefits from the depth and description available through the case study methodology. Ethnography is often used to help describe and interpret human behavior as situated within larger social structures.[3] It typically investigates a particular case or cases to explore complex social constructs to advance theoretical development.[4] I chose ethnography because this method allowed me to consider questions such as how discourses about female sexuality and how the history of policing sex in South Africa manifested themselves in the actual policing of sex workers in Johannesburg. This case study involves five research sites in the three geographic locations.[5] These research sites represent a fraction of the typology of the sex work that is in Johannesburg but are sufficiently unique to highlight the diversity of the industry. I gathered the observational data through field notes, which I recorded the day following each nighttime observation. I also took (minimal) notes during the observation times, as needed.

Initially, I did not plan to interview sex workers for this project and intended to focus on the policing aspect of the interactions, from the police's perspective. However, that quickly shifted as I became informally acquainted with several sex workers in the Rosebank area and later introduced to several more. Maintaining the trust of two groups of participants who are at times antagonistic with each other was challenging, and ethnography requires some form of friendship or intimacy with the research participants because you spend so much time together. Consequently, there is a contradiction in forming close relationships with two groups that are somehow in opposition to each other. Managing both the police and the sex worker relationships required that I focus on one group of participants at a time, recall the appropriate social cues for my audience (such as, lexicon, wardrobe, slang), and deepen the relationships through casual interactions and time spent together. Given the nature of the research, this often happened over drinks and in bars. Working with one group may be interpreted as a form of taking sides. I tried to assure the research participants that my research questions were guiding my approach and that I was not an advocate for one side or the other. This type of communication often happened in casual settings. This relationship building also happened over meals and informal rap sessions, where participants would talk with me about work conditions, salary, family life, and the general challenges of living in Johannesburg. These personal or informal interactions became important ways of maintaining close relationships with the participants as well as obtaining relevant information about other aspects of their lives.

After spending approximately five months in the field building rapport with the police and sex work participants, I began conducting semi-structured interviews with research participants. These included semi-structured interviews with twenty-five police officers focused on their everyday inter-actions with the sex workers, their attitudes about the legal rules concerning sex workers, and their observations about how sex workers are policed. The interviews covered several major research questions, but they also allowed for flexibility in the discussions. This approach allowed the interviews to be open-ended and encouraged the participants to determine the direction of the conversations. Interviews with the twenty-five police members were audio-recorded with their permission and later transcribed by a professional transcription company.

Likewise, I conducted 36 semi-structured interviews with the sex work-ers about their interactions with police officers, their expectations of the po-lice, and their observations about how sex workers are policed. In addition to these thirty-six interviews, I conducted informal interviews during the course of my ethnography with more than fifty sex workers in Johannesburg to build rapport, get a general sense of the working conditions, and introduce myself to sex workers. Although research participants are at times reluctant to be completely forthcoming in interviews, depending on rapport and per-ceived expectations, interviews are helpful in revealing expressed motiva-tions and informal understandings of conduct.

I took copious notes during my interviews with sex workers to ensure accuracy. The semi-structured interviews with sex workers were generally ten to sixty minutes in duration and took place while the sex workers were working. I attempted to be as brief as possible to respect the sex workers' workspace and to avoid interrupting their business transactions. For sex workers, time is quite literally money, and I had to narrowly tailor my re-search questions for the sex workers. Data from interviews with sex workers were generally all handwritten during the interviews, and key points were later transcribed. These interviews were not audio-recorded to encourage trust from the participants.

Longer interviews occurred when sex workers seemed interested in hav-ing a lengthy discussion to share their experiences. I chose a subset of five of the sex worker participants for semi-structured, in-depth interviews, outside of business hours, based on their interest in the project, availability, and their showing up for the interviews. These interviews were helpful in identifying temporal changes in the relationships between the police and sex workers as well as other factors that influence how participants experienced the policing of sex work. The in-depth interviews were each longer than two to seven hours in duration. One of these interviews was audio-recorded with the permission of the participant and later transcribed by a professional transcription company. These interviews explored information outside the scope of my research questions. I was able to gain additional depth about the individual sex workers' stories and their entry into the sex industry. All of these interviews proved helpful in gaining the trust of sex workers because interviewed sex workers would vouch for me on the streets and in brothels when other sex workers were hesitant to speak with me.

I began speaking to sex workers in the Oxford Road area and in central Johannesburg after spending several months patrolling with the police. I would drive around the red-light district in Rosebank on a red scooter and would stop to chat with sex workers who were not actively engaged in any transactions and seemed receptive to me as I slowly drove by. I did this for three months, while I was also patrolling with the police, to allow the sex workers to become familiar with me with the aim of facilitating future introductions. After seeing me on the streets a few times, sex workers began yelling for me to stop while I drove by, and I began to form relationships with the sex workers in Rosebank.

Each research participant was provided with a description of the research project and the parameters of informed consent in the form of an information sheet and informed consent form. Although I made physical copies of these sheets available, all research participants opted to receive this information orally because the sheets of paper would interfere with their working conditions. Both police and sex workers' working environments require mobility, and they were offended when I offered them paper information sheets. Instead, I opted to explain my research study orally. I explained that I was a researcher from Wits and that I was conducting research on the policing of sex workers in Johannesburg. The interviews were topical and designed to cover key issues relating to the research object, while allowing flexibility to build rapport and to address unexpected topics.

All participants were promised confidentiality, and they chose or were provided pseudonyms to aid in masking their identities. I provided all participants in the research information about informed consent before they participated in the study. I fully informed participants about the nature and purpose of the research, and I took additional steps to ensure that the sex workers' identities were protected, including using pseudonyms in written products about the project. All the sex worker participants indicated that their participation in sex work was not coerced and that they knowingly and freely entered into the sex work trade. I also provided ranking officials within the South African Police Service with information regarding confidentiality. However, I informed the polices that although a pseudonym would be used to conceal their identities, it was nevertheless possible that they could be identified given their unique ranking and other identifying information that would be provided in the research report. The real names of participants have not been stored. All participants were at least 18 years of age.

The study incorporates semi-structured interviews with thirty-six sex workers and twenty-five police. While this sample size might seem relatively small, as Docherty and Sandelowski have argued, "qualitative analysis is generically about maximizing understanding of the one in all of its diversity; it is case-oriented, not variable oriented."[6] Accordingly, smaller samples are typical of qualitative research, which is concerned with depth and rich description. "An adequate sample size in qualitative research is one that permits—by virtue of not being too large—the deep, case-oriented analysis that is a hallmark of all qualitative inquiry, and that results in—by virtue of not being too small—a new and richly textured understanding of experience."[7] Qualitative research is concerned with achieving depth and providing description and need not be generalizable.[8]

The sampling for the Hillbrow police interviews was convenience sampling. The ranking captain on the shifts during which I conducted my interviews would introduce me to the officers who were part of the unit that engaged in "visible policing," or another term for on-the-streets patrol work. I would then interview all officers who were willing to participate in the study. I mitigated for the convenience sampling by randomizing the shifts during which I interviewed police officers. After interviewing twenty Hillbrow police officers, I had interviewed most of the officers charged with "visible policing" and complaints. These visible policing officers are the first line of contact for many sex workers in Hillbrow and thus had relevant knowledge regarding my research questions.

By contrast, the Rosebank police station is much smaller, but it took much longer to conduct the interviews there. The Rosebank police repeatedly informed me of their capacity constraints. Accordingly, the interviews there were pushed back on several occasions, and the sampling approach was also convenience sampling. The Rosebank police members were reluctant to participate in semi-structured, pre-scheduled interviews. After much pushback, I managed to conduct semi-structured in-depth interviews with five police officers there. However, during the course of my ethnography, I conducted informal interviews with an additional twelve police members about their duties and their perception of sex work.

The research sampling for sex workers was in large part respondent-driven sampling or snowball sampling. This sampling technique is a form of network sampling driven by the network of existing research participants. It is a sampling technique frequently used to research "hard-to-reach" populations.[9] I also employed targeted sampling and was able to penetrate the sex worker community by becoming a frequent presence in sex work hot spots by cruising around the Oxford Road area in the evening, frequenting brothel hotels during strip shows and sex shows, and becoming a known presence in central Johannesburg.[10]

My participant observation with the sex workers comprised three different approaches corresponding to my three research sites. In Rosebank, I would spend time outside with sex workers when they were in between clients, parking my scooter at a discreet location to avoid interfering with their business. Any evening I was on Rosebank patrol, I would interview every sex worker I encountered within the designated geographic space on which I was focused for the evening. Interviewing the sex workers in their work environment was beneficial because many of their concerns were fresh on their minds as they were working. Additionally, I was able to observe their interactions with each other, and chatting in a group setting among colleagues encouraged sex workers who were hesitant to talk to a stranger to speak up. However, because of the nature of sex work and of my research, I was unable to obtain a truly random sample. Obtaining a random sample for sex workers is challenging, and purposive sampling is generally adopted when researching this "invisible population."[11]

I mitigated for this by interviewing all the sex workers who were present within a given location[12] and regularly switching the location for the evening. This allowed me to obtain some level of randomness in my sample, although the primary sampling technique was convenience sampling. I adopted the same approach in central Johannesburg. I would spend time outside, casually chatting with sex workers and observing as clients interacted with them. I would then conduct semi-structured interviews with sex workers who were interested in participating in the research project. Several of the sex workers I met on the streets had previous experience in brothels and were able to share their insights about working in brothels as well.

I personally transcribed all the ethnographic field notes. This allowed me to fully immerse myself in the topics that were discussed in the previous evening and to begin the process of interpreting the data. In reviewing the data collected during interviews and focus groups, I used critical discourse analysis to decode "the role of discourse in the (re)production and challenge of dominance (or) . . . the exercise of social power by elites, institutions or groups, that results in social inequality, including political, cultural, class, ethnic, racial and gender inequality."[13] Critical discourse analysis provides a mode for interpreting raw data that aims to place the data within their structural context and elucidate what the data reveal about underlying inequality. I reviewed the data frequently and used open coding to pull out themes that naturally arose from the data. These themes provide the organizing structure for this book and are included in many of the subject headings.

Notes

INTRODUCTION

1. See, e.g., Leggett, "A Den of Iniquity?" 21–22.

2. Hillbrow is an inner-city community in Johannesburg, South Africa, with a "reputation as a run-down neighbourhood ridden with drug-dealing, prostitution, slumlord hijacking and violent crime." West-Pavlov, "Inside Out—The New Literary Geographies of the Post-Apartheid City," 7.

3. Building "hijackings" occur when criminal enterprises illegally seize inner-city buildings in Johannesburg and function as the landlords of those buildings in the absence of the lawful landlords. Jacobs, "Building Hijackings on the Rise."

4. Stadler and Dugmore, "'Honey, Milk and Bile': A Social History of Hillbrow, 1894–2016," 444.

5. Leggett, "A Den of Iniquity?"

6. Pieterse, "Cityness and African Urban Development," 208.

7. Robinson, "Thinking Cities through Elsewhere," 4.

8. Ibid.

9. All names of participants in this study, other than the author's name (India), have been anonymized.

10. Brewis and Linstead, "'The Worst Thing Is the Screwing' (1): Consumption and the Management of Identity in Sex Work": "[Sex workers] are selling something which has not been fully commodified and which is usually associated with the non-commercial private sphere, governed as it is by values of intimacy, love and affect. This liminality arguably means that the place where

prostitution happens, whether actual geographical location, part of the body or symbolic location (in terms of its positioning in the prostitute's psyche), is also crucial to the prostitute's sense of self, to their self esteem" (84).

11. Michel Foucault has discussed the role of considering history and conducting an "archeology" of history to reveal a "general of theory of productions" that explains the nature of various discourses. See Foucault, *The Archaeology of Knowledge*.

12. Mbembé and Nuttall, "Writing the World from an African Metropolis," 354.

13. Ibid., 354, 348.

14. Newham, "Tackling Police Corruption in South Africa": "In a study of sex workers in the inner-city area of Johannesburg conducted by the sociologists at the University of Witwatersrand, 16% admitted that they had been forced to perform sexual favours to police members in exchange for not being arrested." (There has been considerable research highlighting the challenges that South African sex workers face: See, for example, Fick & Sex Workers Education & Advocacy Taskforce *Coping with Stigma, Discrimination and Violence*, 12 (noting that "sex workers are vulnerable to violence and that they have to deal with tremendous stigma and discrimination"). Further, Caroline Zulu, a sex worker and advocate, recounts her experience with the police in Daughta, "Sex Workers in South Africa": "The police abuse sex workers, steal our money, demand sex. When the girls are arrested, the police want us to pay 300 Rand to let us free. They say it is a fine for 'loitering.' But they refuse to give us an official receipt for our money or a paper that says we were arrested for 'loitering.' Once we pay, there is no record of the charges, so we can't go to court."

15. Albertyn, "Women and the Transition to Democracy in South Africa," 39, 43.

16. See for example Richter, "Erotic Labour in Hillbrow"; Stadler and Delany, "The 'Healthy Brothel'"; Dunkle et al., "Risk Factors for HIV Infection among Sex Workers in Johannesburg, South Africa," 256; Gardner, "Criminalising the Act of Sex," 328; Hunter, "The Changing Political Economy of Sex in South Africa," 689; Peltzer et al., "Characteristics of Female Sex Workers"; and Rees et al., "Commercial Sex Workers in Johannesburg," 328.

17. Foucault, *The History of Sexuality*, 11.

18. Ibid., 14 ("Forty percent of households are female headed."). "The mean age of marriage for women is twenty-eight years, whereas the majority of women have their first child before the age of twenty-one Fathers often have little or no role in the upbringing of their children. In 1993, some 36 percent of children had absent (living) fathers and 57 percent had fathers who were present. By 2002, the

proportion of children with absent (living) fathers had jumped to 46 percent, while the proportion of present fathers dropped to 39 percent." (internal citations omitted).

19. Morrell et al., "Hegemonic Masculinity/Masculinities in South Africa": "The female homicide rate is . . . highly elevated, at six times higher than the rate worldwide, and at least half of female victims are killed by their male intimate partners. The country also has an alarmingly high level of rate of rape. Fifty-five thousand rapes of women and girls are reported to the police every year, which is estimated to be at least nine times lower than the actual number. In a population-based survey, 28 percent of men interviewed disclosed having raped" (11, 14).

20. Seedat et al., "Violence and injuries in South Africa": "At least half of female victims are killed by their male intimate partners. In 1999, there were an estimated 3797 homicides of women, giving an overall homicide rate (24.7 per 100 000) six times higher than the rate worldwide (4.0 per 100 000)" (1011, 1012).

21. Ibid., 1013.

22. Fick & Sex Workers Education & Advocacy Taskforce, 12 (noting that "sex workers are vulnerable to violence and that they have to deal with tremendous stigma and discrimination").

23. Morrell et al., "Hegemonic Masculinity/Masculinities in South Africa," 11, 12. "The [South African] society is highly patriarchal, with exaggerated racialized, gender inequalities, and the normative use of violence." Ibid., 25.

24. UNAIDS has a commonly adopted definition that describes sex workers as "female, male and transgender adults and young people who receive money or goods in exchange for sexual services, either regularly or occasionally." See, e.g., UNAIDS, *Sex Work and HIV/AIDS*.

25. Harcourt and Donovan, "The Many Faces of Sex Work."

26. Manoek, *Stop Harassing Us!*

27. See, e.g., Mgbako and Smith, "Sex Work and Human Rights in Africa"; and Leggett, "Drugs, Sex Work, and HIV in Three South African Cities."

28. See, e.g., Stadler and Delany, "The 'Healthy Brothel.'"

29. Hoang, *Dealing in Desire*, 2.

30. As Macleod and Durrheim comment in "Foucauldian Feminism: The Implications of Governmentality": "Foucault stressed the importance of formulating and studying the question of power relations in terms of 'power at its extremities . . . where it becomes capillary,' i.e., in the everyday lives, actions and interactions of people" (43; internal citations omitted).

31. See, e.g., South African Commission for Gender Equality, *Position Paper on Sex Work* (January 16, 2013): "The criminalization of sex work harms sex

workers and denies them access to the rights contained in our constitution. Sex workers are subjected to numerous human rights violations, predominately harassment and abuse at the hands of police officers, and are not able to access and exercise legal or labour rights, or social protections" (9). This approach presupposes that sex workers face police harassment because sex work is illegal and that the relationship between sex workers and police is somewhat flat, with police as abusers and sex workers as victims. However, the regulation of sex workers through public nuisance ordinances has a long tradition in South Africa and is connected to understandings of public order and public nuisance (see chapter 1 in this volume) and the ordering of female sexuality in private and public spaces (see chapters 3, 4, and 5). This may well remain the case regardless of the status of sex work as decriminalized or criminalized. For these reasons, the discussion on decriminalization must move beyond blaming the police-oppressor and protecting the sex worker-victim.

32. See Fick and Sex Workers Education and Advocacy Taskforce, *Coping with Stigma, Discrimination and Violence*, which discusses the lived experiences of sex workers and advocates for decriminalization as a means of harm reduction and also for the exercise of sex work choice in line with liberal feminism.

33. Ibid.

34. For a recent view of the value of this approach, see Marks, "Dancing with the Devil?" Marks describes reforms to remilitarize the police service and notes that "new proposals for 'beefing up policing,' are not informed by evidence-based research." She further comments: "Research optimally should feed into social change. Effecting social change is only possible when worldviews come together, especially between unlikely collaborators like police officers and academic researchers. What has this meant in real terms? It has meant being present with the police in good and bad times. It means having to prove yourself as a researcher who is knowledgeable about your field, but also open to learning from the police. It means creating an environment where police and researchers are open to learn from one another" (28–29).

35. Schwartz, "Field Experimentation in Sociolegal Research," 401.

36. See Marks, "Researching Police Transformation," 870.

37. See Wolcott, *Ethnography: A Way of Seeing.*

38. See Morrell et al., "Hegemonic Masculinity/Masculinities in South Africa," discussing the expressions of various forms of South African masculinities, including a Black, urban form. Morrell et al. also comment that "[f]orty percent of [South African] households are female headed." Moreover, the "mean age of marriage for women is twenty-eight years, whereas the majority of women have

their first child before the age of twenty-one. Fathers often have little or no role in the upbringing of their children. In 1993, some 36 percent of children had absent (living) fathers and 57 percent had fathers who were present. By 2002, the proportion of children with absent (living) fathers had jumped to 46 percent, while the proportion of present fathers dropped to 39 percent. . . . The female homicide rate is . . . highly elevated, at six times higher than the rate worldwide, and at least half of female victims are killed by their male intimate partners. The country also has an alarmingly high level of rate of rape. Fifty-five thousand rapes of women and girls are reported to the police every year, which is estimated to be at least nine times lower than the actual number. In a population-based survey, 28 percent of men interviewed disclosed having raped" (14, internal citations omitted). These data provide social context for understanding the gendered history of violence in South Africa, a history relevant for understanding how police officers interact with sex workers.

39. Ibid.

40. At the outset of my research, there were a couple of instances when offended sex workers demanded that I dress "like a lady of the night" before daring to approach them.

41. Shaver, "Sex Work Research."

42. Ibid.

43. Foley, "Critical Ethnography," 469.

CHAPTER 1

1. Davenport and Saunders, *South Africa: A Modern History*, 25–30.
2. Trotter, "Dockside Prostitution in South African Ports," 675.
3. Ibid., 676–77.
4. Ibid., 677.
5. Aderinto, *When Sex Threatened the State*.
6. Trotter, "Dockside Prostitution," 677.
7. Ibid., 676.
8. Ross, *Status and Respectability in the Cape Colony, 1750–1870*, 128.
9. White, *The Comforts of Home: Prostitution in Colonial Nairobi*.
10. Ross, *Status and Respectability in the Cape Colony, 1750–1870*, 128.
11. Trotter, "Dockside Prostitution," 677.
12. Van Heyningen, "Social Evil in the Cape Colony 1868–1902,"171.
13. Trotter, "Dockside Prostitution," 678.
14. Ibid., 675.
15. Ibid., quoting Ross, *Status and Respectability in the Cape Colony, 1750–1870*.

16. Van Heyningen, "Social Evil in the Cape Colony," 171.

17. Stoler, "Educating Desire in Colonial South-East Asia," 36.

18. Bryder, "Sex, Race, and Colonialism," 814.

19. Ibid.: "[T]he provision of prostitutes was thought necessary because sexual passions were heightened in the tropical heat: denied prostitutes, soldiers could turn to rape or, worse, one another: 'The constant haunting fear of homosexuality, the presence of which would undermine the manly adventure of imperial conquest, underscores the whole debate on prostitution throughout this era. . . . In the politics of empire, there was no room for even a hint of the effeminacy assumed to exist among subject men'"; quoting Levine, "Venereal Disease, Prostitution, and the Politics of Empire, 576.

20. Hale, *Freud and the Americans*, 42.

21. Malherbe, "Family Law and 'The Great Moral Public Interests,'" 13–14.

22. Ibid.

23. Foucault, *The History of Sexuality*, vol. 1.

24. Marcus, *The Other Victorians*.

25. Ibid., 5–7.

26. Ibid.

27. Ibid.

28. See, e.g., Ahlberg, "Is There a Distinct African Sexuality?" In discussing the double standard in understanding male and female sexuality during the Victorian era, Ahlberg too comments: "the period is characterized by the strong belief that man's sexual urge is biologically natural while a virtuous woman should be asexual. This rationalized the double standard whereby unchastity was excusable and understandable in men, but unnatural and unforgivable in women. If the man was not sexually satisfied by his virtuous asexual wife, he could use prostitutes" (224).

29. Ibid.

30. Van Heyningen, "Social Evil in the Cape Colony," 173–74.

31. Ibid.

32. See generally Shear, "Not Welfare or Uplift Work," 393, 395.

33. Jochelson, "Sexually Transmitted Diseases in Nineteenth- and Twentieth-Century South Africa," 217.

34. Van Heyningen, "Social Evil in the Cape Colony," 177, 179, 182.

35. Ibid., 179.

36. Trotter, "Dockside Prostitution," 678.

37. Martens, "Almost a Public Calamity," 32.

38. Ibid.: "[I]n 1889 39 'Native women' presented themselves for treatment for syphilis and even for gonorrhea. However, in seeking treatment these women unwittingly risked further ill health. In the 19th century, the principal treatment for syphilis was mercury, and the dose required to eradicate the disease was close to being fatal" (32).

39. See generally Levine, "Venereal Disease, Prostitution, and the Politics of Empire," 580.

40. Levine, "Venereal Disease, Prostitution, and the Politics of Empire," 581.

41. Gardner, "Criminalizing the Act of Sex," 330–31 (internal quotations and citations omitted).

42. Ibid.

43. Levine, "Venereal Disease, Prostitution, and the Politics of Empire," 583, discussing the conditions of Lock hospitals in India.

44. Van Heyningen, "Social Evil in the Cape Colony," 172, 178.

45. Bryder, "Sex, Race, and Colonialism," 818, citing Burton, "White Woman's Burden."

46. Ibid.

47. Hollis, *Women in Public, 1850–1900*, 209, quoting Josephine Butler, *Personal Reminiscences of a Great Crusade* ([1896], 2008).

48. Van Heyningen, "Social Evil in the Cape Colony": "Under this Act these girls had mutinied, and they stated that they had done so to get out of the Lock Hospital before their confinement" (185).

49. Ibid., 195: "The use of the speculum as a diagnostic instrument was still crude and the most usual treatment for syphilis, with heroic dosages of mercury, did more to kill the patients than to cure them."

50. Ibid., 174.

51. Ibid.

52. Ibid., 174–78.

53. Bryder, "Sex, Race, and Colonialism," 818.

54. Malherbe, "Family Law and 'The Great Moral Public Interests,'" 13–14.

55. Martens, "Almost a Public Calamity," 30–31, 34. Martens provides some background on the features of sex work in the Natal: "Prostitution was a feature of Natal town life from the early 19th century. A report on the first sitting of the Pietermaritzburg Magistrate's Court in 1846 condemned 'immorality' and the 'contaminating vices of the canteen.' In the late 1860s Pietermaritzburg citizens witnessed scenes of 'female infamy,' and 'the throngs of children in the streets' told 'what share white men have in the vice that elicits no remark.' . . . In 1890, police

estimated that there were almost 70 prostitutes working in Pietermaritzburg, just over 50 prostitutes in Durban, over 50 prostitutes in Newcastle and 12 prostitutes in Ladysmith. Most of these sex workers were African women, although there were smaller numbers of white, Indian and 'coloured' prostitutes (the latter were usually referred to as 'St. Helenas,' 'Cape women,' or 'Hottentots'"(30-31).

56. Ibid.: "Pietermaritzburg authorities had the most pragmatic approach. Superintendent Fraser had 'no desire to suppress brothels' and so seldom enforced the by-law prohibiting the keeping of brothels in the borough. There were in 1890 'about thirty houses of ill-fame known to the police' in Pietermaritzburg, 10 of which housed white women. Women operated most of these houses and Fraser did not know of a single brothel 'with a bully inside.' Moreover, a significant number of the city's prostitutes lived and worked alone. Superintendent Alexander was far more punitive in his policing of Durban sex workers and he claimed that prostitution and soliciting were prohibited. He reported that there were no brothels in Durban, although there were 'a number of huts occupied by Coolies on the Eastern Vlei, which are here and there let to Kafir girls who carry on prostitution.'"

57. Ibid.

58. Ibid., 27, 36.

59. Ibid.: "The employment of African 'houseboys' who performed 'women's work' in settler homes, as well as African female prostitutes who worked publicly in Natal towns unsettled Whites because they subverted settler notions of appropriate domestic behaviour" (30). See also Atkins, *The Moon Is Dead! Give Us Our Money!*; and McCulloch, *Black Peril, White Virtue*, 149, and Martens, "Almost a Public Calamity," 33, 34, 39-42.

60. Ibid., 49-50.

61. Ibid., 52

62. See, e.g., Police Offences Act, Act No. 27 of 1882.

63. Munro, "Legal Feminism and Foucault," 546, 550.

64. Police Offences Act, Amendment Act No. 44 of 1898.

65. Van Onselen, "Who Killed Meyer Hasenfus?" 1.

66. Cammack, *The Rand at War, 1899–1902*, 4.

67. Van Onselen, "Who Killed Meyer Hasenfus?" 1.

68. Ibid.

69. Cammack, *Rand at War*, 4.

70. Dugmore, "From Pro-Boer to Jingo."

71. Trotter. "Dockside Prostitution," has discussed the influx of White women into the Transvaal during the Mineral Revolution: "In the 1880s, the Mineral

NOTES TO CHAPTER 1   185

Revolution ignited a global migration to the Transvaal gold fields. Diggers, pimps and prostitutes passed through the coastal ports, some never going any further. To cater to this boom, European Jewish pimps trafficked thousands of 'Continental women' (poor European Jews) to southern Africa." When the Boer government tightened its laws against prostitution, many retreated to the coast. "From about 1896 there was an influx into Cape Town of 'continental' women which resulted in a professionalization of the trade and ousted many of the local girls." A brothel explosion ensued (679).

72. Ibid.

73. See Cammack, *Rand at War*, 4.

74. Ibid.

75. Cammack, *Rand at War*, 4.

76. Van Onselen, "Who Killed Meyer Hasenfus?" 1, 3.

77. Ibid.

78. See Harries, "Symbols and Sexuality," 323.

79. Ibid.

80. Ordinance 46 of 1903 § 21(1)(a) (Transvaal), (emphasis added).

81. Act 36 of 1902 §33(1)(a) (Cape); Ordinance 11 of 1903 § 13(1)(a) (Orange Free State); Act 31 of 1903 § 15(1)(a) (Natal).

82. Thompson, "Racial Ideas and Gendered Intimacies" 354.

83. Keegan, "Gender, Degeneration and Sexual Danger," 464.

84. Martens, "Citizenship, 'Civilisation' and the Creation of South Africa's Immorality Act, 1927," 228.

85. Shear, "Not Welfare or Uplift Work," 396.

86. Scully, "Rape, Race, and Colonial Culture," 336, 346.

87. Keegan, "Gender, Degeneration and Sexual Danger," 464.

88. Ibid., 396.

89. Shear, "Not Welfare or Uplift Work," 396.

90. Keegan, "Gender, Degeneration and Sexual Danger," 476 (internal citation omitted).

91. Ibid.: In "the late 1890s in South Africa's urban centres . . . large numbers of European prostitutes [arrived], who, it was feared, were very indiscriminate in the disposal of their favours. After the South African War, a spate of laws was introduced criminalizing their entertaining Black clients. In the Cape, the law was limited to punishing White prostitutes who accepted 'aboriginal natives' as clients, leaving the clients themselves unscathed. In the Transvaal, Natal and Rhodesia, however, legislation was much more stringent, prohibiting all sexual contact between Black men (including 'coloureds') and White women, whether

for gain or not, and imposing heavy penalties on both Black men and White women in such relationships" (464).

92. Ibid., 465.

93. Trotter, "Dockside Prostitution," 679.

94. Shear, "Not Welfare or Uplift Work," 393, 395. See also, Burton, "White Woman's Burden": "Rather than overturning the Victorian feminine ideal, early feminist theorists used it to justify female involvement in the public sphere by claiming that the exercise of woman's moral attributes was crucial to social improvement. . . . The maintenance of racial hegemony was a collective cultural aspiration which feminists tried to use for their own ends" (296).

95. Martens, "Citizenship, 'Civilisation' and the Creation of South Africa's Immorality Act," 226; Martens is quoting Keegan, "Gender, Degeneration and Sexual Danger."

96. Martens, "Citizenship, 'Civilisation' and the Creation of South Africa's Immorality Act," 228. It is worth noting that similar laws have been passed throughout the world, including in the American Colonies of Virginia, Maryland, North Carolina, and Massachusetts as early as 1667, while they were still under British imperial rule. See Sollors, *Neither Black Nor White Yet Both*, App. B. Many of the U.S. prohibitions on interracial marriage persisted until 1967, when the United States Supreme Court outlawed them in *Loving v. Virginia* (1967) 388 U.S. 1.

97. Shear, "Not Welfare or Uplift Work," 398.

98. Ibid.

99. Delius and Glaser, 'Sexual Socialisation in South Africa," 40.

100. See Martens, "Citizenship, 'Civilisation' and the Creation of South Africa's Immorality Act," 224. See also, Klausen, "The Uncertain Future of White Supremacy," discussing the "birth-control movement," which illustrates "how White concern for the survival of South Africa's social order inflected, energized and influenced the politics of fertility during the 1930s." The birth-control movement further highlights how White women's wombs were a contested space for the racialized and gendered morality discourses.

101. Freed, "Summarised Findings of a Medico-Sociological Investigation into the Problem of Prostitution," 53.

102. Ibid., 53–54.

103. Trotter, "Dockside Prostitution," 680.

104. See generally, Ritner, "Dutch Reformed Church and Apartheid."

105. Lewin, "Sex Color and the Law," describing the circumstances that prompted the passage of this statute and noting that "[o]ddly enough, for nearly

three centuries after White settlement had taken root at the Cape, the Afrikaners made no effort to curb miscegenation by law" and allowed interracial marriage even after anti-miscegenation laws prohibiting intercourse had passed (10).

106. Immorality Amendment Act, No. 68 of 1967: "Any person who (a) procures or attempts to procure any female to have unlawful carnal intercourse with any person other than the procurer . . . or (b) inveigles or entices any female to a brothel for the purpose of unlawful carnal intercourse or prostitution or (c) procures or attempts to procure any female to become a common prostitute . . . shall be guilty of an offence."

107. Ibid. (emphasis added).

108. Ibid.: "(1) Any person who knowingly lives wholly or in part on the earnings of prostitution; or in public commits any act of indecency with another person; or in public or in private in any way assists in bringing about, or receives any consideration for, the commission by any person of any act of indecency with another person, shall be guilty of an offence."

109. Freed, "Summarised Findings of a Medico-Sociological Investigation," 53.

110. Trotter, "Dockside Prostitution," 681.

111. Wojcicki, "Movement to Decriminalize Sex Work," 93.

112. See Trotter, "Dockside Prostitution": "[A]t least since the 1960s, relations between sailors and prostitutes have been initiated in rough-and-tumble downtown nightclubs: Although these clubs were often violent places, where sex and drugs were sold, they were some of the few institutions in Cape Town that ignored apartheid legislation. The men and women of all 'races' who went there, just by drinking and dancing together, were breaking the law, and the clubs were frequently raided by the police. Again, we see that dockside prostitution was highly social in its solicitation phase. It was also beyond the law's concern. Though clubs were raided, they were not closed, despite the ceaseless law-breaking. And even with the high levels of violence right in the heart of the city, the clubs were not targets of moral campaigns or police clamp-downs" (682).

113. Wojcicki, "Movement to Decriminalize Sex Work," 94.

114. Ibid., 93, quoting Hilton Watts from the Cape Town *Sunday Tribune*, June 11, 1997.

115. Ibid., 95, quoting NA Debates col 14768 (February 15, 1998).

116. Morrell et al., "Hegemonic Masculinity," 14–15.

117. Van Der Spuy, "Literature on the Police in South Africa," 264.

118. Ibid., 264, 267.

119. Brewer, *Black and Blue*.

120. Whyte, *"Aluta Continua,"* 14.

121. Rauch, "Police Reform and South Africa's Transition," 119, 123.

122. Independent Complaints Directorate, *Investigating Torture*, 12.

123. Ibid., 9.

124. Ibid., 52.

125. Here, I am referring to policing in the Weberian sense, in that the police are acting as the state's arm for the exercise of legitimate force. See Weber, *From Max Weber: Essays in Sociology*.

126. Cawthra, *Brutal Force*.

127. Kynoch, "Apartheid Nostalgia,"9.

128. Adepoju, "Continuity and Changing Configurations of Migration": "South Africans lack trust in the police to maintain law and order. Under apartheid, the police protected whites and oppressed blacks. In the current situation, both groups are disappointed; whites no longer feel safe and blacks want proper police service. The police pay is low and corruption is wide-spread" (17).

129. James, *Money from Nothing*, for example, describes the experiences of middle-class South African individuals, including several police officers, who had to go into debt and were generally "unable to sustain their future dreams with their present income" (15).

130. Ibid.

131. Basdeo, "Curse of Corruption in the South African Police," finding that the salary for "police officials in the SAPS is on par, if not higher than [that for] teachers, nurses and fire fighters" (394).

132. Mbembé Nuttall, "Writing the World from an African Metropolis," 365.

133. Whyte, "*Aluta Continua.*"

134. Kusafuka, "Truth Commissions and Gender," 57.

135. Brogden, "Reforming Police Powers in South Africa," noting that "recent extraordinary events in South Africa, culminating in the election of President Mandela, have major implications for one of the most notorious police forces of modern times" (25).

136. Rauch, "Police Reform and South Africa's Transition," 119.

137. Ibid., 120.

138. Bruce, "Unfinished Business": "[T]he first formal positions on policing issues that emerged from [the ANC's] 1992 policy conference, articulated in the ANC policy document *Ready to Govern*, gave substantial emphasis to police accountability. Not only did this say that the new police service would be 'accountable to society and the community it serves through its democratically elected institutions' but also that policing should be 'based on community support and

participation' and that policing priorities would be 'determined in consultation with the communities they serve'" (1).

139. See Rauch, "Police Reform and South Africa's Transition": "In a speech to the top police commissioners in late 1995, Minister Mufamadi acknowledged that, despite the huge pressures they faced, the police leadership had achieved a great deal. Less than two years previously, the police service was regarded as a possible threat to democracy. 'Today, the relative credibility and legitimacy enjoyed widely by the police service is one of the more clear indicators of the successful transition to democracy which our country has made'" (122).

140. Pigou, "Monitoring Police Violence and Torture in South Africa."

141. Newham, Masuku, and Dlamini, "Diversity and Transformation in the South African Police Service," 20–22.

142. Rauch, "Police Reform and South Africa's Transition": "The new Minister for Safety and Security, Steve Tshwete . . . emphasized the crime fighting role of the police, and ha[d] encouraged a more strong-arm approach to criminals, with far less emphasis on the internal problems of police reform. This discourse ha[d] found favour with the South African public, which is increasingly concerned about crime and a police service which felt disempowered by the period of police transformation following the first election" (123).

143. Brewer, *Black and Blue*, 335.

144. Louw, "Surviving the Transition," describing the increasing crime rate and the perceptions around crime from the 1980s through the political transition in South Africa.

145. Hornberger, "From General to Commissioner to General," 600. Hornberger is citing Pierre Bourdieu, "What Makes a Social Class? On the Theoretical and Practical Existence of Groups," 1987.

146. Hornberger, "Human Rights and Policing": "The pervasiveness of past police practices illustrates what has been described as the 'informal organizational police culture'" (264).

147. Comaroff and Comaroff, "Criminal Obsessions, after Foucault," 800.

148. Rauch, "Police Reform and South Africa's Transition": "Feeling the effects of a devastating post-transition crime wave, the South African public began to demand tougher action against criminals. Recent policy approaches to the problem of crime have largely abandoned any commitment to social crime prevention by the police, attempting to shift this responsibility instead to the 'social' cluster of government departments such as housing, health, welfare and education. The government's two-pronged crime reduction approach now revolves

around sustained heavy policing operations (currently known as Operation Crackdown), and ongoing reform of the criminal justice system. The 'heavy' policing approach is underpinned by an ongoing process of internal police reform, most notably an emphasis on improved service delivery to the public" (125).

149. James, *Money from Nothing*, 15.

150. Foucault, *History of Sexuality*, 1:92.

151. Ibid., 1:93.

152. Hornberger, "Human Rights and Policing," 265.

153. Ibid., 261.

154. Ibid., 270.

155. Foucault, *History of Sexuality*, 1:93.

156. Marks, "Researching Police Transformation," 869.

157. Hornberger, "Human Rights and Policing," 268.

158. Merry, "Transnational Human Rights and Local Activism," notes "the paradox of making human rights in the vernacular: To be accepted, they have to be tailored to the local context and resonant with the local cultural framework. However, to be part of the human rights system, they must emphasize individualism, autonomy, choice, bodily integrity, and equality—ideas embedded in the legal documents that constitute human rights law" (49).

159. Whyte, "*Aluta Continua*," 19.

160. Collier, "Policing in South Africa," 1.

161. Louw, "Surviving the Transition."

162. Hornberger, "From General to Commissioner to General," argues: "The phenomenon of increasing state violence is indeed a threat, but it is also a very popular desire—one that serves to legitimize the estrangement of the law from itself and its formal institutional structures. At the same time, though, just because state violence is desired does not mean it is meted out in the desired way" (612).

163. Quoted in Blomley, "Law, Property, and the Geography of Violence," 124.

164. Ibid.

165. Ibid.

166. Evans, "If Democracy, Then Human Rights?"

167. Christenson, "Using Human Rights Law to Inform Due Process."

168. Blomley, "Law, Property, and the Geography of Violence."

169. Reflecting on the relevant legal norms provides a metric for assessing democratic policing and provides "a three-tiered model that includes '(a) accountability to international standards; (b) accountability to (human rights-based) national, constitutionally based law, either directly through the courts or

through civilian oversight arrangements and internal disciplinary procedures; and (c) accountability to the public or the community." Hornberger, "Human Rights and Policing," 267.

170. Constitution of the Republic of South Africa, Chapter 1, Section 2.

171. Chapter 2, Section 39, states that courts "must consider international law" and "may consider foreign law" when interpreting the Bill of Rights.

172. International Convention on the Elimination of All Forms of Racial Discrimination, art. 2(1)(c).

173. Amnesty International, "Amnesty International Draft Policy on the Protection of Human Rights of Sex Workers."

174. Ibid.: "Systems of oppression such as gender discrimination, racism, socio-economic inequality and legacies of colonial occupation, deny people power and lead to poverty and deprivation of opportunity" (7).

175. *Carmichele v Minister of Safety and Security and Another*, 2001.

176. Chaskalson, "Human Dignity as a Constitutional Value."

177. Chapter 2, Section 12, contains the following provisions:

Freedom and security of the person

(1) Everyone has the right to freedom and security of the person, which includes the right—

(a) not to be deprived of freedom arbitrarily or without just cause;

(b) not to be detained without trial;

(c) to be free from all forms of violence from either public or private sources;

(d) not to be tortured in any way; and

(e) not to be treated or punished in a cruel, inhuman or degrading way.

(2) Everyone has the right to bodily and psychological integrity, which includes the right—

(a) to make decisions concerning reproduction;

(b) to security in and control over their body; and

(c) not to be subjected to medical or scientific experiments without their informed consent.

178. See chapter 4 for a discussion of the Rosebank police station's decision to refrain from arresting sex workers, in order to comply with human rights norms.

179. But see Marks, "Dancing with the Devil?," noting new reforms to remilitarize the police service and "new proposals for 'beefing up policing' [that] are not informed by evidence-based research" (27).

180. South African Police Service, "Human Rights and Policing."

181. South African Police Service, *Policy on the Prevention of Torture and Treatment of Persons in Custody*.

182. See Fombad, "The Constitution as a Source of Accountability": "Today we are haunted by the old demons of authoritarian rule which we had hoped to have exorcized through constitutional reforms and multiparty democracy in the 1990s" (44).

183. Hornberger, "Human Rights and Policing," 271.

184. Woolman and Davis, "Last Laugh"; Sprigman and Osborne, "Du Plessis Is *Not* Dead"; van der Walt, "Justice Kriegler's Disconcerting Judgment"; Cheadle and Davis, "Application of the 1996 Constitution in the Private Sphere"; van der Walt, "Horizontal Application of Fundamental Rights"; Woolman, "The Amazing, Vanishing Bill of Rights." Beyond the law journals, see Davis, *Democracy and Deliberation*; and Cockrell, "Private Law and the Bill of Rights," 3A-3.

185. Kim, "Betraying Women in the Name of Revolution."

186. Vetten, "Addressing Domestic Violence in South Africa."

187. Govender, "Domestic Violence," 663.

188. Human Rights Watch, *Unequal Protection*: "Women attempting to seek police assistance, however, complained to Human Rights Watch that in these cases too they faced bias and obstruction from officials. In some cases, police dismissed complaints, either refusing to believe the woman's allegations or failing to recognize intra family violence as a crime. Police demonstrated a simplistic and biased understanding of the dynamics of rape, a lack of knowledge and experience as to the range of circumstances in which rapes of women occur, or a lack of sensitivity in dealing with rape victims."

189. In chapters 4 and 5, I discuss how understandings about private and public influence the daily policing of sex workers.

190. In *State v Baloyi*, the Constitutional Court held that the state has an affirmative obligation to enact legislative measures that will curtail the incidence of domestic violence. This 2000 case was followed by a series of cases that sought to hold individual state actors accountable for their failure to prevent private acts of violence. The following year, for example, Alix Jean Carmichele brought an action against the Minister of Safety and Security and the Minister of Justice (*Carmichele v Minister of Safety and Security*, 2001). Carmichele was attacked and seriously injured by Francois Coetzee. Coetzee had been awaiting trial for rape and had been released on his own recognizance, although he had a prior conviction for indecent assault. Neither the police nor the prosecutor objected to his release. Coetzee subsequently attacked Carmichele, leaving her with a head injury and a broken arm. Carmichele sought to hold the police and prosecutors

responsible for failing to protect the public against Coetzee. The Cape Provincial of the High Court and the Supreme Court of Appeal reviewed the common law obligations, and both held that the state was under no legal obligation to protect Carmichele. In 2001, however, the Constitutional Court reversed the lower courts' decisions, holding that the common law must be read in accordance with the principles of the Constitution (*Carmichele v Minister of Safety and Security and Others*, paras 18, 19). The Court considered the provisions of the interim Constitution and the Police Act and noted that the police are the primary protectors of the public against acts of violence, especially violence against women and children. The Court remanded the matter, and the lower court found that there was indeed a basis for the action upon consideration of the constitutional normative framework, and in 2003 the Supreme Court of Appeal affirmed this holding (*Minister of Safety and Security and Another v Carmichele*). This case emphasizes the role of the police as protectors in the domestic arena and thereby their role in addressing violence against sex workers. In another case, *Van Eeden v Minister of Safety and Security* (2003), the plaintiff was attacked and raped by Andre Gregory Mohammed, a convicted serial rapist who had escaped police custody. She alleged that by allowing Mohammed to escape from their custody, the police had failed to take necessary steps to protect the public. Following its decision in *Carmichele*, the Constitutional Court of South Africa found that the police had an affirmative duty to prevent Mohammed's escape. The court considered the affirmative obligation of the police to prevent the gender discrimination inherent in violence against women and determined that the police were obligated to prevent Mohammed's escape. A third case, *K v Minister of Safety and Security*, in 2005, involved the issue of vicarious liability. The plaintiff was raped by three uniformed policemen who had offered her a ride home after she was stranded on the streets in the early hours of the morning. The plaintiff brought a delictual claim against the minister, claiming that the minister was vicariously liable for the police officers on duty at the time of the assault. The Constitutional Court found that the minister could be held vicariously liable because the policemen committed the rape during their official duties and those duties include an obligation to protect the public. These officers violated this constitutional obligation and omitted to protect the plaintiff through their conduct.

191. Chapter 4 discusses Hillbrow police station members' involvement in serving as mediators in disputes between sex workers and their clients.

192. In the Criminal Law (Sexual Offences and Related Matters) Amendment Act 32 of 2007, the Sexual Offences Act was amended to more explicitly indicate that this provision of the Act was referring to the activities of the contractor.

193. Several of these conclusions concerning contemporary police practices are drawn from the ethnographic data gleaned during my research, as outlined earlier in the Introduction and discussed in detail in chapters 2, 3, and 4.

194. Mutume, "Gauteng Province Decriminalizes Prostitution."

195. Ibid.

196. Letter from Jean du Plessis, "NGO Submission Regarding Draft Policy Document on Decriminalizing Sex Work."

197. South African Law Commission, *Sexual Offences: The Substantive Law.*

198. South African Law Commission, *Sexual Offences: Adult Prostitution.*

199. Wojcicki, "Movement to Decriminalize Sex Work," 91.

200. Ibid., 89.

201. *National Director of Public Prosecutions v R O Cook*, para 39.

202. *State v Jordan*, paras 24–25.

203. *Egglestone v The State*, para 23.

204. Ibid., para 27.

205. *Kylie v Commission for Conciliation, Mediation and Arbitration and Others*, paras 54–55.

206. *National Director of Public Prosecutions v Lorna M. B.*, para 4.

207. Ibid., para 43.

208. *National Director of Public Prosecution v Geyser*, para 25.

209. Sapa, "Sex Work Should Be Decriminalised."

210. Government of South Africa, Newsroom. "Gauteng Legislature Hosts Provincial Dialogue for Commercial Sex Workers."

211. Sonke Gender Justice, *Decriminalisation of Sex Work*; SWEAT, *Sex Worker Rights Are Human Rights.*

212. South African Law Reform Commission, *Sexual Offences: Adult Prostitution.*

213. Wheeler and Gerntholtz, *Why Sex Work Should Be Decriminalised in South Africa.*

CHAPTER 2

1. Government of South Africa, Newsroom. "Remarks by the Deputy Minister of Police."

2. The Johannesburg Metropolitan Police Department was formed in 2001 by the Johannesburg Metropolitan Council to police local crime in central Johannesburg and to engage in visible policing. See Bénit-Gbaffou, "Unbundled Security Services and Urban Fragmentation."

3. Sanders, "The Risks of Street Prostitution" (internal citations omitted).

4. As Noah Zatz, in "Sex Work/Sex Act," has argued: "criminalization has tended to isolate women from one another (as evidenced by laws making it illegal for a set number of women to live together), encourage dependency on pimps, and cut off mobility between prostitution and other forms of work: 'Prostitutes were uprooted from their neighborhoods and had to find lodgings in other areas of the city and in the periphery. . . . Cut off from other sustaining relationships, increasingly they were forced to rely on pimps for emotional security and for protection against legal authorities. Indeed, the wide prevalence of pimps in the early twentieth century meant that prostitution had shifted from a female- to a male-dominated trade, and there existed a greater number of third parties with an interest in prolonging women's stay on the streets.' The form of prostitution encouraged by this historical process is one in which the subversive potential of prostitution is limited even while the supply of prostitutes is maintained" (301), quoting Judith R. Walkowitz, "The Politics of Prostitution," *Signs* (1980), 128.

5. Howell, "A Private Contagious Diseases Act," 377. See also Lefebvre, *The Production of Space*: "(social) space is a (social) product . . . the space thus produced also serves as a tool of thought and of action . . . in addition to being a means of production it is also a means of control, and hence of domination, of power" (6).

6. Howell, "Private Contagious Diseases Act," 396.

7. Weintraub, "Theory and Politics of the Public/Private Distinction."

8. Freeman, "Feminist Debate over Prostitution Reform": For example, in Toronto, Canada, "in 1988 alone, the city spent $6.3 million fighting prostitution. Yet, 'despite more patrols, dramatically higher conviction rates, and the ongoing massive sweeps (something no other Canadian city had tried before), the police acknowledge that unless there is a raging blizzard the hookers will be out on the street tomorrow'" (82), quoting Wendy Dennis, "Street Fight," *Toronto Life* 85, November 1988, 130.

9. Hubbard, "Sex Zones: Intimacy, Citizenship and Public Space," 51.

10. This aspect of policing is addressed in detail in chapter 3.

11. Van Onselen, "Who Killed Meyer Hasenfus?" discussing, among other points, the collusion of the police and prostitution rings in Gauteng during the Mineral Revolution.

12. Sanchez, "Sex, Law, and the Paradox of Agency and Resistance," 39.

13. Murphy and Venkatesh, "Vice Careers."

14. Hubbard, "Sex Zones," 60.

15. Ibid.

16. Ibid.

17. Ibid.: "The female prostitute, in particular, represents a paradigmatic figure whose legal and social regulation symbolizes the contradictions inherent in
notions of equal citizenship; in many cities prostitutes are forced to work out of
sight, off-street in brothels, massage parlours or private flats where their sexuality
can be commodified with apparent impunity" (58).

18. UNAIDS, *Guidance Note on HIV and Sex Work*, describes controllers as
"power-holding intermediaries between the sex worker and client" (3).

19. As mentioned in chapter 1, all names of the people who feature in my
research have been anonymized.

20. Comaroff and Comaroff, "Criminal Obsessions, after Foucault," 824.

21. Merry, "Transnational Human Rights and Local Activism," 49.

22. Foucault, *History of Sexuality*, 1:92.

23. Here, as earlier, I am referring to policing in the Weberian sense, in that
the police are acting as the state's arm for the exercise of legitimate force.

24. Kotiswaran, "Born unto Brothels," 616 (internal citations omitted).

25. See the section "The Transvaal and the Mineral Gold Rush" in chapter 1;
and Van Onselen, "Who Killed Meyer Hasenfus?"

26. Morrell et al., "Hegemonic Masculinity."

27. Sanchez, "Boundaries of Legitimacy," 543.

28. Aidt, "Economic Analysis of Corruption."

29. Rauch, Shaw, and Louw, *Municipal Policing in South Africa*.

30. A *sjambok* is a leather whip, a tool used by the apartheid police force for
riot control. It is similar to the police baton used by police officers in several
countries.

31. This remark reflects a gendered notion of hygiene consistent with the discourses around sex worker hygiene in the Victorian Era, as will be fully discussed
in chapter 3.

32. Munro, "Legal Feminism and Foucault," 550.

33. Morrell et al., "Hegemonic Masculinity," 12.

34. See, e.g., Jewkes et al., "Transactional Relationships and Sex with a Woman
in Prostitution": "Sex motivated by economic exchange is associated with public health problems, and presents many conceptual challenges for researchers.
Women and men in prostitution are vulnerable to HIV and other sexually transmitted infections, as well as acts of violence from clients, pimps, police and other
parties" (325); Stadler and Delany, "The "Healthy Brothel," noting that "sex workers are extremely vulnerable to HIV infection," and focusing on the provision of
clinical services to sex workers outside traditional clinical settings relating to the
spread of HIV; Dunkle et al., 'Risk Factors for HIV Infection among Sex Workers

in Johannesburg," focusing primarily on the biomedical profile of sex workers as at high risk for HIV infection; Peltzer, Seoka, and Raphala, "Characteristics of Female Sex Workers and Their Attitudes," focusing on sex workers' knowledge of HIV; Rees et al., "Commercial Sex Workers in Johannesburg," examining the HIV status of sex workers in Hillbrow; Scorgie et al., "Socio-demographic Characteristics and Behavioral Risk Factors of Female Sex Workers in Sub-Saharan Africa": "sex work remains an important contributor to HIV transmission within early, advanced and regressing epidemics in sub-Saharan Africa" (920); and Leggett. "Drugs, Sex Work, and HIV." But also see Gardner, "Criminalizing the Act of Sex": "Rather than talk of high-risk and low-risk groups, we should be talking about high- and lower-risk sexual acts. The exchange of sex for money does not spread HIV; unprotected sex with an infected person is what leads to infection. Many of the women who sell sex also have personal partners, and time and time again research has shown that while sex workers may use condoms with the clients, this is not the case with their personal partners, who generally refuse to use condoms. Why then is it often assumed that HIV-positive sex workers got infected in the course of their work?" (328).

35. See Richter et al., "Sex Work and the 2010 FIFA World Cup," arguing that sex workers currently cannot report instances of abuse to the police and are harassed by the police, and that decriminalization will allow sex workers to report instances of abuse to police because their conduct would then be legal. As here, the literature often adopts the narrative of the sex worker as the victim to, in turn, justify decriminalization by reasoning (1) that we must protect the sex worker from the dangers of sex work, and/or (2) that such protection protects the public health by reducing the spread of HIV and opening access. E.g., Richter et al., comment: "Decriminalizing sex work is at odds with the sensibilities of many political and religious leaders and often raises their indignation and ire. Yet watching a population being decimated by HIV should evoke similar responses and elicit strong action based on evidence." However, one must be careful when making this argument. It adopts a framework that deems the sex worker worthy of attention to the extent that we can protect her from her work, and protect society from her contagion. It is well-intentioned research, but it nonetheless reifies past discourses that have been obsessed with the public health profile of the sex worker (as described in chapter 1 of this book).

36. See, e.g., the websites for these two organizations: Embrace Dignity, http://embracedignity.org.za; and New Life Centre 4 Girls, http://www.new lifecentre4 girls.org/.

37. Kapur, "Tragedy of Victimization Rhetoric," 6.

38. Ibid.

39. For a discussion of the weaknesses of so-called carceral feminism or penal feminism, see Bernstein, "Militarized Humanitarianism Meets Carceral Feminism," discussing the militarization of human rights in sex trafficking campaigns; and Chuang, "Rescuing Trafficking from Ideological Capture."

40. The 1996 Constitution, Chapter 2, Section 27, states: "(1) Everyone has the right of access to—a) health care services, including reproductive health care; b) sufficient food and water; and c) social security, including, if they are unable to support themselves and their dependents, appropriate social assistance."

41. SANAC. *The South African National Sex Worker HIV Plan*, 6.

42. Kekana, "72% of Sex Workers in JHB are HIV Positive."

43. Metro police cite several bylaws when approaching sex workers. These bylaws relate to loitering and public decency. The City of Johannesburg Metropolitan Municipality Public Road and Miscellaneous By-Laws, Sections 13 and 14, state:

> 13. (1) No person may loiter or, except when forming part of a queue, congregate on any public road within twenty (20) metres of the entrance to any place of public entertainment so as to obstruct traffic or persons proceeding to, attending at, or departing from such place of entertainment.
>
> (2) No person may, without the prior written permission of the Council tout or solicit a driver of any motor vehicle who parks a motor vehicle at a place of entertainment for the purpose of or under pretext of looking after or watching over the motorvehicle. . . .
>
> 14. (2) No person may on or in view of any public road urinate, excrete, behave in any indecent manner by exposing his or her person or otherwise, make use of any indecent gesture, or commit, solicit or provoke any person to commit any riotous, orderly or indecent act.

CHAPTER 3

1. Clandinin, *Narrative Inquiry*. Narrative inquiry has been defined as "a collaboration between researcher and participants, over time, in a place or series of places, and in social interaction with milieus. An inquirer enters this matrix in the midst and progresses in the same spirit, concluding the inquiry still in the midst of living and telling, reliving and retelling, the stories of the experiences that made up people's lives, both individual and social" (46).

2. Ibid., 47.

3. Ibid., 47.

4. Mathabane, *Kaffir Boy*.

5. Nuttall, "Stylizing the Self," describes Rosedale as "a suburb cum business district where sectors like information technology, retail, fashion, cinema,

restaurants, and travel and tourism have been attracting a trendy and youthful workforce since the late 1980s" (445).

6. Muller, "Financial Main SA's Most Expensive Streets": "Millionaires row in Johannesburg includes Culross Road and Eccleston Crescent in Bryanston, 4th Road in Hyde Park, Coronation Road in Sandhurst and Deodar Road in Atholl; IOL News, "Study Reveals SA's Wealthiest Areas": "Joburg areas dominate the list of wealthiest suburbs with the other top spots going to Bryanston with 31 multi-millionaires, otherwise known as "ultra high net worth individuals" or UHNWI, Hyde Park (26 UNHWIs), and Westcliff (20 UNHWIs)."

7. The police frequently rolled the *r* of the word *prossies*, a shortened version of *prostitutes*.

8. The author has a very basic understanding of spoken Zulu.

9. The police at the Rosebank police station frequently referred to sex workers as "ladies of the night" or "working girls."

10. After approximately three months of joining police on their scheduled patrols, I began patrolling the streets of Rosebank alone to get a sense of the police presence from the outside. I also used this time to quietly observe officers' interactions with sex workers and their clients and to familiarize myself with the sex workers and various hot spots.

11. This lot number is anonymized.

12. Comaroff and Comaroff, "Law and Disorder in the Postcolony," 145 (internal citations omitted).

13. See Hubbard, Matthews, and Scoular, "Regulating Sex Work in the EU": "the state and law may intervene in sex work markets with the intention of tackling gendered injustice, but are perpetuating geographies of exception and abandonment" (137); Gould, "Criminalisation of Buying Sex," acknowledging that Sweden's approach to sex work was driven by fear of foreign prostitutes and the weak liberal tradition in Sweden; and Dodillet and Östergren, "Swedish Sex Purchase Act," discussing the "serious adverse effects of the Sex Purchase Act— especially concerning the health and well-being of sex workers—in spite of the fact that the lawmakers stressed that the ban was not to have a detrimental effect on people in prostitution" (437).

CHAPTER 4

1. Harris, "Xenophobia," discussing how xenophobia is a reflection of the "culture of violence" pervasive in South Africa: "Xenophobia is a form of violence and violence is the norm in South Africa. Violence is an integral part of the social fabric, even although the 'New South African' discourse belies this. Indeed by belying and excluding xenophobia, the 'New South Africa' discourse is able to

define itself as peaceful and tolerant. It is similarly able to coexist with the 'African Renaissance' discourse and to perpetuate ideals of harmony and diversity. But in order to do this, it is necessary that xenophobia is created and represented as a pathology. Consequently, xenophobia as a pathology is central to national discourse. It must be recognized as part of the new nation, and is not separate from the 'New South Africa', even although it is pathologized within and by the discourse" (169). See also Crush et al., *The Perfect Storm*.

2. See chapter 1 for the use of public hygiene discourses to regulate the sex worker's body. While there might be some crime-fighting element in any type of policing, the fact that the police exercised their discretion to police locations with more desirable sex workers reflects that their crime-fighting tasks were not solely, or even primarily, driven by reducing crime. While I relied upon police officers' recollections about the frequency of raids on different brothels, I also reviewed the liquor chief's schedule to confirm that the raids occurred as frequently as the police officers indicated. These logs confirmed the officers' recollections, as did the data I collected from sex workers at the brothels, who recounted the various raids during the course of my research project.

3. Ndaba and Serumula, "Hired Cop Killers Jailed for Life."

4. Cahill, "Feminist Pleasure and Feminine Beautification," comments: "That beauty is a problem for feminist theory is clear. Feminists ranging from Mary Wollstonecraft to Susan Bordo have analyzed the phenomenon of feminine beautification as a crucial and oppressive moment in an overall patriarchal structure" (42) (internal citations removed); also see Davis, "Remaking the She-Devil."

CHAPTER 5

1. Snyder, "What Is Third-Wave Feminism?," comments that "pro-sex feminism usually refers to a segment of the women's movement that defends pornography, sex work, sadomasochism, and butch/femme roles, but it also recuperates heterosexuality, intercourse, marriage, and sex toys from separatist feminist dismissals . . . [and] is heavily influenced by marginalized or nonnormative sexualities—including gay and lesbian, transgender, butch, and sex worker activists—and is devoted to reducing the stigma surrounding sexual pleasure in feminism" (188).

2. Anderson, "Prostitution and Sexual Autonomy," 777.

3. Murray, "Marriage as Punishment."

4. Liberto, "Normalizing Prostitution versus Normalizing the Alienability of Sexual Rights," comments that "the normalization of prostitution and the reduction of sexual autonomy are linked in the way Anderson describes only if prostitution alienates sexual rights rather than preserves them" (138).

5. Halley et al., "From the International to the Local in Feminist Legal Responses to Rape, Prostitution/Sex Work, and Sex Trafficking": "Global governance describes contemporary lawmaking as the product of deep and sustained interaction between states, international organizations, and non-governmental associations. Lawmaking in this mode is characterized by substantial communication in 'networked' form across national borders: networks among governmental sub-units, and networks among NGOs. Global governance is also characterized by ongoing communication between 'official' actors (states and international organizations) and NGOs, in which the latter act as sources of information, guides for 'agenda-setting,' and levers of political pressure" (340). Governance feminism is part of the web of influence on global law-making.

6. Ibid., 341.

7. Cavalieri, "Between Victim and Agent."

8. Halley et al., 'From the International to the Local in Feminist Legal Responses," 338–9.

9. Sexual Offences Act, No. 23 of 1957, as amended in 2007 (as discussed in chapter 1).

10. I use the feminine pronoun here because advocates of this approach are primarily concerned with the problems in sex work that are caused by patriarchy—its violence and its ability to strip women of meaningful choices.

11. Halley et al., "From the International to the Local in Feminist Legal Responses," 338–9.

12. Ibid.

13. For an overview of the various debates concerning the decriminalization of sex work, see Abrams, "Sex Wars Redux," 328–29; and Vance, "More Danger, More Pleasure," critiquing radical feminist approaches to sex work that view women as victims (xvii); and compare them with Barry, *Female Sexual Slavery*; and Dworkin and MacKinnon, *Pornography and Civil Rights*, treating sex work as inherently problematic and violent for women (24).

14. Fick and Sex Workers Education and Advocacy Taskforce, *Coping with Stigma*.

15. Manoek, *Stop Harassing Us!*

16. See Richter et al., 'Sex Work and the 2010 FIFA World Cup," arguing for decriminalization; and Fick and Sex Workers Education and Advocacy Taskforce, *Coping with Stigma*, advocating decriminalization.

17. See, e.g., Boudin and Richter, "Adult, Consensual Sex Work in South Africa," discussing the practical realities of sex work and the need for sex worker autonomy in choosing to engage in body work.

18. South African Commission for Gender Equality, *Decriminalizing Sex Work in South Africa 2013*: "The current legal regime harms the interests of sex workers by denying them their human and constitutional rights to protection as well as preventing access to legal assistance and enjoyment of their labour rights. However the current legal context has led to harassment and abuse of sex workers at the hands of the police" (6).

19. The Commission for Gender Equality *Position Paper on Sex Work* further explains the rationale for its advocacy for sex work decriminalization and, like other sources, relies in part on the narrative that decriminalization will protect the sex worker against police harassment; see the Introduction to this book, n21.

20. African National Congress, *ANC Discussion Paper on Gender Based Violence*, 14.

21. Freeman, "Feminist Debate over Prostitution Reform," 102.

22. Ibid., 105.

23. For example, the *Oxford English Dictionary* defines a *victim* as "a person harmed, injured, or killed as a result of a crime, accident, or other event or action" or "a person who has come to feel helpless and passive in the face of misfortune or ill-treatment."

24. Zatz, "Sex Work/Sex Act," 285.

25. Pateman, *The Sexual Contract*; also see Kesler, "Is a Feminist Stance in Support of Prostitution Possible?"

26. Overall, "What's Wrong with Prostitution?"

27. Satz, "Markets in Women's Sexual Labor."

28. Freeman, "Feminist Debate over Prostitution Reform," 83.

29. Anderson, "Prostitution and Sexual Autonomy," 777.

30. Satz, "Markets in Women's Sexual Labor," 63.

31. Zatz. "Sex Work/Sex Act," 294.

32. See generally, MacKinnon, "Prostitution and Civil Rights."

33. Zatz, "Sex Work/Sex Act," 292, quoting Andrea Dworkin, *Pornography: Men Possessing Women* (Plume 1989), 202.

34. Freeman, "Feminist Debate over Prostitution Reform," 98.

35. Ibid., 86.

36. MacKinnon, "Sexuality, Pornography, and Method."

37. Farley, "Prostitution, Trafficking, and Cultural Amnesia," 110.

38. Richards, "Sexual Autonomy and the Constitutional Right to Privacy."

39. Coalition Against Trafficking in Women, Letter to Amnesty International Board of Directors.

40. Weitzer, "New Directions in Research on Prostitution," 214 (internal citations omitted).

41. Hubbard, "Sex Zones," 53.

42. One of the most influential NGOs in the negotiation of the various UN protocols, Coalition Against Trafficking in Women (CATW), was founded by radical feminist Kathleen Barry.

43. A United Nations conference in 1981 in Nice, France, issued a release stating that "all prostitution is forced prostitution." Fernand-Laurent, *Report of the Special Rapporteur on the Suppression of the Traffic in Persons and the Exploitation of the Prostitution of Others*, 8.

44. Embrace Dignity, http://embracedignity.org.za.

45. New Life Centre 4 Girls, http://www.newlifecentre4girls.org.

46. Davis, "ANC Women's League and the World's Oldest Profession."

47. Embrace Dignity, "Help Us End the Oppression of Prostitution and Sex Trafficking." This 2014 Embrace Dignity petition to the government to end all forms of oppression against women, prostitution, and sex trafficking states: "[O]ur concern is the lack of understanding of the harms of the prostitution and its links to sex trafficking. Without addressing prostitution and all forms of commercial sexual exploitation, our effort to end gender oppression and sexual violence will continue to be undermined."

48. See Parliament of the Republic of South Africa, Select Committee on Petitions and Executive Undertakings: Content of Embrace Dignity Petition.

49. See, e.g., Crenshaw, "Mapping the Margins."

50. Nussbaum, "Whether from Reason or Prejudice."

51. Crenshaw, "Mapping the Margins."

52. Foucault, *History of Sexuality*, 1:5.

53. Kapur, " Tragedy of Victimization Rhetoric," 36.

54. Bernstein, "The Sexual Politics of the 'New Abolitionism,'" 137.

55. Kempadoo, "Women of Color and the Global Sex Trade," 40.

56. Kempadoo, "Globalizing Sex Workers' Rights," 233.

57. McClintock, "Screwing the System": "The moment of paying a female prostitute is structured around a paradox. The client touches the prostitute's hand in a fleeting moment of physical intimacy in the exchange of cash, a ritual exchange that confirms and guarantees each time the man's apparent economic mastery over the woman's sexuality, work, and time. At the same time, however, the moment of paying confirms precisely the opposite: the man's dependence on the woman's sexual power and skill. Prostitutes stand at the flash points of

marriage and market, taking sex into the streets and money into the bedroom. Flagrantly and publicly demanding money for sexual services that men expect for free, prostitutes insist on exhibiting their sexwork as having economic value" (72).

58. Trotter, "Dockside Prostitution."

59. Munro, "Legal Feminism and Foucault," 547.

60. See, e.g., Chung, Tucker, & Takeuchi, "Wives' Relative Income Production and Household Male Dominance."

61. Bernstein, "For and against Marriage."

62. McClintock, "Screwing the System," 70.

63. Shrage, "Should Feminists Oppose Prostitution?"

64. De Marneffe, "Avoiding Paternalism."

65. Ibid.

66. Sanchez, "Boundaries of Legitimacy," 544.

67. Ibid., 545.

68. Munro, "Legal Feminism and Foucault," 549.

69. Zatz, "Sex Work/Sex Act," 277.

70. See Trotter, "Dockside Prostitution."

71. Zatz, "Sex Work/Sex Act," 301, 279–80.

72. Kotiswaran, "Born unto Brothels," 579.

73. Ibid.

74. Klasen and Woolard, "Surviving Unemployment without State Support."

75. Sanders, "The Risks of Street Prostitution," 1704.

76. Ibid., 1708.

77. Foucault, *History of Sexuality*, 1:6.

78. Merry, "Transnational Human Rights and Local Activism," discusses how human rights laws have been translated to local contexts through the process of vernacularization, which allows global norms to be "adapted to local institutions and meanings" (39).

CONCLUSION

1. Rees, "Commercial Sex Workers in Johannesburg."

2. Albertyn, "How South Africa Could Become the First African Country to Decriminalize Sex Work": "If history is to be our guide, then public health arguments are powerful motivators for reform. Many hope that the combination of public health and human rights will underpin progressive law reform in this area to accelerate the decriminalization of sex work."

A NOTE ABOUT METHODOLOGY

1. I chose this approach because, as Julia Hornberger writes, "research methodology that looks at the everyday work of policing is more likely to be attuned to capturing de facto realities of sovereignty than a methodology operating within the formalized and institutionally reified version of the police as seen, for example, from a perspective of international relations." (Hornberger, "Human Rights and Policing: Exigency or Incongruence?")

2. See generally Gomm et al. (eds), *Case Study Method: Key Issues, Key Texts* (2000).

3. See generally Brewer, *Ethnography*, (2000).

4. Krefting, "Rigor in Qualitative Research," 214–222, 215.

5. The five general research sites are (1) Rosebank Police Station, (2) Oxford Road, (3) Hillbrow Police Station, (4) Hillbrow brothels, and (5) central Johannesburg. However, there were actually multiple corners on Oxford Road, six brothels in Hillbrow, and multiple street corners in central Johannesburg. The study was thus a relatively fluid multisite case study.

6. Docherty and Sandelowski, "Focus on Qualitative Methods," 179.

7. Ibid., 183.

8. Ibid.

9. Johnston & Sabin, "Sampling Hard-to-Reach Populations with Respondent Driven Sampling," 38.

10. Shaver, "Sex Work Research," 296.

11. Ibid.

12. I would define location by selecting certain street corners on which to focus. This would frequently mean focusing on street locations on Oxford Road that were between Houghton and Rosebank Mall or between Thrupps Shopping Centre and Rosebank Mall.

13. van Dijk, "Principles of Critical Discourse Analysis," 249–50.

Bibliography

BOOKS, ARTICLES, AND POLICY PAPERS AND STATEMENTS

Abrams, Kathryn. "Sex Wars Redux: Agency and Coercion in Feminist Legal Theory." *Columbia Law Review* 95 (1995), 304-76.

Adepoju, Aderanti. "Continuity and Changing Configurations of Migration to and from the Republic of South Africa." *International Migration* 41:1 (2003), 3-28.

Aderinto, Saheed, *When Sex Threatened the State: Illicit Sexuality, Nationalism, and Politics in Colonial Nigeria, 1900-1958.* University of Illinois Press, 2015.

African National Congress. *ANC Discussion Paper on Gender Based Violence.* 2012.

Ahlberg, B. M. "Is There a Distinct African Sexuality? A Critical Response to Caldwell." 64:2 *Africa* (1994), 220-242.

Aidt, Toke S. "Economic Analysis of Corruption: A Survey." *The Economic Journal* 113 (2003), F632-52.

Albertyn, Catherine. "Debate around Sex Work in South Africa Tilts towards Decriminalisation." *The Conversation*, May 15, 2016.

Albertyn, Catherine. "How South Africa Could Become the First African Country to Decriminalize Sex Work." *Newsweek*, May 16, 2016. https://www.newsweek.com/south-africa-decriminalize-sex-work-460261.

Albertyn, Catherine. "Women and the Transition to Democracy in South Africa" *Acta Juridica* (1994), 39-63.

Amnesty International. *Amnesty International Draft Policy on Sex Work.* ORG 50/1940/2015. July 7, 2015.

Anderson, Scott A. "Prostitution and Sexual Autonomy: Making Sense of Prohibition and Prostitution." *Ethics* 112 (2002), 748–80.

Atkins, Keletso. *The Moon Is Dead! Give Us Our Money! The Cultural Origins of an African Work Ethic, Natal, South Africa, 1843–1900.* Heinemann, 1993.

Barry, Kathleen. *Female Sexual Slavery.* Prentice-Hall, 1979.

Basdeo, Vinesh. "The Curse of Corruption in the South African Police: A Rot from Within." *South African Journal of Criminal Justice* 23 (2010), 385–400.

Benjamin, Walter. "Critique of Violence." In *Reflections: Essays, Aphorisms, Autobiographical Writings,* trans. Edmund Jephcott. Schocken Books, 1978.

Bénit-Gbaffou, Claire. "Unbundled Security Services and Urban Fragmentation in Post-apartheid Johannesburg." *Geoforum* 39 (2008), 1933–50.

Bernstein, Anita. "For and against Marriage: A Revision." *Michigan Law Review* 102 (2003), 129.

Bernstein, Elizabeth. "Militarized Humanitarianism Meets Carceral Feminism: The Politics of Sex, Rights, and Freedom in Contemporary Antitrafficking Campaigns." *Signs* 36 (2014), 45–72.

Bernstein, Elizabeth. "The Sexual Politics of the 'New Abolitionism.'" *Differences* 18:3 (2007), 128–51.

Blomley, Nicholas. "Law, Property, and the Geography of Violence: The Frontier, the Survey, and the Grid." *Annals of the Association of American Geographers* 91 (2003), 121–41.

Boudin, Chesa, and Marlise Richter. "Adult, Consensual Sex Work in South Africa—The Cautionary Message of Criminal Law and Sexual Morality." *South African Journal on Human Rights* 25 (2009), 179–97.

Brewer, John. *Black and Blue: Policing in South Africa.* Oxford University Press, 1994.

Brewer, John. *Ethnography.* McGraw-Hill Education (UK), 2000.

Brewer, John. "The Police in South African Politics." In *South Africa: No Turning Back,* ed. Shaun Johnson. Palgrave Macmillan, 1988.

Brewis, Joanna, and Stephen Linstead. "'The Worst Thing Is the Screwing' (1): Consumption and the Management of Identity in Sex Work." *Gender, Work & Organization* 7:2 (2000), 84–97.

Brogden, Mike. "Reforming Police Powers in South Africa." *Police Studies* 17 (1994), 25.

Bruce, David. "Unfinished Business: The Architecture of Police Accountability in South Africa." Paper written on behalf of the African Policing Civilian Oversight Forum Policy. November 2011, 1.

Bryder, Linda. "Sex, Race, and Colonialism: An Historiographical Review." *International Historical Review* 20 (1998), 806-22.

Burton, Antoinette M. "The White Woman's Burden: British Feminists and the Indian Woman, 1865-1915." *Women's Studies International Forum* 13:4 (1990), 295-308.

Cahill, Ann J. "Feminist Pleasure and Feminine Beautification." *Hypatia* 18 (2003), 42-64.

Cammack, Diana. *The Rand at War, 1899-1902: The Witwatersrand and the Anglo-Boer War.* University of Natal Press, 1990.

Cavalier, Shelley. "Between Victim and Agent: A Third-Way Feminist Account of Trafficking for Sex Work." *Indiana Law Journal* 86 (2011), 1409.

Cawthra, Gavin. *Brutal Force: The Apartheid War Machine.* Vol 247. International Defence and Aid Fund for Southern Africa, 1986.

Chaskalson, Arthur. "Human Dignity as a Constitutional Value." In *The Concept of Human Dignity in Human Rights Discourse*, ed. David Kretzmer and Eckart Klein. Springer, 2002.

Cheadle, Halton, and Dennis Davis. "The Application of the 1996 Constitution in the Private Sphere." *South African Journal on Human Rights* 13 (1997), 44-66.

Christenson, Gordon A. "Using Human Rights Law to Inform Due Process and Equal Protection Analyses." *University of Cincinnati Law Review* 51 (1983), 3.

Chuang, Janie A. "Rescuing Trafficking from Ideological Capture: Prostitution Reform and Anti-trafficking Law and Policy." *University of Pennsylvania Law Review* 158 (2010), 1655.

Chung, Grace H., M. Belinda Tucker, and David Takeuchi. "Wives' Relative Income Production and Household Male Dominance: Examining Violence among Asian American Enduring Couples." *Family Relations* 57 (2008), 227-38.

Clandinin, D. Jean. "Narrative Inquiry: A Methodology for Studying Lived Experience." *Research Studies in Music Education* 27 (2006), 44-54.

Coalition Against Trafficking in Women. Letter to Amnesty International Board of Directors, July 17, 2015. https://catwinternational.org/action/no-ai-policy-full-decriminalization-sex-trade/.

Cockrell, Alfred. "Private Law and the Bill of Rights: A Threshold Issue of 'Horizontality.'" In *Bill of Rights Compendium.* LexisNexis South Africa, 2001.

Collier, Paul M. "Policing in South Africa: Replication and Resistance to New Public Management Reforms." *Public Management Review* 6 (2004), 1-20.

Comaroff, Jean, and John Comaroff. "Criminal Obsessions, after Foucault: Post-coloniality, Policing, and the Metaphysics of Disorder." *Critical Inquiry* 30 (2004), 800.

Comaroff, Jean, and John Comaroff. "Law and Disorder in the Postcolony." *Social Anthropology* 15:2 (2007)133–152.

Crago, Anna-Louise, and Jayne Arnott. "Rights Not Rescue: A Report on Female, Trans, and Male Sex Workers' Human Rights in Botswana, Namibia, and South Africa." Open Society Institute, November 2008. https://www.open societyfoundations.org/uploads/b8bcb899-0ed2-425c-b5ad-acea33c4dc77/ summary_20081114.pdf.

Crenshaw, Kimberlé. "Demarginalizing the Intersection of Race and Sex: A Black Feminist Critique of Antidiscrimination Doctrine, Feminist Theory and An-tiracist Politics." *University of Chicago Legal Forum* (1989), 139–167.

Crenshaw, Kimberlé. "Mapping the Margins: Intersectionality, Identity Politics, and Violence against Women of Color." *Stanford Law Review* 43 (1991), 1241–99.

Crush, Jonathan, David McDonald, Vincent Williams, Kate Lefko-Everett, David Dorey, Don Taylor, and Roxanne la Sablonniere. *The Perfect Storm: The Reali-ties of Xenophobia in Contemporary South Africa.* Idasa and Southern African Research Centre, 2008.

Cunningham, Stewart. "Reinforcing or Challenging Stigma? The Risks and Ben-efits of 'Dignity Talk' in Sex Work Discourse." *International Journal for the Semiotics of Law* 29 (2016), 45–65.

Davenport, Rodney, and Christopher Saunders. *South Africa: A Modern History.* 5th ed. Macmillan, 2000.

Davis, Dennis. *Democracy and Deliberation.* Juta, 1999.

Davis, Kathy. "Remaking the She-Devil: A Critical Look at Feminist Approaches to Beauty." *Hypatia* 6 (1991), 21–43.

Davis, R. "The ANC Women's League and the World's Oldest Profession." *Daily Maverick*, May 12, 2012.

De Marneffe, Peter. "Avoiding Paternalism." *Philosophy & Public Affairs* 34 (2006), 68–94.

Delius, Peter, and Clive Glaser. "Sexual Socialisation in South Africa: A Histori-cal Perspective." *African Studies* 61 (2002), 27–54.

Docherty, Sharron, and Margarete Sandelowski. "Focus on Qualitative Methods: Interviewing Children." *Research in Nursing & Health* 22:2 (1999), 177–185.

Dodillet, Susanne, and Petra Östergren. "The Swedish Sex Purchase Act: Claimed Success and Documented Effects." Presentation at the international workshop *Decriminalizing Prostitution and Beyond: Practical Experiences and Challenges.* The Hague, March 2011.

Du Plessis, Jean. Letter from Jean du Plessis, Chief Executive Officer of The House, to Mr Sylvester Rakgoadi. "NGO Submission Regarding Draft Policy Document on Decriminalizing Sex Work" (28 July 1996).

Dugmore, Charles. "From Pro-Boer to Jingo: An Analysis of Small Town English-Language Newspapers on the Rand before the Outbreak of War in 1899." *South African Historical Journal* 41 (1999), 246-66,

Dunkle, K. L., M. E. Beksinska, V. H. Rees, R. C. Ballard, Ye Htun, and M. L. Wilson. "Risk Factors for HIV Infection among Sex Workers in Johannesburg, South Africa." *International Journal of STD & AIDS* 16 (2005), 256-61.

Dworkin, Andrea, and Catherine A. MacKinnon. *Pornography and Civil Rights: A New Day for Women's Equality*. Organizing Against Pornography, 1988.

Embrace Dignity. http://embracedignity.org.za.

Embrace Dignity. "Help Us End the Oppression of Prostitution and Sex Trafficking." December 10, 2014. http://pmg-assets.s3-website-eu-west-1.amazonaws.com/160302Embrace_Dignity.pdf.

Evans, Tony. "If Democracy, Then Human Rights?" *Third World Quarterly* 22 (2001), 623-42.

Farley, Melissa. "Prostitution, Trasfficking, and Cultural Amnesia: What We Must Not Know in Order to Keep the Business of Sexual Exploitation Running Smoothly." *Yale Journal of Law & Feminism* 18 (2006), 109-44.

Fernand-Laurent, Jean. *Report of the Special Rapporteur on the Suppression of the Traffic in Persons and the Exploitation of the Prostitution of Others*. UN Doc. E/1983/7 and Corr. 1–2 (1983).

Fick, Nicolé, and Sex Workers Education and Advocacy Taskforce. *Coping with Stigma, Discrimination and Violence: Sex Workers Talk about Their Experiences*. 2005.

Foley, Douglas E. "Critical Ethnography: The Reflexive Turn." *International Journal of Qualitative Studies in Education* 15 (2002), 469-90.

Fombad, Charles Manga. "The Constitution as a Source of Accountability: The Role of Constitutionalism." *Speculum Juris* 2 (2010), 41-65.

Foucault, Michel. *The Archaeology of Knowledge*. Pantheon Books, 1972.

Foucault, Michel. *The History of Sexuality*. Vol. 1. Trans. Robert Hurley. Pantheon Books, 1978.

Freed, Louis F. "The Summarised Findings of a Medico-Sociological Investigation into the Problem of Prostitution in Johannesburg." *South African Medical Journal* 22:2 (1948), 52-56.

Freeman, Jody. "The Feminist Debate over Prostitution Reform: Prostitutes' Rights Groups, Radical Feminists, and the (Im)possibility of Consent." *Berkeley Women's Law Journal* 5 (1989), 75-109.

Gardner, Jillian. "Criminalising the Act of Sex: Attitudes to Adult Commercial Sex Work in South Africa." In *The Prize and the Price: Shaping Sexualities in South Africa*, ed. Melissa Steyn and Mikki van Zyl. HSRC Press, 2009.

Gomm, Roger, Martyn Hammersley, and Peter Foster, eds. *Case Study Method: Key Issues, Key Texts*. Sage, 2000.

Gould, Arthur. "The Criminalisation of Buying Sex: The Politics of Prostitution in Sweden." *Journal of Social Policy* 30 (2001), 437-56.

Govender, Michelle. "Domestic Violence: Is South Africa Meeting Its Obligations in Terms of the Women's Convention? Notes and Comments." *South African Journal on Human Rights* 19 (2003), 663-78.

Government of South Africa. "Gauteng Legislature Hosts Provincial Dialogue for Commercial Sex Workers." November 14, 2014. http://www.gov .za/gautenglegislaturehostsprovincialdialogueforcomemrcialsexworkers -17november2014.

Government of South Africa, Newsroom. "Remarks by the Deputy Minister of Police, Ms MM Sotyu (MP) at the National Sex Work Symposium." August 23, 2012. https://www.gov.za/remarks-deputy-minister-police-ms-mm -sotyu-mp-national-sex-work-symposium.

Hale, Nathan G., Jr. *Freud and the Americans: The Beginning of Psychoanalysis in the United States, 1876–1917*. Oxford University Press, 1971.

Halley, Janet E., Prabha Kotiswaran, Hila Shamir, and Chantal Thomas. "From the International to the Local in Feminist Legal Responses to Rape, Prostitution/Sex Work, and Sex Trafficking: Four Studies in Contemporary Governance Feminism." *Harvard Journal of Law and Gender* 29 (2006), 335-423.

Harcourt, C., and B. Donovan. "The Many Faces of Sex Work." *Sexually Transmitted Infections* 81:3 (2005), 201–206.

Harries, Patrick. "Symbols and Sexuality: Culture and Identity on the Early Witwatersrand Gold Mines." *Gender & History* 2 (1990), 318-36.

Harris, Bronwyn. "Xenophobia: A New Pathology for a New South Africa." In *Psychopathology and Social Prejudice*, ed. D. Hook and G. Eagle. University of Cape Town Press, 2002.

Hoang, Kimberly Kay. *Dealing in Desire: Asian Ascendancy, Western Decline, and the Hidden Currencies of Global Sex Work*. University of California Press, 2015.

Hollis, Patricia. *Women in Public, 1850–1900: Documents of the Victorian Women's Movement*. Rev. ed. Routledge, 2013.

Hornberger, Julia. "From General to Commissioner to General—On the Popular State of Policing in South Africa." *Law & Social Inquiry* 38 (2013), 598-614.

Hornberger, Julia. "Human Rights and Policing: Exigency or Incongruence?" *Annual Review of Law and Social Science* 6 (2010), 259–83.

Hornberger, Julia. "'My Police—Your Police': The Informal Privatisation of the Police in the Inner City of Johannesburg." *African Studies* 63 (2004), 213–30.

Hornberger, Julia. *Policing and Human Rights: The Meaning of Violence and Justice in the Everyday Policing of Johannesburg*. Routledge, 2011.

Howell, Philip. "A Private Contagious Diseases Act: Prostitution and Public Space in Victorian Cambridge." *Journal of Historical Geography* 26 (2000), 376–402.

Hubbard, Phil. "Sex Zones: Intimacy, Citizenship and Public Space." *Sexualities* 4 (2001), 51–71.

Hubbard, Phil, Roger Matthews, and Jane Scoular. "Regulating Sex Work in the EU: Prostitute Women and the New Spaces of Exclusion." *Gender, Place and Culture* 15 (2008), 137–52.

Human Rights Watch. *Unequal Protection: The State Response to Violent Crime of South African Farms*. August 2001. http://www.hrw.org/reports/2001/safrica2.

Hunter, Mark. "The Changing Political Economy of Sex in South Africa: The Significance of Unemployment and Inequalities to the Scale of the AIDS Pandemic." *Social Science & Medicine* 64:3 (2007), 689–700.

Hunter, Mark. *Love in the Time of AIDS*. Indiana University Press, 2010.

Independent Complaints Directorate. *Investigating Torture: The New Legislative Framework and Mandate of the Independent Complaints Directorate*. Republic of South Africa, 2010.

IOL News. "Study Reveals SA's Wealthiest Areas." August 29, 2012. https://www.iol.co.za/news/south-africa/study-reveals-sas-wealthiest-areas-1371969.

Jacobs, Lea. "Building Hijackings on the Rise." *Private Property*, April 30, 2015. https://perma.cc/5QT3-8WRZ.

James, Deborah. *Money from Nothing: Indebtedness and Aspiration in South Africa*. Stanford University Press, 2015.

Jewkes, Rachel, Robert Morrell, Yandisa Sikweyiya, Kristin Dunkle, and Loveday Penn-Kekana. "Transactional Relationships and Sex with a Woman in Prostitution: Prevalence and Patterns in a Representative Sample of South African Men." *BMC Public Health* 12 (2012), 325.

Jochelson, Karen. "Sexually Transmitted Diseases in Nineteenth- and Twentieth-Century South Africa." In *Histories of Sexually Transmitted Diseases and HIV/AIDS in Sub-Saharan Africa*, ed. Philip W. Setel, Milton Lewis, and Maryinez Lyons. Greenwood Press, 1999.

Johnston, Lisa G., and Keith Sabin. "Sampling Hard-to-Reach Populations with Respondent Driven Sampling." *Methodological Innovations Online* 5:2 (2010), 38–48.

Kapur, Ratna. "The Tragedy of Victimization Rhetoric: Resurrecting the 'Native' Subject in International/Post-colonial Feminist Legal Politics." *Harvard Human Rights Journal* 15 (2002), 1–38.

Kaufman, Carol E. "Reproductive Control in Apartheid South Africa." *Population Studies* 54 (2000), 105–14.

Keegan, Timothy. "Gender, Degeneration and Sexual Danger: Imagining Race and Class in South Africa, ca. 1912." *Journal of Southern African Studies* 27 (2001), 459–77.

Kekana, Masa. "72% of Sex Workers in JHB are HIV Positive." Eye Witness News, March 11 2016. http://ewn.co.za/2016/03/11/72-percent-of-sex-workers-in-JHB-are-HIV-positive.

Kempadoo, Kamala. "Globalizing Sex Workers' Rights." *Canadian Woman Studies* 22:3-4 (2003), 143–150.

Kempadoo, Kamala. "Women of Color and the Global Sex Trade: Transnational Feminist Perspectives." *Meridians* 1:2 (2001), 28–51.

Kesler, K. "Is a Feminist Stance in Support of Prostitution Possible? An Exploration of Current Trends." *Sexualities* 5 (2002), 219.

Kim, Suzanne A. "Betraying Women in the Name of Revolution: Violence against Women as an Obstacle to Democratic Nation-Building in South Africa." *Cardozo Women's Law Journal* 8 (2001), 1.

Klausen, Susanne. "The Uncertain Future of White Supremacy and the Politics of Fertility in South Africa, 1930–1939." http://www.kznhass-history.net/files/seminars/Klausen2002.pdf.

Klasen, Stephan, and Ingrid Woolard. "Surviving Unemployment without State Support: Unemployment and Household Formation in South Africa." *Journal of African Economies* 18 (2009), 1–51.

Klug, Heinz. "Law Under and After Apartheid: Abel's Sociolegal Analysis." *Law and Social Inquiry* (2000), 657–77.

Kotiswaran, Prabha. "Born unto Brothels—Toward a Legal Ethnography of Sex Work in an Indian Red-Light Area." *Law & Social Inquiry* 33 (2008), 579–629.

Krefting, Laura. "Rigor in Qualitative Research: The Assessment of Trustworthiness." *American Journal of Occupational Therapy* 45:3 (1991), 214–222.

Kusafuka, Ayumi. "Truth Commissions and Gender: A South African Case Study." *African Journal on Conflict Resolution* 9:2 (2010), 45–67.

Kynoch, Gary. "Apartheid Nostalgia: Personal Security Concerns in South African Townships." *South African Crime Quarterly* 5:3 (2003), 7-10.

Lefebvre, Henri. *The Production of Space*. Blackwell,1991.

Leggett, Ted. "A Den of Iniquity? Inside Hillbrow's Residential Hotels." *South African. Crime Quarterly*, No. 2 (2002), 19.

Leggett, Ted. "Drugs, Sex Work, and HIV in Three South African Cities." *Society in Transition* 32:1 (2001), 101.

Levine, Philippa. "Venereal Disease, Prostitution, and the Politics of Empire: The Case of British India." *Journal of the History of Sexuality* 4 (1994), 579-602.

Lewin, Julius. "Sex Color and the Law." *Africa Today* 10, No. 6 (1963), 9-12.

Liberto, Hallie Rose. "Normalizing Prostitution versus Normalizing the Alienability of Sexual Rights: A Response to Scott A. Anderson." *Ethics* 120 (2009), 138-45.

Louw, Antoinette. "Surviving the Transition: Trends and Perceptions of Crime in South Africa." *Social Indicators Research* 41 (1997), 137-68.

MacKinnon, Catherine A. "Prostitution and Civil Rights." *Michigan Journal of Gender & Law* 1 (1993), 13-31.

MacKinnon, Catherine A. "Sexuality, Pornography, and Method: Pleasure under Patriarchy." *Ethics* 99 (1989) 314-46.

Macleod, Catriona Ida, & Kevin Durrheim. "Foucauldian Feminism: The Implications of Governmentality." *Journal for the Theory of Social Behavior* 32 (2002), 41-60.

Malherbe, Vertrees C. "Family Law and 'The Great Moral Public Interests' in Victorian Cape Town, c.1850–1902." *Kronos: Southern African Histories* 36 (2010), 7-27.

Manoek, Stacey-Leigh. *Stop Harassing Us! Tackle Real Crime!: A Report on Human Rights Violations by Police against Sex Workers in South Africa*. A project of the Women's Legal Centre, Sisonke, and the Sex Workers Education and Advocacy Taskforce (SWEAT). 2012.

Marcus, Steven. *The Other Victorians: A Study of Sexuality and Pornography in Mid-Nineteenth-Century England*. Routledge, 2008.

Marks, Monique. "Dancing with the Devil? Participatory Action Research with Police in South Africa." *South African Crime Quarterly*, No. 30 (2009).

Marks, Monique, "'Researching Police Transformation: The Ethnographic Imperative." *British Journal of Criminology* 44 (2004), 866-88.

Marks, Monique. "Transforming Robocops? A Case Study of Police Organisational Change." *Society in Transition* 31 (2000), 144-62.

Martens, Jeremy C. "'Almost a Public Calamity': Prostitutes, 'Nurseboys,' and Attempts to Control Venereal Diseases in Colonial Natal, 1886–1890." *South African Historical Journal* 45 (2001), 27–52.

Martens, Jeremy. "Citizenship, 'Civilisation' and the Creation of South Africa's Immorality Act, 1927." *South African Historical Journal* 59 (2007), 223–41.

Mathabane, Mark. *Kaffir Boy: The True Story of a Black Youth's Coming of Age in Apartheid South Africa*. Macmillan, 1986.

Mbembé, Achielle, and Sarah Nuttall. "Writing the World from an African Metropolis." *Public Culture* 16 (2004), 347–372.

McClintock, Anne. "Screwing the System: Sexwork, Race, and the Law." *Boundary 2* 19:2 (1992), 70–95.

McCulloch, Jock. *Black Peril, White Virtue: Sexual Crime in Southern Rhodesia, 1902–1935*. Indiana University Press, 2000.

Merry, Sally Engel. "Transnational Human Rights and Local Activism: Mapping the Middle." *American Anthropologist* 108 (2006), 38–51.

Mgbako, Chi, and Laura A. Smith. "Sex Work and Human Rights in Africa." *Fordham International Law Journal* 33 (2010), 1178.

Morrell, Robert, Rachel Jewkes, and Graham Lindegger. "Hegemonic Masculinity/Masculinities in South Africa: Culture, Power, and Gender Politics." *Men and Masculinities* 15 (2012), 11–30.

Muller, Joan. "SA's Most Expensive Streets." *Financial Mail*, November 13, 2013.

Munro, Vanessa. "Legal Feminism and Foucault—A Critique of the Expulsion of Law." *Journal of Law and Society* 28 (2001), 546–67.

Murphy, Alexandra K., and Sudhir Alladi Venkatesh. "Vice Careers: The Changing Contours of Sex Work in New York City." *Qualitative Sociology* 29 (2006), 129–54.

Murray, Melissa. "Marriage as Punishment." *Columbia Law Review* 112 (2012), 1–65.

Mutume, G. "Gauteng Province Decriminalizes Prostitution." Interpress Service, November 7, 1997. http://www.ipsnews.net/1997/11/south-africa-gauteng-province-decriminalizes-prostitution.

Ndaba, Baldwin, and Rabbie Serumula. "Hired Cop Killers Jailed for Life." IOL News, May 28, 2015. http://www.iol.co.za/news/crime-courts/hired-cop-killers-jailed-for-life-1.1864863#.VabANJNViko.

New Life Centre 4 Girls. https://newlifecentre.co.za/.

Newham, Gareth, Themba Masuku, and Jabu Dlamini. "Diversity and Transformation in the South African Police Service." Center for the Study of Violence and Reconciliation, 2006. http://www. csvr. org. za.

Newham, Gareth. "Tackling Police Corruption in South Africa." Research report written for the Centre for the Study of Violence and Reconciliation, June 2002. http://www.csvr.org.za/docs/policing/tacklingpolicecorruption.pdf.

Nussbaum, Martha C. "'Whether from Reason or Prejudice': Taking Money for Bodily Services." *Journal of Legal Studies* 27:S2 (1998), 693–723.

Nuttall, Sarah. "Stylizing the Self: The Y Generation in Rosebank, Johannesburg." *Public Culture* 16 (2004), 430–52.

Overall, Christine. "What's Wrong with Prostitution? Evaluating Sex Work." *Signs* 17 (1992), 705–24.

Parliament of the Republic of South Africa, Select Committee on Petitions and Executive Undertakings. Content of Embrace Dignity Petition and Existing Legal Framework on Sex Work. March 2, 2016. http://pmg-assets.s3-website-eu-west-1.amazonaws.com/160302content.pdf.

Pateman, Carole. *The Sexual Contract.* Stanford University Press, 1988.

Peltzer, Karl, Phillip Seoka, and S. Raphala. "Characteristics of Female Sex Workers and Their Attitudes in Semi-urban Areas in South Africa." *Curationis* 27 (2004), 4–11.

Pieterse, Edgar. "Cityness and African Urban Development." *Urban Forum* 21 (2010), 205.

Pigou, Piers. "'Monitoring Police Violence and Torture in South Africa." Paper presented at the International Seminar on the Indicators and Diagnosis on Human Rights: The Case of Torture in Mexico. Convened by the Mexican National Commission for Human Rights, 2002.

Rauch, Janine. "Police Reform and South Africa's Transition." In *Crime and Policing in Transitional Societies*, Mark Shaw et al. [Conference proceedings.] University of the Witwatersrand, 2000.

Rauch, Janine, Mark Shaw, and Antoinette Louw. *Municipal Policing in South Africa: Development and Challenges.* Monograph No. 67. Institute for Security Studies, 2001.

Rees, Helen, Mags Beksinska, Kim Dickson-Tetteh, R. C. Ballard, and Ye Htun. "Commercial Sex Workers in Johannesburg: Risk Behaviour and HIV Status." *South African Journal of Science* 96:6 (2000), 283–84.

Richards, David A. J. "Sexual Autonomy and the Constitutional Right to Privacy: A Case Study in Human Rights and the Unwritten Constitution." *Hastings Law Journal* 30 (1978), 957–1018.

Richter, Marlise. "Erotic Labour in Hillbrow: Sex Work, Johannesburg's 'Den of Iniquity' and HIV/AIDS." *Health Systems Trust* (2008), 1–24.

Richter, Marlise, Matthew Chersich, Fiona Scorgie, Stanley Luchters, Marleen Temmerman, and Richard Steen. "Sex Work and the 2010 FIFA World Cup: Time for Public Health Imperatives to Prevail." *Globalization and Health* 6 (2010), 1-6.

Ritner, Susan Rennie. "The Dutch Reformed Church and Apartheid." *Journal of Contemporary History* 2 (1967), 17-47.

Robinson, Jennifer. "Thinking Cities through Elsewhere: Comparative Tactics for a More Global Urban Studies." *Progress in Human Geography* 40 (2016), 3-29.

Ross, Robert. *Status and Respectability in the Cape Colony, 1750–1870: A Tragedy of Manners*. Cambridge University Press, 1999.

SANAC. *The South African National Sex Worker HIV Plan, 2016–2019*. Pretoria, South Africa, 2016.

Sanchez, Lisa E. "Boundaries of Legitimacy: Sex, Violence, Citizenship, and Community in a Local Sexual Economy." *Law & Social Inquiry* 22 (1997), 543-80.

Sanchez, Lisa E. "Sex, Law, and the Paradox of Agency and Resistance in the Everyday Practices of Women in the 'Evergreen' Sex Trade." In *Constitutive Criminology at Work: Applications to Crime and Justice*. SUNY Press, 1999.

Sanders, Teela. "The Risks of Street Prostitution: Punters, Police and Protesters." *Urban Studies* 41 (2004), 1703-17.

SAPA. "Sex Work Should Be Decriminalised." IOL News, May 16, 2013. http:// www.iol.co.za/news/crime-courts/sex-work-should-be-decriminalized-1 .1516936#.Va_9DBNViko.

Satz, Debra. "Markets in Women's Sexual Labor." *Ethics* 106 (1995), 63-85.

Schwartz, Richard D. 'Field Experimentation in Sociolegal Research.' *Journal of Legal Education* 13 (1961), 401-10.

Scorgie, Fiona, Matthew Chersich, Innocent Ntaganira, and Antonio Gerbase. "Socio-demographic Characteristics and Behavioral Risk Factors of Female Sex Workers in Sub-Saharan Africa: A Systematic Review." *AIDS and Behavior* 16 (2012), 920-33.

Scully, Pamela. "Rape, Race, and Colonial Culture: The Sexual Politics of Identity in the Nineteenth-Century Cape Colony, South Africa." *American Historical Review* 100 (1995), 335-59.

Shaver, Francis M. "Sex Work Research: Methodological and Ethical Challenges." *Journal of Interpersonal Violence* 20 (2005), 296-319.

Shear, Keith. "'Not Welfare or Uplift Work': White Women, Masculinity and Policing in South Africa." *Gender & History* 8 (1996), 393–415.

Shrage, Laurie. "Should Feminists Oppose Prostitution?" *Ethics* 99 (1989), 347–61.

Sollors, Werner. *Neither Black Nor White Yet Both: Thematic Explorations of Interracial Literature.* Oxford University Press, 1997.

Sonke Gender Justice. *Decriminalisation of Sex Work: Policy Development & Advocacy.* http://www.genderjustice.org.za/policy-development-advocacy/decriminalisation-sex-work/.

South African Commission for Gender Equality. *Decriminalizing Sex Work in South Africa 2013: Official Position of the Commission for Gender Equality.* 2013.

South African Commission for Gender Equality. *Position Paper on Sex Work.* January 16, 2013.

South African Law Commission. *Sexual Offences: Adult Prostitution.* Issue Paper 19, October 2002.

South African Law Commission. *Sexual Offences: The Substantive Law.* Discussion Paper 85, October 1999.

South African Law Reform Commission. *Sexual Offences: Adult Prostitution.* Discussion Paper 0001/2009, Project 107, 2009.

South African Law Reform Commission. *Sexual Offences: Adult Prostitution.* Project 107, June 2015. http://www.justice.gov.za/salrc/reports/r-pr107-SXO -AdultProstitution-2017.pdf.

South African Police Service. "Human Rights and Policing."

South African Police Service. *Policy on the Prevention of Torture and Treatment of Persons in Custody.* 1999.

Snyder, R. Claire. "What Is Third-Wave Feminism? A New Directions Essay." *Signs* 34 (2008), 175–96.

Sprigman, Chris, and Michael Osborne. "Du Plessis Is *Not* Dead: South Africa's 1996 Constitution and the Application of the Bill of Rights to Private Disputes." *South African Journal on Human Rights* 15 (1999), 25–51.

Stadler, Jonathan, and Sinead Delany. "The 'Healthy Brothel': The Context of Clinical Services for Sex Workers in Hillbrow, South Africa." *Culture, Health and Sexuality* 8 (2006), 451–63.

Stadler, Jonathan, and Charles Dugmore. "'Honey, Milk and Bile': A Social History of Hillbrow, 1894–2016." *BMC Public Health* 17 (2017), 444.

Statistics South Africa. Census 2011. https://www.statssa.gov.za/publications/P03014/P030142011.pdf.

Stoler, Ann. "Educating Desire in Colonial South-East: Foucault, Freud, and Imperial Sexualities." In *Sites of Desire/Economies of Pleasure: Sexualities in Asia and the Pacific*, ed. Lenore Manderson and Margaret Jolly. University of Chicago Press, 1997.

SWEAT. *Sex Worker Rights Are Human Rights*. http://www.sweat.org.za/.

Thompson, Debra. "Racial Ideas and Gendered Intimacies: The Regulation of Interracial Relationships in North America." *Social & Legal Studies*, 18 (2009), 353–71.

Trotter, Henry. "Dockside Prostitution in South African Ports." *History Compass* 6 (2008), 673–90.

UNAIDS. *Guidance Note on HIV and Sex Work*. 2009.

UNAIDS. *Sex Work and HIV/AIDS: Technical Update*. 2002.

Urban Development Zone. https://www.joburg.org.za/work_/UrbanDevelopmentZone.

Vance, Carole S. "More Danger, More Pleasure: A Decade after the Barnard Sexuality Conference." In *Pleasure and Danger: Exploring Female Sexuality*. Pandora Press, 1992.

Van Der Spuy, E "Literature on the Police in South Africa: An Historical Perspective." *Acta Juridica* (1989), 262.

Van der Walt, J. "Horizontal Application of Fundamental Rights and the Threshold of the Law in View of the Carmichele Saga." *South African Journal on Human Rights* 19 (2003), 517–40.

Van der Walt, J. "Justice Kriegler's Disconcerting Judgment in *Du Plessis v De Klerk*: Much Ado about Direct Horizontal Application (Read Nothing)." *Tydskrif vir die Suid-Afrikaanse Reg* 4 (1996), 732.

Van Dijk, Teun A. "Principles of Critical Discourse Analysis." *Discourse & Society* 4:2 (1993), 249–283.

Van Heyningen, Elizabeth B. "The Social Evil in the Cape Colony 1868–1902: Prostitution and the Contagious Diseases Acts." *Journal of Southern African Studies* 10:2 (1984) 170–97.

Van Onselen, Charles. "Who Killed Meyer Hasenfus? Organized Crime, Policing and Informing on the Witwatersrand, 1902–8." *History Workshop Journal* 67 (2009), 1–22.

Vetten, Lisa. "Addressing Domestic Violence in South Africa: Reflections on Strategy and Practice." Expert Paper for the Expert Group Meeting, *Violence against Women: Good Practices in Combating and Eliminating Violence against Women*. UN Division for the Advancement of Women, Vienna, May 17–20, 2005.

Weber, Max. *From Max Weber: Essays in Sociology*. Oxford University Press, 1946.

Weintraub, Jeff. "The Theory and Politics of the Public/Private Distinction." In *Public and Private in Thought and Practice: Perspectives on a Grand Dichotomy*, ed. Jess Weintraub and Krishan Kumar. University of Chicago Press, 1997.

Weitzer, Ronald. "New Directions in Research on Prostitution." *Crime, Law and Social Change* 43 (2005), 211–235.

West-Pavlov, Russell. "Inside Out—The New Literary Geographies of the Post-Apartheid City in Mpe's and Vladislavić's Johannesburg Writing." *Journal of South African Studies* 40:1 (2014), 7.

Wheeler, Skye, and Liesl Gerntholtz. *Why Sex Work Should Be Decriminalised in South Africa*. Human Rights Watch and SWEAT. August 2019. https://www
.hrw.org/sites/default/files/report_pdf/southafrica0819_web_0.pdf.

White, Luise. *The Comforts of Home: Prostitution in Colonial Nairobi*. University of Chicago Press, 1990.

Whyte, Elmari. "*Aluta Continua*: The Struggle Continues in South Africa—Against Violent Crime." *Dialogue e-Journal* 7 (2011), 1–30. https://citeseerx.ist
.psu.edu/viewdoc/download?doi=10.1.1.576.1175&rep=rep1&type=pdf.

Wojcicki, Janet M. "The Movement to Decriminalize Sex Work in Gauteng Province, South Africa, 1994–2002." *African Studies Review* 46:3 (2003), 83–109.

Wojcicki, Janet. "'She Drank His Money': Survival Sex and the Problem of Violence in Taverns in Gauteng Province, South Africa." *Medical Anthropology Quarterly* 16 (2002) 267–93.

Wolcott, Harry F. *Ethnography: A Way of Seeing*. Alta Mira Press, 1999.

Woolman, Stu. "The Amazing, Vanishing Bill of Rights." *South African Law Journal* 124 (2007), 762–94.

Woolman, Stuart, and Dennis Davis. "The Last Laugh: *Du Plessis v De Klerk*, Classical Liberalism, Creole Liberalism and the Application of Fundamental Rights under the Interim and Final Constitutions." *South African Journal on Human Rights* 12 (1996), 361–404.

Zatz, Noah D. "Sex Work/Sex Act: Law, Labor, and Desire in Constructions of Prostitution." *Signs* 22 (1997), 277–308.

TREATIES AND INTERNATIONAL INSTRUMENTS

African Charter on Human and Peoples' Rights, 1986. OAU Doc. CAB/LEG/66.6.

Protocol to the African Charter on Human and Peoples' Rights on the Rights of Women in Africa. OAU Doc. CAB/LEG/66.6, Sept. 13, 2000.

UN Convention against Torture and Other Cruel, Inhuman or Degrading Treatment or Punishment. G.A. Res. 39/46, 1987.

UN Convention on the Elimination of All Forms of Discrimination against Women. G.A. res. 34/180, 1979.

UN Declaration on the Elimination of Violence Against Women. G.A. res. 48/104, 1993.

UN International Covenant on Civil and Political Rights. G.A. res. 2200A (XXI), 1966.

UN International Convention on the Elimination of All Forms of Racial Discrimination. G.A. res. 2106 (XX), 1965.

UN Protocol to Prevent, Suppress and Punish Trafficking in Persons, Especially Women and Children. A/RES/55/25, 2000.

UN Rules for the Treatment of Women Prisoners and Non-custodial Measures for Women Offenders. A/RES/65/229, 2010.

UN Universal Declaration of Human Rights. G.A. Res. 217 A, 1948.

UN Vienna Convention on the Law of Treaties, 1969.

US Victims of Trafficking and Violence Protection Act of 2000 (VTVPA). Public Law 106-386.

LEGISLATION AND STATUTES

Act 31 of 1903 § 15(1)(a) (Natal).

Act 36 of 1902 §33(1)(a) (Cape).

Constitution of the Republic of South Africa, 1996.

Criminal Law (Sexual Offences and Related Matters) Amendment Act 32 of 2007.

Criminal Procedure Act, No. 51 of 1977.

Domestic Violence Act, No. 116 of 1998.

Immorality Act, No. 5 of 1927.

Immorality Act, No. 21 of 1950 (amended in 1957).

Immorality Amendment Act, No. 68 of 1967.

Immorality Amendment Act, No. 57 of 1969.

Immorality Amendment Act, No. 2 of 1988.

Morality Act, No. 36 of 1902.

Ordinance 11 of 1903 § 13(1)(a) (Orange Free State).

Ordinance 46 of 1903 § 21(1)(a) (Transvaal).

Police Offences Act, No. 27 of 1882 (Cape).

Prevention and Combating of Trafficking in Persons Act, No.7 of 2013.

Prohibition of Mixed Marriages Amendment Act, No, 21 of 1949.

Sexual Offences Act, No. 23 of 1957.

South African Police Service Act, No. 68 of 1995.

Union Bill 350, No. 553 of 1913.

CASE LAW

Carmichele v Minister of Safety and Security 2001 (4) SA 938 (CC).

Carmichele v Minister of Safety and Security and Others (310/98) 2001 (1) SA 489 (SCA) (2 October 2000) paras 18, 19.

Egglestone v The State 2008 ZASCA 77 (A).

Ex Parte Minister of Safety and Security and Others: In Re S v Walters and Another 2002 (4) SA 613 (CC).

Govender v Minister of Safety and Security 2001 (4) SA 273 (SCA).

Government of the Republic of South Africa v Basdeo and Another 1996 (1). SA 355 (5).

Jordan v State 2002 (6) SA 642 (CC).

K v Minister of Safety and Security 2005 (9) BCLR 835 (CC).

Kylie v Commission for Conciliation, Mediation and Arbitration and Others 2010 (4) SA 383 (Labour Appeal Court of South Africa).

Macu v Du Toit 1983 (4) SA 629 (A).

Matlou v Makhubedu 1978 (1) SA 946 (A).

Minister of Safety and Security and Another v Carmichele (533/02) (2003) ZASCA 117; (2003) 4 All SA 565 (SCA) (14 November 2003).

National Director of Public Prosecution v Geyser 2008 ZASCA 15 (CC).

National Director of Public Prosecutions v Lorna M. B. 2009 (2) SACR 547 (Durban and Coast Local Division).

National Director of Public Prosecutions v R. O. Cook Properties (Pty) Ltd. 2004 (03) SA 260 (CC) para 39.

R v Sibande 1958 (3) SA 1 (A) at B.

Raloso v Wilson and Others 1998 (1) BCLR 26 (NC).

Rex v Christo, 1917 OPD 420.

Rex v Dikant, 1948 (1) SA 693 (OPD).

Rex v V, 1951 (2) SA 178 (EPD).

Rex v Weinberg, 1916 OPD 653.

State v Barnard 1986 (3) (SA) 1 (A).

State v Baloyi 2000 (1) SACR 81 (CC).

State v F 1975 (3) SA 167 (TBD).

State v Horn 1988 SA 46 (AD) at 59 (S Afr).

State v Jordan 2002 (6) SA 642 (CC).

State v Makhwanyane and Another 1995 (2) SACR 1 (CC).

State v Martinus 1990 (2) SACR 568 (A).

State v Mogohlwane 1982 (2) SA 587 (T).

State v Van Wyk 1967 (1) SA 488 (A).

Sex Worker Education and Advocacy Task Force v The Minister of Safety and Security et al. Case No. 3378/07 2009 High Court of South Africa (Western Cape).

Index

Dalling, D. J., 45–46
Delius, Peter, 39–40
domestic violence, 85–86, 192–
    193n190; as private, 53, 65; in South
    Africa, 64
Domestic Violence Act (DVA), 64, 72,
    86–87
Donovan, B., 6
Duarte, Jesse, 66
Durban (South Africa), 22–23, 29–30,
    184n56
Dutch East India Company, 22, 25
Dutch Reformed Church, 42
Dworkin, Andrea, 137

Embrace Dignity, 140–141, 149,
    203n47
employment, sex work as, 136; con-
    tracts, 148; economic value of,
    203n57; financial freedom of, 145;
    as form of labor, 146; as means of
    economic gain, 150–151, 165; sex
    or gender discrimination, 61; sex
    work as solely work, 150
England, 26–28. See also Britain
ethnography, 2, 11, 99, 130, 169–175;
    legal, 12
Europe, 24

family life, impact of sex work on, 7
Farley, Melissa, 138
female sexuality, 22, 27, 31, 35, 46, 139,
    160, 179n31; disciplining of, 21;
    double standard, 182n28; exercis-
    ing power over, 129, 150; private
    expression of domesticity, 148;
    public expression of, 89; regula-
    tion of, 32, 162

feminism, 2, 136, 141, 151, 164, 186n94;
    pro-sex, 200n1. See also carceral
    feminism; radical feminism
Foley, Douglas, 20
Foucault, Michel, 8, 25, 143, 148, 150,
    178n11, 179n30; and power, 55–56,
    149
Freeman, Jody, 136

gender, 4–5, 10–11, 21–22, 38, 43,
    65, 123, 151, 166; discrimination,
    60–61, 191n174; essentialism, 94;
    identity, 61; inequality, 30, 140;
    South Africa, 8; violence, 53,
    192–193n190
gender and sex work: Black male sex-
    uality, 34–36; carceral feminism,
    143–144; female empowerment,
    142; femininity and masculinity, 4;
    feminist debate around, 5–6; 130;
    feminist gaze, 5; gender equality,
    179–180n31; hierarchical status
    and male gaze, 119; male experi-
    ence reduced to, 137; male sexual
    immorality, 37; men's perception
    of women, 136–137; patriarchal or-
    der in, 73, 137; power over female
    sexuality, 129–130; sex or gender
    discrimination, 61; sexual objecti-
    fication of women, 137; as survival
    strategy by marginalized women,
    146; as violence against women,
    137. See also radical feminism
Gibraltar, 27
Glaser, Clive, 39–40
global governance, 201n5
Global South, 142
Gombong, 24

radical feminism, 5, 46, 136, 140–141, 149; criticism of, 139, 146; intersectionality, lacking in, 142; male sexual hegemony, reinforcing of, 146; partial criminalization, support of, 134; sex, and economic struggles, 133; sex work, abolition of, 138–139, 164–165; theory of asymmetry, subscribing to, 137; universal sisterhood, fiction of, 143; v. sex workers, 149; Western, middle-class, White agenda of, 139, 142; women's choices, little regard for, 137–138

radical progressive perspective, 6

rape, 86–87, 152, 180–181n38, 192–193n190

Rauch, Janine, 53

research methodology, 13–14, 113–114, 169–175

Rex v Christo, 39

Rex v. Dikant, 39

Rex v V., 41–42, 138

Rex v Weinberg, 39

Rhodesia, 185n91

Robinson, Jennifer, 2

Rood, W. H., 40

Rosebank, 11, 17, 19, 50, 147, 155, 158, 165, 198n5, 199n9, 199n10; bribes, 107, 109, 111–114, 117, 147, 163; clients, focus on, 111–112, 116–117; clients, extorting of, 107–110, 147; "freebies," seeking of, 109; human rights language, adopting of, 105, 109–110, 116–117, 162–163; lawfare, 116–117; Oxford Road, 10, 99–101, 104–105, 108, 110–111; police abuse of power, 109–110; police corruption, 108, 116; police station, 101–102; policing of, 102–108, 130; poshness of, 99–100; research methodology in, 174–175; sex work in, 98–99, 101, 104–105, 108, 114, 132–133, 160, 162, 166; sex workers and police, interactions between, 104–107

R v Sibande, 43, 87

Safari, 82

sampling methods, 173–175

SANAC, 163

Sanchez, Lisa, 72

Sanders, Teela, 71–72, 152

Satz, Debra, 136–137

Schwartz, Richard, 12

settler colonies, 22

sex slavery, 138

sex trafficking, 66, 140–141

sexuality, 10–11; deviant sexualities, policing of, 25; double standard, 182n28; and patriarchy, 5; power relations, 148, 150

Sexual Offences Act (1957), 41–42, 45–46, 65–68, 88, 193n192

sexual Puritanism, 140, 147

sex work: abolition of, 141, 147, 152, 164–165; advocates of, 148; definition, 6; changing lives, ability to, 149; diverse clientele, 75–76; double standard, 24–25; as encouraged and feared, 24; essentializing, 46, 137; geography of, 71–72, 74, 76; liminal space, 3–4, 133; pro-sex stance, 132; as public nuisance, 162, 179–180n31; resistance, 161; as sexual transaction, 150; spatialization of, 118; subordination, 133, 136–137; Swedish approach to, 110, 117, 134, 147, 165; terminology, 17;

CPSIA information can be obtained
at www.ICGtesting.com
Printed in the USA
LVHW032006110423
744071LV00003B/481

9 781503 629745